JN119209

白い本

篠田守男
上野オサム

The White Book

Morio Shinoda / Osamu Ueno

October 9, 2021 First edition, 1st printing

Author: Morio Shinoda, Osamu Ueno

Illustration: Morio Shinoda
Photo: Osamu Ueno
Taku Tamehiro (P12, P492)
Mathematical formula: Naoki Wada
Image supervision: Masami Suzuki
Editing: Takahiko Honda
Book design: TWworks
Translation: IT Automatic Translation

Publisher: Takahiko Honda
Publisher: Gallery Station Inc.
Asakusabashi, Taito-ku, Tokyo 111-0053
Iijima Building, 1-23-5 Asakusabashi, Taito-ku, Tokyo
Phone: 03-3865-0088
Fax: 03-3865-0233
URL https://www.g-station.co.jp
Printing and binding: Vector Printing Co.

$$\mathcal{H} = \sum_{n=1}^{N-1} + \sum_{n=N}^{\infty}$$

幸せを表現する数式

2020年8月30日

Theorem 1. 幸せ $\mathcal{H}$ は一つずつの積み上げによる部分とその延長では得られない部分からなり、それぞれを有限和と無限和で以下の方程式で表現した。

$$\mathcal{H} = \sum_{n=1}^{N-1} + \sum_{n=N}^{\infty} \tag{1}$$

$\sum_{n=1}^{N-1}$：一つ一つ積み上げる項、論理、物質的豊かさ、サイエンス等　(2)

$\sum_{n=N}^{\infty}$：積み上げでは満たせない項、直観、精神的豊かさ、アート等　(3)

幸せの方程式というお題をいただいて、(1) の式をイメージしました。つまり有限と無限の構造であり、表現したいのは有限の N をいくら大きくとっても無限には届かないが、無限を得るためにはその部分の有限が必要という構造です。

似たような構造は生活の中のいろいろな場面で見かけます。人は幸せに向かって物質的に足りないもの (2) を積み上げていきますが、それだけをいくら積み上げても足りず、足りないものを数えるのをやめて足るを知ることで幸せになれる。
物質的な豊かさと精神的な豊かさの例を上げましたが、サイエンスとアートも幸せに対して同じような関係だと思います。

数学者・和田尚樹

和田尚樹（わだなおき）1986年生まれ。京都大学、ロシアのサンクトペテルブルク・ステクロフ数学研究所で数学を学び、京都大学大学院情報学研究科を2009年に修士課程早期修了、2013年に博士後期課程単位認定退学。現在は、株式会社VALUESで企業や官公庁におけるデータ活用支援に従事している。

目次

第1章　篠田守男

第2章　上野オサム

前書き

篠田守男

これは約四十年まえに考えていたのですが、本屋さんの書棚に真っ白い本が一冊あったら1番目につくじゃありませんか！いろんな出版社に提案したのですが誰もとりあってくれませんでした。それをこの本で扱ってみたいと思います。

三十年前の記憶は肉体化しているが四十年前は歴史的な知識になってしまうと思っている。例えば天皇の歴代を三十年で区切っていくと肉体化された記憶が浮かび上がってくるということである。
故にファッションなどは三十年前を探ればデザインとして継承されていく。ところがアートでは個の世界であり、ある種の発明のようなところがある。三十年前ではパクってもすぐバレてしまうので四十年以前であればバレにくいのである。この白い本は彫刻がついた本である。または彫刻に本がついたともいえる。そして上野オサムとの共著である。普通共著というのは同じ概念、または同軸上のコンセプトによって問題を提議するものであるがここでは全く無作為にならなんとなくつながっているようにも見える不思議な本であり、奇態な本といえる。

まあ読んでみてご覧なさい。

前書き

上野オサム

「誰がために鐘が鳴る」（アーネスト・ヘミンウェイ）

この白い本の、白いという空間認識は、私の空白をどう認識するのかを問う、白なのかもしれない。

近代という時代の幕開けは、空白の地図の認識と語る、ユヴァル・ノア・ハラリ氏。

人間至上主義の今、篠田氏が40年前に発した、認識空間が開花する時なのかもしれない。

篠田氏の発想空間アートは、早すぎるのか？

それとも、ＩＴ時代の的外れ者なのか？

私という存在は、経験認識の個としての広がりが、次世代へと続くのか？

空間の白いという心の隙間を、貴方はこの本を通じ、どう表現されるのか？

「あなたに問いたい」

白い世界への招待状。

上野オサムが初めてFaceBookに登場した。僕は以前からあらゆる個人的な情報をFBに流している。一つの情報で世界中に届くからである。まったく便利な世の中になったもんだ。彼は理由はわからないが何故か拒否していた。僕は個展の案内から、くだらない独りごとにいたるまでFBをつかっている。Twitterはまったくといっていいほど使わない。さしたる理由もないので、それで通用してきたのでそれはそれでいいと思っている。おそらく上野オサムもそんな理由でFBをつかわなかったのかもしれないが、囁きでは短すぎて情報交換などできるはずがない。それがすごく最近FBに登場したものだから驚くと同時に、僕にとっては非常に便利になったことは否めない。

理由はこれだ！　数分してLINE上に送られてきた写真をみて合点した。長い釣竿を肩に行く日も釣果のなかったヘミングウエイそのもの。さらに彼の前書きをみてガッテン承知の助と。

篠田

@Taku Tamehiro

第1章

篠田守男

女性の目と彫刻

女性を語るには先ず、自分が男であるというはっきりした自覚を常に持ちながら進めないと焦点がぼけてしまう恐れがある。それは女性が同じ人間として身近にありながら、広角レンズをとおして眺めた遠近法のように遥か彼方に存在しているからである。生物学上では類・科・目とそれぞれが雌・雄二つのピラミッドがあって、その一つのピラミッドの頂点にある我々男性は他方の頂点にある女性を理解するために、雄の犬を理解し、――私は女性と理解しあうよりもはるかに雄犬の方が互いにコミュニケーションできるように思えるのだが――且つ雄の豚、さらにアメーバに至るまで山を下り降りて平地を横切り、速やかに隣の山に移り、遺伝子組み換えの門を開き、爬虫類の雌を理解しつつ遥かな頂点を極めて、はじめて人類の女性をも多少なりと理解できると考える。世によくいう女は子宮でものを考えるという俗説も男が雄のピラミッドの中で考えた一人よがりの理論なのではないか。このように女性の目という表題も、あくまでも男性の目をとおしての女性的視点であって女の目そのものではない。

編集者がどのようなねらいでこの表題を私に向けたのか判らないが、私はむしろ男の目、女の目というところにこだわってみたい。即ち男が作るもの、また女が作るもの、そしてそれを鑑賞する男と女、これらを私の目をとおして見てみたいということである。冒頭に雄雌二つのピラミッドと比喩したが、ワイニンゲルが個体としてみた男と女が、理念としての男性と女性との混合組成であるとしたように、この二つにはそれぞれ微妙なグラデーションを作っている。非常に個人的、内的作業である芸術の創造は、このグラデーションの作用するところが大であるといえる。

芸術の学生にこのような課題を与えたことがある。それは、「諸君はアートというものを一切考えずに諸君の個人的趣味に徹して立体物を作りなさい」というものであった。ここに表れたものは、幾度くりかえしても男と女では異なるある種の特徴がみられたことである。それは誰が見ても女または男の作ったものであると理解できる、いわば生理に近い部分で作られたような特徴が表れたことである。かつて女流作家というとき、男と同じであるということが前提としてあった。そこで、あえて女流という形容詞をつけていた。これは女でありながら男と同じようにという含みをもっていた。これが一九六〇年代のウーマン・リブを経て男女平等が確立され、そして一九八〇年初頭から再び女流時代を迎えるのであるが、ここでいう女流とは前者と趣を異にしている。それは前者が男をダーゲットにしていたのに対して女が女であることを基盤にして芸術が生まれているところにある。これは一九七〇代の後半からでてきたインスタレーション・アート——本来は取付け、設備、装置といった意味から転じて、数点の作品を組み合わせて装置化する——とあいまってにわかに脚光をあびた。これらの女流作家たちに共通するところは、従来の非常に男性的な彫刻に対して、クラフトや手芸の領域を彫刻のなかに取り入れてきたことである。一九七〇年代にアメリカ西海岸でピーター・ボーカスを頂点にして陶芸家たちが陶製の彫刻をつくりパンク・アートとよばれた時代があったが、今の女流作家たちの作品はそれ以上にクラフト的であり、趣味手芸的である。しかし素材やディテールは手芸的であってもアートとしてなかなかの説得力をもっている。一九八一年にニューヨークのブルックリンにあるプロジェクト・スタジオ・ワン（P・S・1）で新しい芸術家たちを集めて展覧会を開催したことがある。このP・S・1は年度毎に新進の作家たちを選び、そこで助成金をだして、その会場で彼らに制作させ年度末にその場で発表させるというシステムをとっている。この会場で女流作家として印象に残ったのはテオドラ・スキピタレス、リディア・ハン、ナンシー・グロスマン、シーラ・クライン等であった。この他ニューヨークで活躍しているリンダ・ペングレスやリラン等にこの年再開することができたのだが、この人たちも女性的発想のなかから作品を生みだしている作家たちである。その後、このような欧米の女流作家たちの影響をうけて日本でも堤展子、寺田真由美、広田美穂、瀬戸富恵といった新人たちが育ってきた。これらのいわゆる女らしい芸術は今や世界的傾向の一つである。そして特徴的なところはいずれも趣味手芸的形態を巨大化することによって別の意味をもたせているところである。

私はながい間メカニックとよばれるような彫刻を作っている。非常に細密な機械部品を組み上げたメカニカルな機械的作品という評価をうけてきた。しかし、女性の目から見ると非常にセクシーであるという多くの答えがかえってくるのである。前者はあきらかに男性の目であるが、後者のコミュニケーションのなかには、私の内面にある女性的グラデーションの一部が女性鑑賞者と結びついたとみるべきであろうか。事実、私はアルミという無機質な素材の表面を変えるために相当な神経を費やして触覚化しようとしている部分がある。ほとんど機会によって制作されるなかで、唯一の手仕事はこの部分である。かつてヨーロッパに滞在したときに初めてミケランジェロの彫刻にふれて、それまでグラビアなどで見ていた作品と全く異なる、なめるように作られた大理石の石像に驚かされたと同時に、そのホモ的なまでの男性像の色っぽさに感動した思いがある。私の肉体の一部に微かに存在していたホモ的要素がにわかに拡大されてきて、ミケランジェロをもとめてヨーロッパ中を訪れた思い出がある。この旅は芸術を鑑賞するというより誠に不純な、変則的な欲望を満たす旅行になってしまったが、このなかでダビデの美少年を見、バッカスの色っぽさに感嘆したのである。そして思いはルネッサンス時代にまで逆行してミケランジェロが同性愛の対象として男像を作っているような不徳な考えにまで及んだ記憶が鮮明に残っている。確かにフィレンツェにあるバッカス像のふくよかな肉体やルーブルにある瀕死の奴隷像のあの衣服をたくしあげた手つきや、わずかに腰をひねって内股にまげられた脚のポーズは男性同性愛者の美少年の姿である。

ハイパー・リアリズムの作家で女性のお尻を描き続けるジョン・カセールは更に屈折した生理から生みだされる芸術であろう。数年前ニューヨーク滞在中にこのカセールに会う機会があり、制作上の話のなかで面白いことをきいた。これは彼の描く美しいお尻のモチーフはお尻を描くためではなく、絹やサテンの下着を際立たすための素材にすぎないのである。女性の下着や薄手のナイロン生地のコレクションには、その量といい質といい目をみはるものがあった。更にカセールの選択のなかに、ある種の一貫性があることにきづくのである。それは布の手触りなのである。その手触りをキャンバスのうえに視覚化することに、ほとんどカリスマ的に情熱を注いでいるのである。フェティシズムである。これにあたいしてアレン・ジョーンズは非常に直視的に女というものを見ている。表面は女へのサディズムという形態をとっているが、女性にたいする愛の変形とみることができる。それは一九六九年にミラノのギャラリエ・ミクロがだした出版物、アレン・ジョーンズ・フィギュアーズを見ると明らかである。内容はジョーンズの作品と共に彼がそれまで集めてきた雑誌の切り抜きや広告、ポスターの類を収録した一種のピクトリアル・マガジンであるが、その切り抜きのなかにしばしば登場するのが、一九四〇年代にアメリカでビザール・コミックとして活躍したカートゥーニスト、アーニー・スタントンであり、ジーン・ビルブリュウであった。彼らのカートゥーンは女性をサディスティックに扱いながら、それが戯れとも思えるように愛情に包まれているのである。アレン・ジョーンズは自ら述べているように作品のモチーフとしてほとんどこの二人から影響を強くうけている。

共にサディスティックなテーマをモチーフとする作家に、今度は逆に女の側から男を見る女流作家ナンシー・グロスマンがいる。ジョーンズの明るい、むしろユーモアともとれるサディズムにたいしてグロスマンのそれは異常性に満ち満ちている。ほとんどの作品が男性像であり、頭部だけの作品が多く、それも頸部がなく西瓜のようにゴロっと展示されたものが多い。等身大の作品でも膝から下や腕の肘から先がなかったり、まあ、一種のトルソーとも見ることができるが、それもいわゆる古典的トルソーのプロポーションではない。表面的にはかならず黒のなめし皮を張り、ジッパーでつなぐという凝りようである。
このようななかに、なにか男と女の本質的な差異を見るのである。更に彫刻ではないが、空山基のロボットのイラストレーションのようにスティールの硬質なテクスチャーが逆に女の姿態とあいまってエロティシズムを助長させるという男の感性、また写真家、権藤新也もフランス版ZOOMに紹介された、生とも死ともつかない、生と死のあいだを浮遊するような写真表現、これらを私という男の目から眺めてきたわけであるが、さて、読者にとっては如何であろうか。

「カミーユ・クローデル・アルバム」より（発行：アプト　インターナショナル株式会社）昭和62年

まちや展シンポジウム草案

司会鈴木―この度は、「てらまちこころまちまちや展」にご来場頂き、ありがとうございます。これより展覧会同時開催イベントである、シンポジウム「町家でアートを語ろう…この町にあるもの、あったもの」を行いたいと思います。早速ですが坂本先生お願いいたします。

坂本先生―シンポジウムのトップバッターということで、少し町家の話をさせて頂きます。実は、金澤町家継承活用研究会という会がありまして、そこでは金沢で空き家になっている町家の保全や改修をして町家を積極的に活用していこうという活動を行っています。今回の展覧会会場となったこの場所も、そんな町家の一つです。また「金澤町家」という固有名詞を、一般的には無い言葉ですけれど、この言葉を作りまして、金沢の戦前の木造住宅を大事にしていこうという主旨でやっております。町家はもともと商人とか職人の住居ということで、この家もそれに属しますね。ただ、今いるこの建物は昭和の初期にできたものでそんなに建築としては古くはない、古くはないという言い方はあれかな、古いですけど町家としては古くないですね。ですから、二階もそうですけど、天井が高いのが特徴です。もっと古いものになると、天井が非常に低い町家が多くあります。昔は二階をつくってはいけないというお触書が回って、それで二階に隠れ部屋のようなものをつくって使っていたというような、そんな時代もありました。それから、武士系、武家屋敷とか足軽の住居ですね、これは、金沢だと長町辺りに行くとありますよね。周りが土塀とか門で囲われている、ああいう種類の武士系の町家、それから、他には近代和風といったつくりの町家、これは西洋文化が日本に入ってきて、建築様式とか技術が入ってきた昭和戦前くらいのものを指しています。その他に、茶屋系という町家もあったりしますが、そういったものを総称して「金澤町家」と呼んでいます。そもそも町家自体は現代の言葉でタウンハウスあるいは店舗併用住宅といった感じで、今でも街中に行くと結構ありますよね。下にショップが入って上に人が住んでいるという、そういうスタイルの江戸時代の建物のことを町家と言います。金沢の平均的な町家は、間口が三間半から四間くらいで、中に入ると土間があって、その奥に六畳くらいの部屋が縦につながっていて、部屋の横には「通り土間」といって土間の延長があって、土足で入っていくところがあるといった感じです。金沢の場合、昔は間口の間数で税金が決まっていたのでそういった寸法で納まっていたということですね。それで一階がお店で、一階の奥と二階が住居というのが基本です。それから町家には座敷とか仏間がありますが、そういうところには床の間があって、昔の言ってみればディスプレイ空間ですね、四季折々のものを飾ったり掛け軸を飾ったりする空間があります。このディスプレイ空間ですけど、ここは家の一番聖域というか重要な場所で、当然家の中には神棚があるんですけど、もう一つの家の神様が居ると言われていた場所でもあります。それから、店をたたんでしまった家を、「しもたや」という言い方もします。また、「通り土間」あるいは「通り庭」とも言いますが、そういったものがなぜ作られたかというと、勿論色々な使い方はあるのですが、昔は水周りが後ろにあって、排水は全部後ろ側に流していたんですね。その汚物を外へ運ぶ通路として利用されたのがこの「通り土間」なんですよ。だからそこを板敷きにするわけにはいかなかった。だけど今は、下水管が道路側に通るようになって、表側に水洗トイレをつけたりして、表側に下水を通すようになったことで、そういった通路も要らなくなったんですね。それから、大店の町家では「土蔵」があったりもします。その他にも、北陸では「セド」という、奥の方に少しひらけた外の空間があって、そこで洗濯物を干したりとか子供が遊んだりとか仕事をしたりとかそういった場所がありました。そして、もう一つ重要なのが「中庭」です。大体四間ごとに一箇所くらいずつ庭があるのですが、昔の家は軒を連ねていたので、隣から光が漏れてこないんですね。だから自分の家にそういった庭をつくらないと光が入らないのですよ。他にも通風口といった役割もありました。風を通す、まぁ煙突みたいなものですね。あとは、とくに北陸ですと雪を捨てなければならないでしょ。山のように雪が積もるので、昔は積もったのでそれを捨てる場所として中庭を使っていたということです。このように町家には多種多様なつくりがあることを分かって頂けたと思いますが、そこには当然様々な人の手が入っているわけですね。大工さんもそうだし、左官屋さん、畳屋さん、ふすまを作る建具屋さんとか瓦屋さんとかたくさんの職人さんが入って一つの空間を作っている、そういう意味では町家自体が共同作業の作品だということは言えると思います。最後になりますけど金沢の町家は徐々に数が減ってきているのが現状です。平成十一年にはおよそ一万一千棟あった町家が、去年の春で九千五百棟に減ってしまっているのですよ。年間で計算すると約三百戸の家が壊されてしまっています。駐車場になったり、新しく建て替えられたりしています。今日の町家をどういう風に感じ取って頂けるかわからないですけど、町家のこの空間は、本当に日本建築の特徴的なもので、融通無碍というか自由自在な空間だと思うんですね。襖を全部取っ払うとどーんと大きな空間が目の前に現れたり小さな空間があったりとか、そういう融通無碍と、それから周りの気候や風土や季節とかそういったものとも非常に結びついている空間が町家なんですよ。今回の展覧会を通して、町家を何かこう新しい発見の場として皆さんにも考えて頂けたらいいなと思いました。以上です。ありがとうございました。

司会井上——一言で町家といっても、様々な違いや特色があって、金沢には金沢の町家があり、京都には京都の町家があるのですね。しかもそれぞれにもまたつくりの違いがある。とても勉強になりました。坂本先生ありがとうございました。

では次に、天徳院の荒井源空和尚様からお話を頂戴したいと思います。よろしくお願いいします。

荒井和尚—門外漢の私がお話しするというのは非常に場違いかと思ったりしてるんですが、よろしくお願いします。先ほど町家の保存、維持管理について坂本先生よりお話がありましたが、町家同様、天徳院についても維持管理ということが難しいんですよね。ご存知の方もあるかと思いますが、天徳院は、八千坪、約二万四千平米くらいの敷地の中に、建物とそれぞれお堂がありまして、そして樹木が植わっている、そういう環境の中に在るわけです。もう彼此三百数十年前から現連としてあるわけですが、あの古い建物を維持管理するというのは大変なことで、私が関わってからもう三、四十年経ちますが、例えば修繕するにしても壊してしまうわけにはいきませんから、当然前と同じようなものにしなければならないし、保たなければならない。最近は技術もかなり進歩してきたんでしょうけども、古いものを直して保存するということについては、非常に難しいわけですよ。そういう事もあったりして苦労しているところですが、同時に、この仏教文化あるいは伝統文化というのでしょうか、寺院建築の保存というのが貴重なことになってきているのも事実です。しかし財政問題が入りますのでなかなか思うようにはいかないのが現状です。そのような状況の中で、天徳院をどうしていくのか、どのように護持していくのかということなんですが、やっぱりこれはお寺である限りは大勢の方が出入りすることが大事なんですね。本来お寺というのはそういう不特定の方が大勢入って、そして自分なりの心を癒し、お互いにこう、和む、集うというか、そういう場所であったわけですね。また、お寺の中には仏像があったり、仏画があったりします。こういう仏像仏画が、やっぱり仏教としての役割を果たしているわけですね。まぁ、そういうことがいわゆる人間社会の中にあってそれなりの位置を占めているというか、役割をしているんじゃないかなと思っています。それともう一つ、この天徳院は前田家三代藩主利常侯が奥方のために建てたお寺なんですよ。これは一つの権力ですね、前田家という大きな権力でもって、あるいは、そのバックには徳川幕府という大きな権力がありますから、そういった権力のなかで建てられたものですね。それが当然仏教を広める事によって、良民いわゆる人々の心を癒すと同時に管理するんですよ。さらに天徳院の場合は、多くの寺院の統括という役割も前田家から与えられた、というか命令されたんですね。当然そこには政治があったりもしたわけです。またお寺には檀家がいるのですが、その檀家の中には町家に住んでいる人々もいます。町家とお寺との関係というものもそういう点でも結びつくんじゃないかと思います。いずれにしても伝統ある建物なり仏像なりそういったものを維持管理するというのは、はっきり言うとお金がかかるんですね、苦労してます。どうしたらこれを維持できるかと。実は内輪話なんですが、ある時には、全部壊してしまって山の奥に移転しようじゃないかとか、庭をつぶしてしまってマンションを建てようとか、いろんな意見が出たりしていました。それから山門がございますが、今、金沢市の文化財になっているのですが、これも百万石文化園ですか、江戸村というのがありまして、涌波、湯涌の奥にですね、そこへもっていこうじゃないかという話が出たことがあるんですよ。そういう風にして天徳院にも危なっかしいことがいっぱいあったんです。それを死守するというのが大事なことなんですね。もっていかれないように、もっていかないんだったら今度は守らなければならない、壊れたらあるいは修繕しなければならないということで、なんというかイタチごっこというかそういうことがずうっと付きまとってきました。でないと文化財が守れないんですね。私も市のあるいは県の行政に何度も足を運んでこういう文化財に財政的な援助をしてくださいよということを言いました。けどね、やっぱり行政側は当然県民市民の生活そのものが直接関わってきますから、そちらの方を優先して伝統文化財を補助するのがなかなかできないというのが現状であります。

さて、もう一つ私がお話ししたいのは、木造建築の重要さについてです。これはおそらく私の想像というかまだ勉強浅学ですが、おそらく日本の在りし前からと言いますか、ずっと累積され、進化していったのがこういう木造建築だろうと思うのです。そしてそれはやはり日本独特のものだろうと思っています。この日本独特の木造建築物をやっぱりどうしても守っていかなきゃいけないし、そこに住んでいる市民県民が豊かな精神文化を育んでいくためにも大事なんじゃないかなと思っております。そういう点でもお寺には重要な役割があると思うんですよ。また、一般の町家にしても一般の家屋にしても木造建築というものは落ち着いた空間が生まれるんではないかなと思っております。そして、その環境があるいは環境のあり様というのが人格形成にとっても非常に重要だと考えております。それを証明するといったわけではないんですが、私どもの天徳院幼稚園の状況をお話しますと、園内には自然をできるだけ取り込んでいるんですよ、そのため園内の中に植わっている樹木あるいは草花等々に子供たちが直に触れて毎日生活ができるのです。それから園舎、子供たちが学び遊ぶところも木造にしました。そしてできるだけ自然に触れるような環境設定をして、子供たちが自ら取り組んでいけるものを作っていくことが大事じゃないかと考えているんです。たしか生理学者だったと思いますが、子供たちが木造の中に生活する重要性を言っておりまして、それは何故かと言いますと、ベータ波とか何とかいう波が木から発散されるんだそうです。それが子供の、とくに幼児の子供たちの生理状況に非常にいい作用を及ぼすんだという説を聞きました。ということは私どもの幼稚園の園舎の木造ということは間違いなかったなと思うんです。それからもう一つ、私は常々子供たちには本物を与えたいと考えているんです。できるだけ最高のものを与えなきゃいけないなと。これは子供人権宣言にも出てますが、近い将来子供たちが日本の国を背負って立つわけですから、そういう力を彼らが育んでいくだろうと思っております。それでちょっと証拠品があります。今ここに秋刀魚の絵とチャボの絵とそれからもう一枚は印象画があるのですが、これは六歳の子供が描いたんですよ。秋刀魚については本当の秋刀魚を目の前にして写生しスケッチするわけですね。それからチャボについては毎日飼育していますから、チャボに触れているわけです。ときには抱いたりもして育てている。そういう生活をずっと繰り返していますから、その中で彼らが観察してそれを表現する力が生まれる気がするわけですね。印象画についても、長い物語なんですが、ロシアの民謡民話を題材にしたものを子供に読ませましてね、それぞれ自分の印象に残ったものを描かせるのですよ。まぁ六歳児ですから十分な形ではないと思いますが、しかし彼らなりに構図、あるいは色彩等の表現は非常に率直素直で面白いと思ってるんです。というのは何が言いたいのかというと環境が子供の育ち、とくに人間にとっては非常に大事なんじゃないかと思うのです。私はそういう点でも自然とか木で作ったものを、そういったものを大事にして、そして子供たちに触れるようにしていきたいと思っております。先ほど申したように木というのは非常に心を和ませます。それはいわゆる理屈抜きでですね、とくにわれわれの人間の生活の中にそれを取り組んでいくことが大事なんじゃないかなと思っております。とりとめないことをお話しましたけども、一応一区切りを付けます。失礼します。ありがとうございました。

司会井上―ありがとうございました。この幼稚園児の描いた作品にはすごく驚かされたんですが、僕もちょっと機会がありまして幼稚園に絵を教えに行くアルバイトなんかをしているんですけども、すごく上手でその差にびっくりしてしまいました。本当に環境というのは大事だなと。それでは続きまして篠田先生からよろしくお願いいたします。

篠田先生―金沢美大で大学院の彫刻を担当しております彫刻家の篠田守男です。実はこの企画書を頂いたときは、私の名前が最後にあって、前には建築家の先生や江戸文学の先生等がいらっしゃるから、他の先生方の専門的御講義を拝聴して、素人の感想と少ない知識をちょっと披露しようかなと思っていたら、なんとごまかされました。(笑) 私は町家とか建築は部外者なものですから、一応私なりの考えで披露させて頂きます。
今回はホワイトボードに書いたように、「町家の発生」、「日本の裏の文化」、「日本建築の空間」、「住むということ」という4つのキーワードをもとに話したいと思います。

I　町家の発生

ではまず、町家の発生ですが、町家の前身というのは農家なんですね。どういうことかというと、農家には入り口に近いところに「前土間」といって労働のための牛馬を飼っているところがあって、士農工商というカースト制度のなかで商人は一番下位にあるのですが、町家ができるようになってから、ここで商品を並べて商うようになったのですよ。とくに室町時代に町家が建てられ始め、家を連ねるようになってからは、土間に商品を並べていたものを、玄関を広くして商品を陳列するようになったのです。また、農家時代の「前土間」は、先ほど坂本先生から伺ったように、表から裏へ抜ける「通り土間」とつながっていて、日本では平安時代の頃から神社仏閣や城下町のメイン通りは多くが東西に位置していましたから、南北にあたるこの「通り土間」は風の通路としても最適だったわけですね。後には、この土間が生活の機能として重要な役割を果たすようになり、商家独特の構造を作り上げていったともいえます。例えば、台所、食材保存、収納といった生活の機能としての部分と、生きるうえでのゆとりといいますか、人との交流の場としての座敷という内部空間と完全に分離した場ができあがっていったのですね。また、この頃から板の間に座畳（※現在の座ぶとん）だったものから敷畳となり、現在の日本家屋の原型ができたと思います。ここでは、西洋のような機能別空間ではなく、多様性のあるマルチプル・スペースが完成したのです。つまり、寝る時はベッドルームであり、接待のときには心地よい応接空間になるといった具合ですね。その後、床の間ができ、そのあたりから美術が関わってきたと思います。それも固定されたものではなく、季節に合った掛け軸やそれに伴った生花や料理といったように、その家の主人の品格というものまで表すようになって、これは接客のみならず、その主人が作り上げた文化といえるでしょう。今風にいえば、作者と同時に鑑賞者でもあり、他人に対して作り手と受け手が対等になったということですね。しかもそれが一点の作品というのではなく、トータルな作品、いわばインスタレーションともいえるのです。そこにいる人間のファション、動き、所作にいたるまで作品であり、空間であり、季節という自然と共にあったわけですね。しかし今日、われわれはこの素晴らしい生活文化を舶来主義によって放棄してしまったのではないでしょうか。と思えるのですよ。

話は変わって、美大にも講演会で二度お越しいただいた千葉成夫という興味ある評論家がいるのですが、非常に極論を持っていて、彼によると、「日本人というのは単一民族ではなくごった煮であり、どこから来てどこで発達したか分からん。」と言うのです。これは実にその通りだと思います。次は私の持論ですが、北はアイヌ人がいてその中にはロシア人の血が入っているかもしれないし、南の長崎ではポルトガル人やオランダ人の血が入っているだろうと思うのです。

筑波大学の定年後、私は長崎大学に二年勤務したのですが、昼の三時頃市電に乗ると女子高生が大勢乗ってきて、見ると皆、宮沢リエみたいなんですよ。私の学生にも宮沢系が何人かいて、「君等の先祖にはオランダ系かポルトガル系が入っているだろう?」という質問をするのですが、異口同音に、「いや、私たちは純粋日本人だ。」というのです。殆ど気がついていないのです。西欧では先祖の名前を自分の名前に入れていますね。ピカソなど非常に長くて、まるで落語の寿限無ですよ。ことほど左様に千葉成夫の日本民族ごった煮説に、私も納得するわけです。

Ⅱ　日本の裏の文化

次に日本の裏の文化についてです。先ほどのごった煮から生まれた日本固有の文化というのを、私は「裏文化」と呼ぶのですが、表をおさえることによって裏の美が滲んでくるといった感じで、例えば世阿弥の風姿花伝にも出てくる、「秘すれば花」という有名な文章がありますが、隠すことによって滲んでくる美学というのかな。それで中国から伝わってきた仏教建築はすごく華やかで、東照宮なんかはまさにその最たるものなのですが、建築家たちはどぎついと言って批難するのです。まぁ、もっとも桂離宮以後の話ですが、その桂離宮でさえもそんなに有名ではなかったのに、ドイツの建築家ブルーノ・タウトによって世界的建築になったわけです。何が言いたいかというと、桂離宮はまさに日本の「裏文化」なのですよ。

ブルーノ・タウト（Buruno-Taut 1880-1938）は１９３３年から四年間、仙台、高崎に居を構えて日本各地を旅し、日本古来の道具を発掘していったわけです。桂離宮は八條宮智仁の別荘として建てられたのですが、まず第一期は１６２０年から１６２５年にかけて造られて、それが現在の古書院です。第二期には１６４５年から１６４８年に中書院、新書院、松琴亭、笑意軒等御茶室が建てられていったのです。この離宮はもてなしの場でもあったはずなのに、その導入部は誠に質素なもので、やんごとなき人物の家とは思えないのですよ。さらには一歩玄関に招かれ進むほど家主の心づかい、心配りといったものが見えてこない。でも不思議なことになぜか心が和むのです。更に進めば幅2間の長い廊下がありますが、左手に丸竹をくんだ月見台があって、手摺もない誠にシンプルなものなのです。更に驚かされるのは長さ十五、六間の廊下は先端に行くに従って一尺ほど狭められているのです。つまりパースがついているわけです。その目的は、回遊式庭園と呼ばれる桂離宮の庭園を、建物から見る際のヴューにあるのですよ。建物は桂川の氾濫を避けて高床式になっているので目線の高さが通常の二倍強になります。接客の場合、今の応接間にあたる部屋が一番奥にあり、そこに至るまでの回廊から、ですから今言ったような目線で庭園が鑑賞できるわけです。一見しただけでは分からないのですが、そこには充分に客に楽しんでもらいたいというサービス精神が込められているのですね。また、帰る際には当然逆パースになるので、長さを短く感じさせるのです。実は、このような配慮がいたるところに施されているのですよ。

もう二、三例をあげますと、厠の手前の手摺は、廊下に立って見ると直線に見えるのですが、匡から見ると微かに手摺の桟が角度をもっており、その延長上にちょうど扇の要のように地中の一点に集点を結ぶという構造になっているのです。まだあります。中書院の居間にある棚にはわずかながら奥行きにパースをもたせ、空間を感じさせる効果を備えています。これを桂棚といって、修学院離宮の化粧殿にある霞棚と並んで日本三棚と呼ばれています。この日本なになにとか、近江八景というような先人の美の指導者たちが唱えたことを、一般庶民もその美に賛同し、生活に取り入れてきたんですね。日本の古い寺や民家、町家なんかがそれです。これらの心地よい美というのは、何も日本人だけではなく、黄金分割とか、音楽でいえば、殆どド、ミ、ソの和音でなりたっているモーツァルトの曲の心地よい響きなんかもそうです。ある音の研究者は、自然の音、例えば木々のふれあい、竹笹のふれあう音はすべてド、ミ、ソの和音であると言い切っています。美と感じる感覚は人間の生理の領域との関わり合いにおいて、振動の琴線に共鳴するのかもしれませんね。

Ⅲ　日本建築の空間

さて次に日本建築の空間についてですが、１９０３年にアメリカで岡倉天心が、翻訳ではなく天心自身が英語で書いた「The Book of Tea」という有名な本を出版しました。その影響を大きく受けたのが、建築家のフランク・ロイド・ライト（Frank-Loyd -Wright 1867-1959）で、彼は、それまでゴシック風な住宅建築を作っていたのですが、１９０６年のシカゴのユニティ・チャーチを初めとして、１９０９年のシカゴ・ロビー邸や東京帝国ホテル等といった、それまでの平面的フロアーだったものから、日本家屋の踏み石や縁側、本間、床の間といった同一空間内での高低差に着目し、西洋建築内に様々な高低差もつフロアーを設計するようになったのですよ。これはさらにエーロ・サーリネンやルイス・カーン等に影響を与え、エール大学のポール・ルドルフによってスキップ・フロアーとして概念化されて、第二次世界大戦後のアメリカ建築に大きな示唆を与えることになるわけです。これはちょうど絵画において浮世絵が印象派の画家たちに影響を与えたように、建築においてもこのようなエポックがあったのですね。

Ⅳ　住むということ

最後に住むということについてですが、このことについて語る前に面白いエピソードを一つ御披露したいと思います。万国博覧会が最も情報の発信地であった頃の話ですが、１８８９年パリ万博が開催されて、エンジニアだったグスターフ・エッフェルの作ったエッフェル塔が当時のパリジャンたちから非難ゴウゴウというときの話です。１８８７年2月14日、ですからエッフェル塔建設中の新聞、「ル・タン」紙の孫引きですが、「パリの街は、一介の機械製造人の異様にして拝金主義的な思いつきに、これ以上長くつき合うことによって、取り返しのつかないほど身を汚し、醜くなろうというのであろうか?何となれば、エッフェル塔は、商業主義的なアメリカでさえ欲しそうにないものであり、疑いなくパリの恥だからである。〈中略〉われわれの万国博覧会を訪れにやって来たとき、外国人は驚いてこう叫ぶだろう。〝なんたることだ！フランス人はあれほど褒めそやされている彼らの趣味をわれわれに示すために考え出したのが、このおぞましい代物なのか？〟と」最後の〝このおぞましい代物なのか？〟のくだりは私がとくに強調したかったセンテンスですが、この反対運動に共した人たちの中には、ギー・ド・モーパッサン、シャルル・ガルニエ、アレクサンドル・デュマ・フィス等もいたのですよ。ロラン・バルトはそのことを彼のエッセイで、「中でもモーパッサンは、しばしばエッフェル塔のレストランで昼食をしたが、しかし彼はここが好きだったわけではない。〝ここはエッフェル塔が見えないパリの唯一の場所だからだ〟と彼は言っていた。実際、パリで、エッフェル塔を見ないようにするためには無限に多くの注意を払わなければならない。」と語っているのです。まぁ、バルトは一見反対者に思えるのですが、後には「私と、塔を見ていることがわかっている私のすべての友人たちを、パリ越しに結びつけてくれている。〈中略〉エッフェル塔は、友情に満ちているのである。」とも言ってたりして。このことは私の「住む」ということの中で大きく関わってくるのですよ。例えばエッフェル塔のレストランで食事をしているモーパッサンに思いを馳せると、大変心地よかったんだろうとか。私はあまり名所旧跡を訪ねるのが好きではないのですが、何度目かのパリで、弟子二人を連れていったことがあります。そのうちの一人が若い女の子で、どうしてもエッフェル塔を見たいというので、つきあったのですが、外観はモーパッサン同様、どこにも美どころか醜悪であるとしか感じませんでした。しかし内部に入るや一変したのですよ。その構造体の美しさなんかは目をみはるものでした。たぶんモーパッサンは私同様に内部の美に心地よかったんでしょう。

ここで本題に入らねばなりませんが、結論から言ってしまうと、住むと見るでは次元が異なるのです。東の茶屋街では観光客がひきもきりませんが、どこをどう探索しようが、見るという次元を越すことはできません。「住む」というのは、その空間の中で良くも悪くも呼吸しながら生きることなのです。私は

1990年に、茨城県の新治村に千坪の土地を購入し、建坪二百坪という巨大な彫刻を作って住もうと考えたんです。その人工物というか、とにかく周囲の自然とともに完璧なエコ循環を作って、外観は芸術作品なので充分に鑑賞に値するはずですよね。だからこれは全体が一つの作品であり、内部の部分も独立した作品であるというナノ彫刻、もしくは分子彫刻と考えていました。これは最初に申し上げた町家にしても桂離宮にしても私は同じことだと思うのですよ。「全体と部分」、彫刻でいえば、全体を見て一点の作品として見るのですが、住居規模のスケールになると、全体と部分が総合的に鑑賞できるわけです。このことを逆に捉えれば、作り手にとっては相当繊細な神経と強力な造形力が必要となってくるのですよ。最後になりましたが、「住む」というキーワードの中で最も私が興味を持ち、お伝えしたかった話をしたいと思います。筑波大学時代に調査を行ったのですが、「奇械館」といって、まぁこの名前は幸村先生の命名で、当時の美術手帖にもその記事を載せましたが、まさに奇っ怪な建物です。ホームレスのような老人がひとりで生活をしているのですが、川のほとりに鉄骨構造の、といっても勿論クズ鉄を回収してきては作り続けているのですが、三階建てくらいのスケールで、どこの階にも区切りがなくて、内部を巡っているうちに最上階の展望台に出てしまうという。しかも日々増殖する建築なんです。沖縄海洋博のときに菊竹清訓等が唱えた〝メタボリック・アーキテクチュア〟という理論がありますが、この素人老人の奇械館は、まさにそのコンセプトを具現化しているものでした。勿論、違法建築で行政の指導を無視して作り続けていたのですが。自分の土地で作れば、ロサンジェルスのワッツ・タワーのように世界的素人建築として有名になるであろうと思われるのに、誠に惜しまれます。

以上、少し長くなりましたがここら辺で話を終わらせて頂きます。ありがとうございました。

司会井上―はい、何かどんどん篠田ワールドに引き込まれてしまいましたが、町家、お寺、建築と話もたくさん出たところで、続きまして太田先生と高橋先生に、今こうやってお三方にお話頂いたことを踏まえて何かお話して頂けたらなと、一言でも二言でもよろしくお願いします。ではまず太田先生よろしくお願いします。

太田先生—三人の方々にお仕事を押し付けたかたちで私は逃げ回ってましたら、それがシンポジウムとしては結果的に良かったということで、あの本当にありがとうございました。こう見ますと美大の関連する先生、学生さんも含めて、その他にも存じ上げない方もいらっしゃるようですので、ここまでに至った経過も含めてですね、ちょっと簡単にご説明をして御礼を申し上げたいと思います。ご存知の方もいると思いますが、金沢美大には十一年十年ちょっと前からドクターコースが設けられまして、美大系の大学としては大変珍しく、上から下まで一貫つまり学部から修士、博士まで教育できるということが整備ができて、それ以降、そこでせっかくなんだからパワーアップするためにどんなことができるか毎年試行錯誤的に地域との繋がりということをキーワードに、入ってきたドクター一年生に向けて教員も一緒に努力しながらやってきたという不思議な授業があるんですね。地域美術研究、地域美術なんとかと地域をつけてともかくそういう努力をしてまいりました。今年幸い八人の新ドクターさんが入られてですね、マンパワーというのはすごいもので、少ない年ですと三人くらいの年もあったのですがこれだけの方がいるんだったら少し今までと違うようなこともできるかな、つまり問題提起をしてそれに多角的に実働して調査とかですよ、そしてそれをまとめてさらに作品につなげることができないのかなということを教員のほうはかなり欲張りに考えました。というのはこの授業を何年かやってみて、こちらが問題を出してそれに多少の努力をして頂いてレポート出して頂いて成績をつけるというのはドクターの授業としてはおかしいなというのは私には少なくともあって、ほかの先生方も何かそれだけじゃないのにしたいなという思いがあったんだと思うんですね。それで提起をしました。その際に、まぁそれぞれ六人、ここに今日はおられないお二人の工芸関係の先生もその枠に入っておられますのでかなりたくさんの教員がそこにコミットするわけですが、それぞれの関心のありようが違うのがまたすごく良いんですね。いろいろな、勝手に言います教員も学生も、そしてそれじゃあ何をしようかということで、今年は主として四月から秋九月くらいまでに大きくある問題に即して実働して、その後それを踏まえて作品に何とかつなげようということにしたのですが、本当にいい形になりました。いろいろ言った中に十年位前東京から金沢に来た時に町家が戦災を受けなかったから、町家がすごく残っていて魅力的だなということと、私はだいたい歩いて四十分かけて学校に行くんですね。たくさんの道を歩いていくので毎日同じ道を歩くのが嫌な人間なんです。行きと帰りも必ず違えるというくらいこう変化を求めて歩くので、そうするとその町家の間に不思議な空間があって広見と言われているらしいんですよ。広見と町家というのは人間空間だなと思って魅力的な町だというのを感じていたので、広見をちょっと勉強してみませんかという提案をしました。広見を選べばやっぱり金沢という町、町家という空間それを見ていくことになるので他の先生方もそれぞれに問題提起をしながら学生さんと、えっとあれはいつでしたかね、調査実際に始めたのは？

司会井上―まだ春、夏前とかだったと思いますね。

太田先生―ゴールデンウィーク明けには町に飛び出して、坂本先生が地図を用意してくださって、双眼鏡、それから足固めもしてとかいろんなことをしながら町に出て何回か調査をしてきました。そういった中で実は、これはもう市長さんに感謝しなきゃいけないんですが現実的には事務の方といったらいいんですかね、そんなに熱心にやっているんだったら少し予算付けてあげるから展覧会をしたらという形で書類を出したのは私じゃなくて田嶋さんとか皆さんが協力して出したわけですがそうしましたら取れちゃったんですよね。わずか二十万円なんですが、良くこの展覧会にこぎつけてくれたと思います。それプラスアルファで坂本先生が努力してくださって、また別のところから支援をいただいたようですが、ほんのわずかな資金を元に、まぁ材料費はほとんど出てないといろんな足は出てる、足も手も頭も出てるとは思いますが、ともかく今日のこの展示にこぎつけたということはあります。先輩後輩含めて、町の方もこの展示にお見え、あるいは様子を見に駆けつけてくださったこと、大変感謝いたします。どうもありがとうございます。話を町家に収束しなければいけないですが、ちょっと一つだけ今日の作品も含めてですね、広見と町家に関心があるというその経過はわかって頂けたと思うんですが。少し芸術学的な側面からお三方のおっしゃったことも踏まえて一つ二つまあまとめて言う形で申しあげたいと思うのですが、ちょっと古い地図を持ってきたけど、金沢の古地図というものが玉川図書館にあるので、関心ある方はぜひ見に行って頂きたいんですけど、そういうのを見ますとね、町家って本当に犀川のこっち側方なんかにはほとんど無いんですよ。犀川はだって城下町二つの川の間にこう人の住む町空間が広がっているんですね。江戸中期から戦前までが金沢の町の中の町家が、安定して展開していった好機であろうという風に思われます。で、その町家が進展していく中で生活空間共同体として、いろんな形での協力体制が今で言えば何でしょうね、何とか校区という呼び方がありますよね、学校単位での地域連帯がすごく強い町だし、思うんですが、そこの空間の要所要所に広見と呼ばれる空間ができてきたらしいんですね。これはあの前期皆さんと文献なんかを読んで、坂本先生がまぁ基本的に文献を持ってきて下さったんですが、まだまだ研究が進んでなくて、というか進みにくくてですね、なかなかわかりにくい。いつからできて、いくつあって、何のためにどんな形して、全てがはっきりとはでないんですが、私から見ると今でもこの町に確然とそれは存在しているんですよ。で、そのことは焼けなかったからそれが生きているかどうかはともかく、空間として存在するんですね。ということは、かつてそれをそこを必要とした人間がそれを利用し、そして今でもそれが保存されているということは、何かしら非常に人間の基本共同体として基本になるものと繋がるものを、そこに秘めているんだろうと今も私は思っている。で、この町家を今ここで話している町家はそばに広見が無くて、これからこの町家はどこの広見と繋がってたかというのは、私的の問題として今投げかけられているんですが、町家自体ひとつこう話を戻しますと、今日本の家を取り上げている本を見ますと、木と漆喰でできた家が最高という一つの価値観がありますよね。町家はまさにそうなわけです。木と漆喰と紙と、もう一つなんですか土間ですか、そういう生の素材でできている。かつ生きた人間が生活するにおいて基本的な生活とそれから社会共同体としての必要な空間ですね、そういうものを全部備えてきたもの、ですからそこで皆さんが展示、すごい直感力を美大の方は、今日の作品には反映されていると思うんですね、つまり素材そのものをいかにこの素材で、そのものでそれを、素材を基本にして人間が作り上げてきた空間の中で活かせるかということを、ぴたっとこう直感的に今日何人かの方がおっしゃったと思うんですが、こういう風になるとすぐ陰影礼賛とか言うんですが、そこまで抽象化しなくてもいいですけど、私これ、あの結構駄目だと思うんですよね、もうちょっとね光そのものに敏感になって頂けるそういう空間だと思う、素材そのものは皆さんの作品の質をあらたに問い、そして作品を作らせたようにですね、かつての人間空間の光が作品をもう一つこう浮かび上がらせる力になると思うので、光そのものをもう少し、あの昔に帰ればいいという風には全然思っていません、今もこの空間にふさわしい光って何だろうと考えて頂ければ。今の美術館ってホワイトキューブと言われていますよね。そうじゃなくてこの町家が町家の素材空間と呼んだらいいようなそこにふさわしいような光と作品、それを人間に回帰していく、素材に回帰していくそういう空間。非常にこれから可能性のある、自然を大事にしてお子さんたちを大事に、幼いお子さんを育てていらっしゃる天徳院さんのあの作品、あれ見てびっくり仰天ですよね。おのずとそういう感性が養われて、そういう生活空間にいることでああいう作品ができるんだという実例を先に見せられてしまったような。あの方々がみんな美大に来ていただければどんなに良いかと思うのですが。ちょっと最後はとりとめも無い感じではありますが私の実感です。いい作品を見せて頂いて本当にありがとうございました。

高橋先生—高橋です。僕もいっぱい話あるんですが、手短に最後に話をさせていただくということにしますが。その今まで皆さんのお話なんかも含めてですけど、作品と空間、具体的には町家が空間になるわけでしょうけども、そのあと環境と人間みたいな、入れ物とその中身みたいな簡単に言えばそういうことになると思うんですけど、まあ相互に関係しあっている問題ですよね。個人的に僕が思うには、なんていうかぁ文脈の中でメタがどう成立するかみたいな問題で、ずっと個人的には思ってるんですけど。まぁこう言うとまたちょっと面倒くさそうな話なんですが、どういうことかと言いますと、昨日、坂本先生なんかに一緒についてきて、作品の搬入を見てたんですけど、町家のその並びっていうのは本当にこうなんていうのかな〝まちや〟っていう全体がこの町家のメタ、メタというのは超越ということで、超越の反対は内在というか、ともかく〝まちや〟なんですね。何をやろうとその中で見ると町家にしか見えない。で、あのポスターが今日はちょっと大きめのポスターありますけど、昨日は小さいパンフレットとかを貼ってただけですよね。あれを貼ってただけじゃちょっと何をやっているのかわからないというか、それこそ町家のパワーが強くてですね、例えばこのホワイトボードがあるので、ここに手書きでいいから、やってますとかって書けばどうかとか昨日思ったんですけども、多分それを書いてみても外から見ても町家に埋没してしまうというか。妙な町家の、町並みというか寺町の力があるなあと昨日の段階では思ってました。今日見るとわりともう少し、そこにイーゼル風ななんかあれで看板が出ていて。まあメタの話に戻るとそのメタっていうのはつまり、作品、一個作品があるとしますよね。作品があることとそれ自体とそれからその作品が作品ですよとアピールしている、そのアピールがメタなわけですよ。で、この展覧会、展覧会の会場ですよとアピールしているそういう要素が昨日の段階で見つからなかったんですけど。もう町家のパワーにおされている。今日はまあある程度何ていうのかな、これだけ人がいれば外からまあ何かやってるなとまあわかるでしょうけど。そういう何か作品ですよというようなものが、どんな風に成立するのかというか。美術館というのは基本的に作品を作品ですよという風に見せるシステムだろうと思うんですけど、それで抽象的な話のように見えますけども、これ多分具体的に一個一個の作品についてそういうことが、皆さんの作品について言えるかなぁと、そういうことを今日はとりあえず大雑把なこととしては思ってました。畳の部屋で作品を鑑賞しようとするというのは、こう普段やっぱり立って作品を見るということが多いと思うんですけど、座って作品見るみたいなこと、実はちょっと二週間くらい前に大阪でも同じような民家で展覧会をやっていてたまたま出張がてら行ったんですけどそこでも畳の上に座って、作品のレベルはもちろんこちらの方がはるかに高いと思いますけど、その時にも感じたんですけど。一つだけいいのが大阪にもありましたけど。とりあえずそのことと、後もう一つは太田先生の最後の話と同じなんですけども、天徳院幼稚園の子供たちの絵画にはびっくりしたということを付け加えさせて頂きました。まあそんなところです。

司会鈴木――ありがとうございました。先生方、天徳院の和尚さんありがとうございました。それではこれをもちまして、シンポジウムを終了したいと思います。

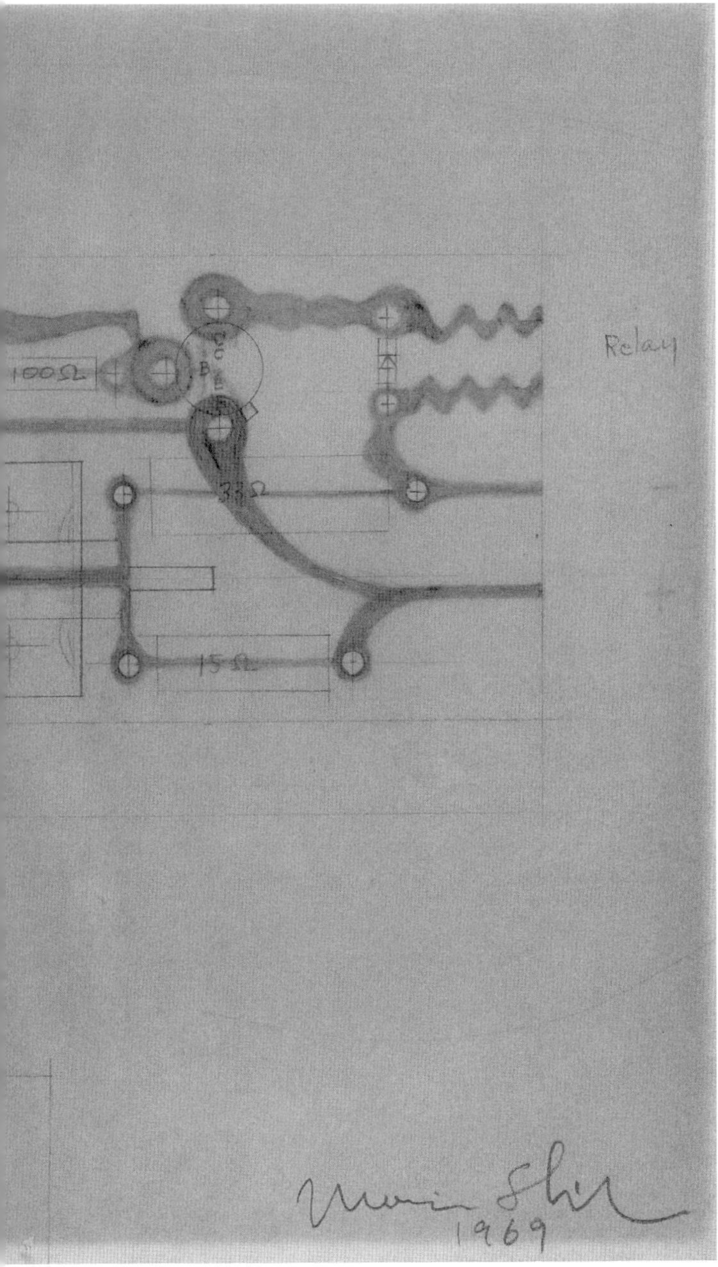
Relay
C
B
E
100Ω
33Ω
15Ω
1969

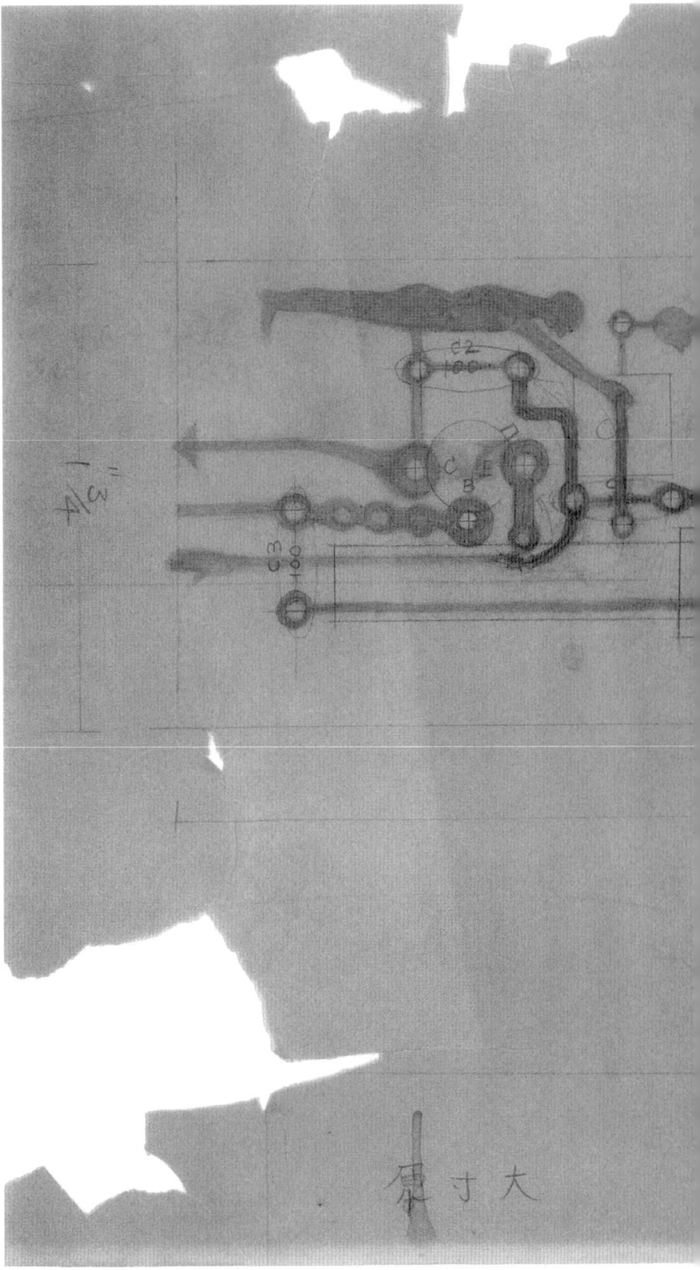
原寸大

Who's who in Tsukuba

筑波大学芸術学系教授　篠田守男

新治村の山林1000坪を取得、新治彫刻プロジェクトとして工作物を構想。9月上旬にはモデル完成。イギリスのトランス・ワールド・インターナショナルのテレビ部門が終日撮影に。

愛車　ポルシェ歴25年　血液型　AB型

作品の所在　ほとんど欧米の美術館。近隣では国立近代美術館（竹橋）、東京都美術館、宇都宮市の栃木県立美術館に

■快適性とは

クーラーがまず嫌い。暑いときには汗を、寒いときはガクガタ震えてという生活。公務員宿舎のセントラルヒーティングはめったに使わない。

■密閉度

アルミサッシュとコンクリートの建物では、冬場閉めてしまうと、外で何が起こっているかも。

■隙間風

東京では、木造の古い家。隙間風は入るわ、雨が降れば音がするわ。そういう生活が僕にとって夢。

■土地

この年になるまで、自分の土地を持ったことなし。いつ自分がその環境から離れるかもしれないという思いから。

■ギリギリの線

しかし、あと五十年生きられるかどうか。もうどこでもいい、とにかく自分の世界を実現して、たとえ五年でも十年でもそこで生きたい。

■新治プロジェクト

山林はそのままへ地上二十メートルに彫刻としての工作物をつくり、そこに文字どおり自然と共棲して住もうと。

■アイディア

ここで僕が営む日常が、ひょっとしたら、世界中の人々に、何かのアイディアを提供するのでは。

■アイデンティティ

僕が生まれたころ、目黒にもまだど

ぷ川があった。蝉が取れた。柵のない崖っぷちがあった。怪我もした。小さいときから、ここは危険だと発見しながら育った。

■今や

余りに便利。自分にとって何が危険かがわからなくなつているのでは

■父

長野県生まれ。昔、庄屋までやった農家の次男坊というと、まず養子に。

■母

岐阜県生まれ。五歳ぐらいで東京に出、その後父と一緒に。

■その長男

母方の姓。岐阜に行くと篠田姓は結構たくさんある。

■兄弟

四人。二番目と四番目が日支事変のころ、薬もくになくて、肺炎で夭折。

■五歳下

三男は、僕の影響で武蔵野美術学校を出、グラフィックデザイナーとして、一人前。東京で僕よりはるかに稼ぐ。

■勤労動員

中学生時代、旋盤で、零戦の足を削

る。

■父の死

終戦の一カ月後、僕の十四歳のとき、腸チプスか何かで。四十五歳。

■遺言

これからは英語の時代になる、とにかく英語の学校へ行けと。

■柱

母親が働き、僕は中学から大学まで、食糧の買い出しや炊事で母親を助けた。

■生活感

日本が負けてこれからどうなるという時、夢などなかった。窮乏生活も当たり前という……

■英文学

イギリス文学専攻、チョーサーを選んで一応卒業論文まで書いたが。

■中退

英語がしゃべれるどいうだけで、ちゃほやされた時代。これじゃ自分はだめになると。

■バイト

講和条約前、多少でも英語ができると、いい働き口あった。通産省終戦連絡部で、法案を英訳して司令部の

許可をとる仕事があり、雇員として
その事務に当たった。

■講和成立後

そのセクションはなくなったが、雇員でも公務員だから首にできない。ジェトロ（海外貿易振興会）への配属を密かに望んでいたが、上司が勝手に産業工芸試験所へ。

■図書館

試験所は、世界じゅうの研究者や作家を呼んで講演会を開き、一般の人に普及するのが目的だった。図書館には、アート、デザイン関係で最先端の世界じゅうの雑誌が全部。——
必死で事務を片づけ、もっぱら図書館に。

■みそっかす

周りには、芸術家や建築家が一杯。職員の八〇%が、千葉大工学部の図案科か今の芸大出身。見よう見真似で遊ばせてもらっているうち、その道に。

■好奇心

見ていることは好き。今でも、工事現場など一時間見ててもあきない。

■コンペが山ほど

デザインという言葉がない時代。日本が戦争に負けて金稼ぎをするには、日本のものをよその国に売って儲けるしかない。通産省では輸出振興策をメインのプロジェクトとして押し出し、地方の物産会、工業会は、競って賞金を出して図案を募集。

■賞金

黒板に貼られた賞金額は、一等五万円、二等が三万円、まず僕の給料に匹敵する額だった。

■三等専門

専門家たちは必死で一等を。僕は小遣い稼ぎで三等狙い。コンスタントに毎月一つは。

■意匠部へ

部長さんから、「お前は学校は違うけれども、才能がある。おれのところに来い」と。

■初めて本職の触強

それまでは外部で見ていただけ。システマティックにものを見ていない。「こんなの図面じゃない」と係長に怒られながら、基礎をたたきこまれた。

■仕事

自分で設計したものを持って、秋田とか山形に行き、職人さんに試作品をつくってもらう。それをさらにモダンに、外国へ輸出できるように再設計して彼らのためにプロモート

■一九六〇年代

彫刻を始めて五、六年の頃、発注芸術家と言われたことも。イメージが再現できれば、自分の手を経なくてもいい。図面を書いて、必要なところは鋳物屋さんなどに発注。できてきたものを、僕はただ組み立てるだけ。

■六畳一間

みんながアトリエを持っている時代、下宿に図面テーブル一つで、アトリエも機械も道具も必要としなかった。

■アメリカ出張

半分視察みたいなもの。大体、部課長が。ところが、語学ができない、家族と離れて異国の地でノイローゼになる。一方、向こうからは、もっと若い人で語学力があるのを寄越さないと勉強にならんじゃないかとクレーム。

■テスト

「じゃ、だれでもいい、我と思わん者は手を上げよ」と。僕も、だめでもともとと図々しく。外人の先生が来て、会話から何からやったら僕がトップ。たった一人選ばれて渡米。

■シカゴ美術学校

世界的な美術館の中で、本物を見ながらの授業。ものすごい勉強になった。

■恩師

ない。むしろ環境が。

■酒歴

親父は一滴もだめ。母親は、お屠蘇でひっくり返るほど。僕も、学生のころは全然飲んでいない。お役人になった途端に飲まされた。特にデザインのほうに配属されてから。

■マイペース

深酒もしないかわり、宴会でも必要以外は飲まない。ただ、飲みたいときは、ウィスキー一本ぐらいすぐ。

■節度

飲まないときは、一週間一滴も。頭で決めないで、飲みたくないときは飲まない、食べたくないときは食べない。節度正しい生活はだめ。

■胃腸が丈夫

翌日に持ち越すことはまずない。一晩寝るともうカラッと。

■落ち込んだら

自宅に籠もって、地球上で、こんなおれみたいな運の悪い男はいないと、飲まず食わずで、二日でも三日でも考えこむ。「結構底までいっちゃうと、翌日普通であってもね、きのうよりはいいやみたいなところがあって」

■タバコ

ピースのライト、一日八十本。前は、両切りの缶ピーだった。「今、どこへ行っても売ってないから。かといって、害のあるものを一年分まとめて缶で買っておくというのもね」

■夢

新治プロジェクトとして私設の美術館ができたら、死ぬまでに一回でいい、世界じゅうの美術館にある自分の大型の作品を一堂に並べてみたい。

■無題

作品には番号のみ。写実ならともか

く、抽象の場合、題名をつけると、先入観をもって見られる。

■番号順

ただ、順番に。今構想中の作品は5801。

■著書

『快楽宣言』(南天子画廊出版部)——一九七二年、日本で初めて個展をやったとき。

■老眼鏡

若いときは、遠視。四十過ぎたら急に度が進み、眼鏡なしではいられないほどに。母親は八十五歳で矍鑠。眼鏡もかけずに新聞を。

■健康

「病院に一泊したいという願望があるくらい」

■一冊の本

芥川龍之介『侏儒の言葉』

■示唆を受けた人

ヘンリー・ミラー、バクミンスター・フーラー。

■好きな言葉

哲学者エピキュールの「苦痛こそ快楽」

■快楽

怖いというのは快楽。怖いというものがないと、避けるという概念も生まれない。今まで日本人は貧しかったから、今みたいに全部コンピューターで快適にという時代を迎えた。しかし、いつかは、自分で体を動かさないと生活できないようなことを考えるようになる。だだ、人間は、社会が変わるほど長生きできない。やはり自分でやるよりほかは……。

■妥協

生活の場では八〇%までは妥協。ただ、それで終わっていくのはあまりにも寂しい。やはり僕なりの世界が……。

■筑波大教授

構成専攻。総合造形コース。英語でプラスチック・アート・ミックスドメディア。今までは彫塑、石彫、木彫とか素材で分かれていたが、メディアそのもので分けようと。

■学生の卒後は

芸術家に。あるいは、電通のような代理店、デザイン関係の会社。建築関係とか、美術館の学芸員にも。

「筑波の友」第39号（1989年10月15日発行）

Porsche

風を切るから柔らかい造形「ポルシェ356」。

ポルシェ356――奇妙な疼きが腹の底から湧いてくるのを男なら感じるに違いない。この車が生まれた頃男たちが求めていたのは、単なるスピードではなかったらしい。未完成のメカニズムに見る不思議な美しさ、時代の匂い。あらためて人の心をくすぐる。

現在、シュツットガルトのポルシェ本社中枢では、超需要の車を作るか否かで結論が出ないでいる。超需要とは文字通り生涯壊れない車である。設計はすべて完了して、ゴー・サインを待つばかりなのだが、これが完成すると当然収入減になるのは明らかである。

しかしその前向きな姿勢が私は好きだ。わが国でも古来〝使い込む〟という考えがあり、長い年月を経て使い込まれたものはその商品価値をも高める。昔嫁入り衣装の打掛は絹をしなやかにするために、嫁入り前から寝間着として使用し、嫁入り当日には、美しい艶を出すといわれていた。製品の完成というのは、それが製造されたときよりも、使い込まれて完成に近づくともいえる。

私のポルシェ３５６ＳＣ１９６４は26年を経て益々完成に近づいている。そして20数年も生活を共にしていると、肉体化して完全に身体の一部となってしまっている。

その後９１１Ｔ１９７２の中古を入手したが、さりとて肉体の一部を切り離す訳にもいかず、２台になり、更には１９８４年９１１カレラによって3台になってしまった。こうなると子どものようなもので離れることができない。普通の車のように年毎に人相が変わらないところが誠に有難い。20年30年と乗っていると、旧い写真などにふれるとき思い出もひとしおだが、自分だけ老いていくのをみるとゾッとする。学生時代に乗せてあげた教え子など再会すると、もう、すっかり家庭をもって子どもなどがいたりして、タイプ・スリップしてしまったようで、数え子も自分の子どもと車を見比べて奇妙な感傷にひたるのである。

また、植物が人間に反応するように車も数十年も共にしていると反応をしめす。聞こえる所で、〝この頃衰えたかな〟とでも言おうものならすぐ反応し、フケが悪くなったりする。読者は信じられないかもしれないが、何度も遭遇しているのは事実である。

篠田守男（筑波大学芸術学系教授）

1000字の伝言板

幻想の「空奇館」。
彫刻家・篠田守男

ここ数年来、自分の住処（すみか）について考えています。住居は、個人の住宅といえども様々な制約、法的な規制があります。そして、個人の住生活や家族構成によるプライベートな制約によってもがんじがらめに縛られています。私のような、いわゆる家族、家庭というものを持たない、また将来も持つことはあり得ないという人間にとっても、家を建てようと思うと、住宅という一般概念にとらわれて、制約に対する妥協点をスタートに選んでしまいがちです。

原点は、私一人が生きるために完全に機能する住処。しかもそれが生涯にかけて何よりも快適であらねばならないという原則論をふまえて、幻想のように頭の中で構築していって出来たのが「空奇館」という住宅であります。奇妙な空間を持つオブジェ的住宅といいましょうか、住めるという機能を持つ彫刻といいましょうか、そんな意味あいを託して付けた名前なのです。自分の空間的欲望と、肉体に見合った最小限の運動量を必要とする構造と、感覚的自然ではなく物理的自然ともあえて共存するという三つの観点から個条書きしていったものを組み替え、組み合わせという作業を何度も通過させて、気がつくとこのような奇妙な家が出来上がっていました。

さて、皆様をこの空奇館へ御案内いたしましょう。車で北土浦というＩＣを降りると筑波山の右手の山の中腹に薄い萌黄色の館が見えるはずです。車を降りられて50メートルも行くと村道がふたてに分かれる交点の林が空奇館の入り口です。一歩林にふみいると白い50段ほどの階段がそびえ立っています。これは、どうしても登って頂かなくてはなりません。それも最小限の運動の一つであるからです。ただ、お気をつけ頂くのは、最初の階段幅が3メートルに対して上段で1メートルと狭くなっていることです。上段までで高さ8、9メートルはあり、手すりがありませんので落ちたら命の保証はありません。登りきったところで、階段として独立させるためと次の運動量の消化の目的で、母屋へのアプローチとの間に50センチの隙間を設けてあります。これは私が80歳を迎えた時にどうにか飛べるであろう距離を算出したもので、この寸法の決定に一番苦心しました。老化して飛べなくなった時、橋桁の下に住む浮浪者のように家を失ってしまうからです。さあ、思いきって飛んでください。アプローチのほうは3メートル幅がありますので落ちることはありません。思いきって飛んでくださ い。アプローチのほうは3メートル幅がありますので落ちることはありませんのでご安心ください。建物に向かって、このアプローチも先細になっています。これはまわりの自然を充分に満喫して頂くために遠近法を利用して距離を長く見せています。お帰りの節は逆に短く感じるはずです。途中左手に茶室のにじり口のような小さい入り口がありますが、この建物は私の作品とコレクションを展示した私設の美術館です。もしその方面に興味のある方はぜひご覧くださ い。ここでは隙間が1メートルとなっていますが、にじり口のうわてに手をかけて懸垂の要領でひとふりすれば、館のポーチに降りられます。もし、し損じてもここまでくると地面が3メートルとの高さですし、下にはプッシュもありますので、ちょっと足をくじくぐらいですみます。中は吹き抜けで、金属パイプが天井から床まで走っていますので、これを滑り降りてください。ただし、戻りもこのパイプを利用して頂く以外に出口がありませんので、体力に自信のない方はご遠慮ください。この建物は空間として私が最も力を注いだところで、内部の局面をトポロジカルに設計してあり、床に立たないといとこの不思議な空間は見えてこないのです。もう、ここまで来られれば、母屋は問題ありません。恐怖と運動量は反比例して増減するから、馴れによってあなたのエネルギーは増すはずです。最後になぜこんな家を作ったかといいますと、私にとって生活は恐怖であり、快楽であり、肉体や精神の研鑽の場でもあり、なによりも便利、合理をとりのぞき、夏は暑く冬は寒い生活をしたかったからなのです。

「翼の王国」（全日空）１９８８年６月

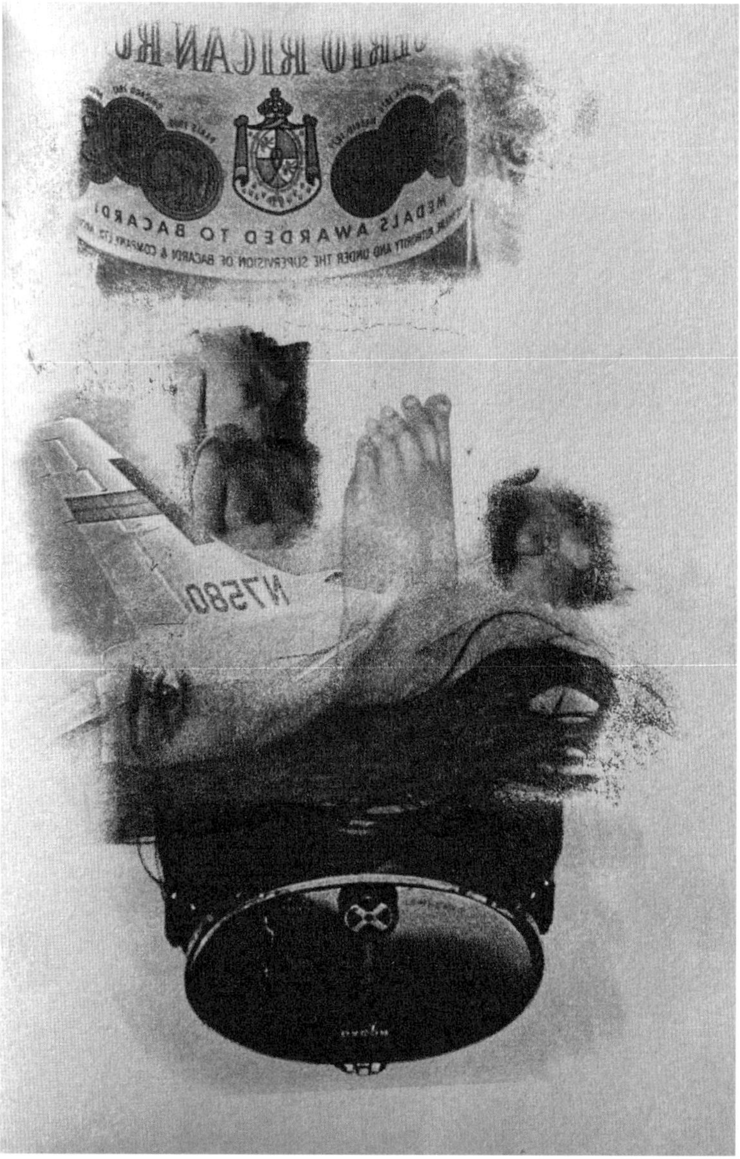
MEDALS AWARDED TO BACARDI
N7580

田園散歩

あのモニュメントは、昭和41年の田園都市線開通記念として制作したものです。当時、人々の関心は月に向かっていて、これからの時代を予感して「宇宙ファミリー」をテーマに制作にとりかかりました。ちなみに、人類が初めて月面に立ったのは、それから3年後のことです。

以前は、いまロータリーになっているところが池で、その池の中に50メートルくらいを埋め、夜、水中に照明をあてて小波が立つとモニュメントが光るという発想でした。ところが管理が大変というこどもあり、駅前にショッピングセンターができたときに池を小山にして、イチョウを植え、現在の形に造りかえたんです。

この作品は、10メートルもの高い作品をひとつの鋳物でこしらえるという、技術的にも画期的なものでした。12本造って、その中の6本がファミリーとして駅前に立っているわけです。

東急沿線・街の情報誌「THE GROWING」vol.9　1990年7月

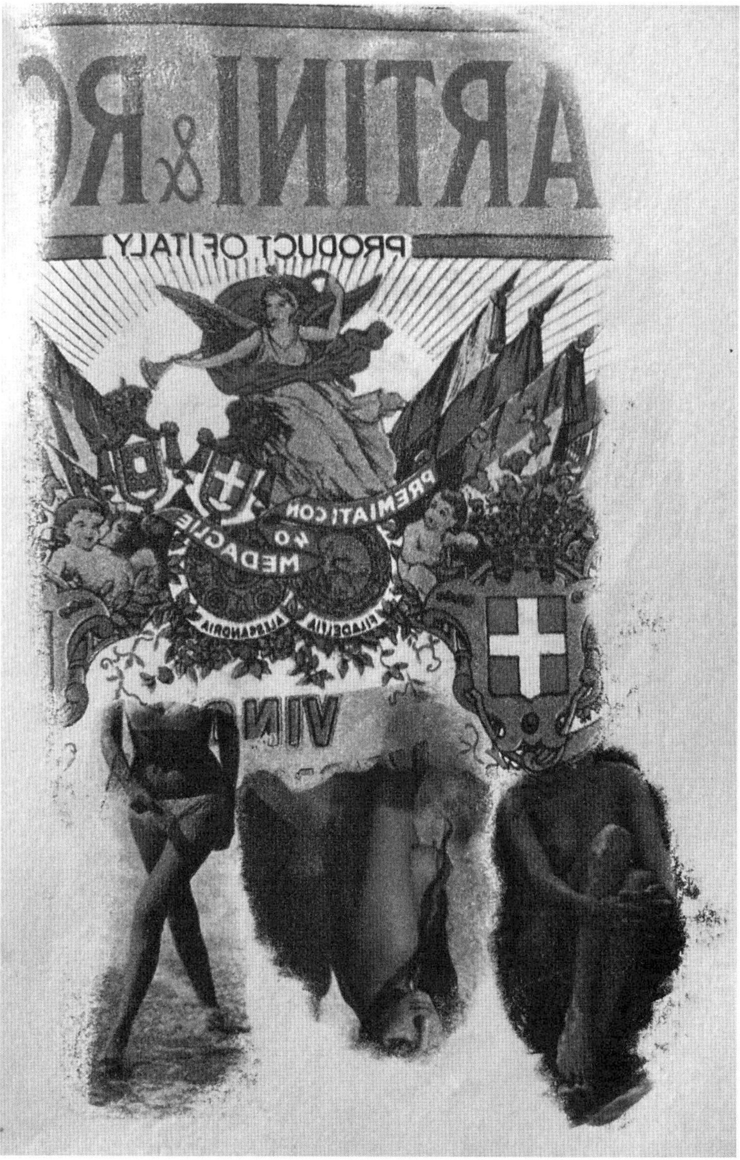
PRODUCT OF ITALY
PREMIATI CON
40
MEDAGLIE

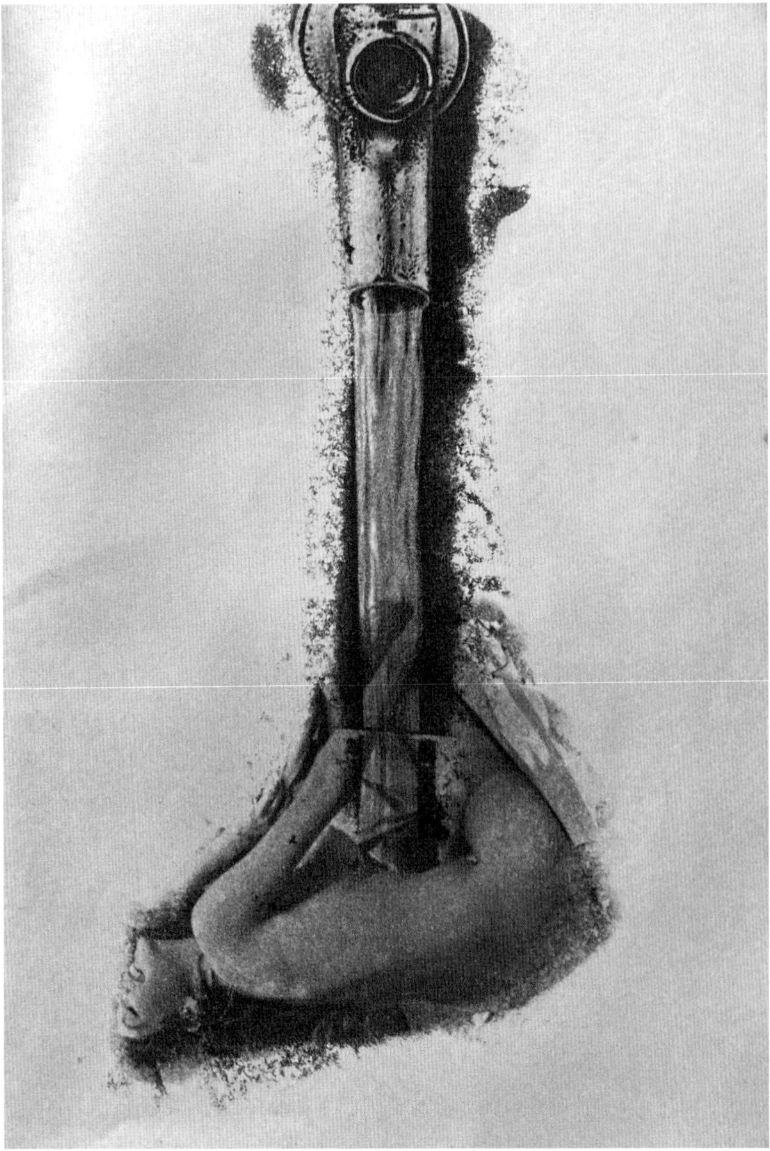

空間幻想

右利き左利きの空間

1950年代後半に住宅公団が、実験的に独身者向けの鉄筋コンクリートによる本格的なアパートを東横線の日吉につくったことがある。当時はアパートといえば木造2階建ての安普請と決まっていた時代であるから、コンクリート打放しの建築は相当モダーンなものなので、当時の若者の気を引くに十分であった。無理すれば初任給でどうにか入居できる範囲であったと記憶する。ただし3・5坪のワンルームでわずかな流し台とガス台にシングルベッド。バス、トイレは共同棟という、今でいえば刑務所のような作りであった。1棟5階建て100戸。競争率は結構高かったが私は見事当選して入居することになった。この種の同サイズのワン・ルーム・アパートは天井を支える支持壁と間仕切り壁が一つおきに配置され、この支持壁に設備が組み込まれるので、隣どうしは対象形にならざるを得ない。設備関係が右に位置するか左にあるかで空間がまるで異なるのである。正しくは空間感覚に相異がみられる。右利き、左利きにも関連がありそうだが、私には、左に設備、右がノッペリという空間が少なくとも数センチ広く感じられる。これはちょうど映画館に入ってリラックスする座席の位置が右よりだったりするのと共通する空間感覚かも知れない。

空間生活

私は戦後の40年間に日本で12カ所、アメリカで13カ所、住居を転々としたが、借家住まいにはそれなりの利点がある。特に私のような仕事では制作の内容に合わせて、該当する工場の近くに引っ越したり、必要な環境を求めて移転したりすることが多い。私は若い頃からボヘミアン的なところがあり、1カ所に定着してしまうのが、何か未来が薄まるようで転居を重ねていたような気がする。ひどい時は所番地が気にいって越したこともある。それに建物に神経質にならなくてもすむ自由さがある。アメリカの大学からいきなり招請がきてホイホイでかけられたのも持ち家のない根無し草の故である。

現在、私が住んでいるところは学園都市の公務員宿舎であるが、いわゆるブロック建築ではなく瓦屋根の2戸建て2階建てで、リビングとダイニングが4段のスキップ・フロアーで高いほうの天井は5メートルという吹き抜けになっている。このわずか4段の高低差が住むものにどれ程の有効空間と安らぎを与えてくれるか計り知れないものがある。お役人の設計にしては大拍手を送りたい。このように作りに変化があると面白いのは、外観は何十軒もまったく同じ作りではあるのだが、住んでいる人間の家族構成にもよるが、同じ公務員で何故にかくも違うかと思わせるほど異なるのである。

これは家具の趣味とか物の多少とかによる違いではなく、空間が異なるのである。物の置かれ方、色彩の扱われ方等によって同じ体積を持つ空間が変化してしまうのである。これを私は空間コミュニケーションと呼んでいるが、人は生活を始めると無意識のうちに自分なりの空間をつくりあげている。カニは甲らに似せて穴を掘る。

ハンガリー生まれの画家、彫刻家、デザイナーであったモホリ・ナギは「空間は人間の感覚体験のリアリティであり、空間の知覚は人間の生理的機能である」といったように住宅内部の空間も住んでいる人間に左右される。住みごこちの良さとはこの空間を個人的に、積極的に取り入れることだと思う。ドイツの心理学者メッツガーは平面に対して高さ寸法は4分の1短くすることによって同じに見える、と証明している。これは実際の空間より4分の1余分に利用できるということである。空間も重力に支配されるのか?さらに色、パターン、形状等の心理学的空間利用を加味することによって住宅空間も相当変化させることが可能になると思われる。

『S&E』No7　1990年秋　三井不動産パンフ

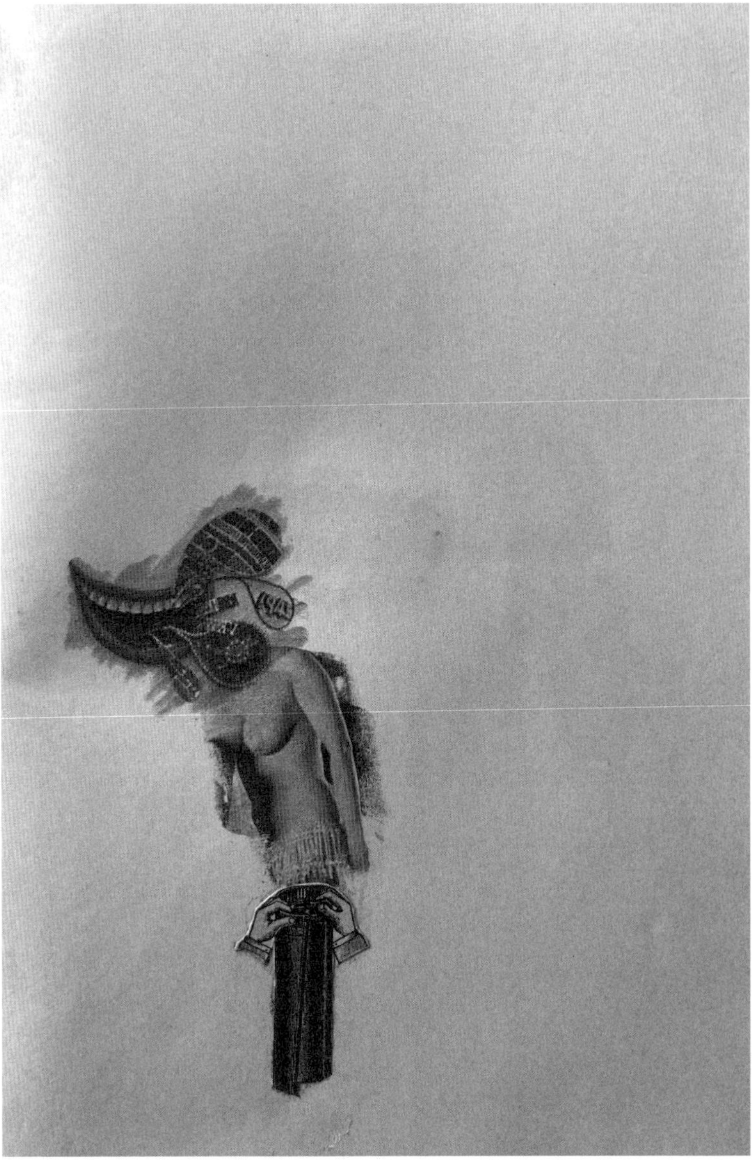

インスピレーション

91年7月24日〜8月31日

「篠田守男・ドキュメント展」

〈純粋彫刻〉を生み出すアート思想

日本の代表的彫刻家・篠田守男氏。一貫して発表し続ける吊り構造を取り入れた金属彫刻『TC（テンションとコンプレッション）』を通じて、氏のアートに対する姿勢や思いを、作品の良き理解者である中原洋氏と語っていただいた。

特別対談　篠田守男×中原洋

繊細な触覚でいち早く時代を読むアーティスト

中原：篠田さんは、バックミンスター・フラーの影響を受けたとおっしゃっていましたが、ニューヨークで出会ったコレクターが言っていたことで、実は僕もそう思っていることがあるんです。「アーティストの側にいると、彼等がどういうふうに時代を変化していくかということを一番早く捉える人達だ」と彼女が言ったんですね。そこでフラーという人を考えると、彼は〈宇宙船地球号〉で、地球の未来を読んだ人だと思うんです。篠田さんは、それをアーティストという世界の中に持ち込んで、一番先鋭的に表現したんじゃないかと、勝手に思っているいるんですよ。地球上で暮らす人間の社会関係にはバランスがありますよね。そのテンション、緊張関係のような危ういバランスみたいなものを、60年代に捉え、表現したのが篠田さんじゃないかなと思っているんです。

篠田：60年代に、ダリがまだ元気な頃「自分の髭は宇宙からのアンテナだ」と言ってる時代があったんですよ。その時にたまたま僕の作品を見て「篠田のテンションは、一種の俺のアンテナに近いよ。」とある雑誌で語ったというのを聞いたことがあるんです。奇しくも今中原さんが言われたアーティストは触覚を持っているのというのと、ダリが髭をはやしたというのと共通して面白いなと、ふっと思い出しましたね。

中原：ウィリアム・ウェグマンというアーティストがいるんですが、彼のペインティングは全部死滅した生物の絵なんですよ。彼はコンセプチュアルアーティストなんですが、ある種のエコロジストだなと思ったんです。エコロジストという言い方は正しくないですが、今の状況の中で、地球がどういう風に変わっていくか。人間は死滅していくのではないかみたいなね。そういうところへまで彼は考えているように思えるんです。アーティストの仕事というのは、そういう未来を読む触覚だというところがかなりあるんだと思うんですよね。

篠田：僕の場合は、人の巡り合いが非常に運がよかったなと思うんです。マックス・エルンストにしても、メレット・オッペイハイム、バックミンスター・フラーといったある時代時代のパイオニア的存在の方に会ったことが、非常に刺激になり、自分の中で栄養になっていますね。フラーの講演から発想した58年の作品が、テンションのスタートなんです。パオロ・ソレリからも影響を受けましたね。彫刻家や美術家から受ける刺激というのは、50年代で私の中ではすでに終わっていて、それ以降はフラーから始まって、ほとんど建築ばかり見てましたね。アメリカ初期の、ルイス・カーンとかエーロ・サーリネンとかほとんどアメリカ中を駆けずり回っていたことがあったんです。

中原：かつて建築というのはアートと一体となって存在していたと思うんですよね。1920年代のニューヨーク・アール・デコの建築というのは、エントランスを入っていくと、彫刻があり、壁画があって、「あっ、美しい」と思ってしまう。だけど、今の建築を見ていて、必ずしもアートとマッチしているとは思えない。あの辺までが、建築とアートが一番幸せにきた時代なのかなと。

篠田：I・M・ペイの1982年の講演で、彼と4人のアーチストが共同企画で進めている建物のプロジェクトの説明があったんです。建物は私、インテリアはあなたということではなくて、D・フレヴィンというアーチストも参加していたんですが、彼が光りを使ってこうしたいという提案をし、それをもとにして建築家が、そのためにはこういう部屋が必要だというような、同時にスタートして進めていくんです。中から外へ広がっていく。

中原：非常に珍しい企画ですよね。なかなか興味深い。

篠田：私の場合だと、既に建物は出来ていて、それにくっつける、いわゆるモニュメントですね。今度の展覧会のパンフレットにも書いたことですが、モニュメントって一体なんだろうということが最近、特に今度の展覧会で一番疑問になっていることなんです。

作品自体がメッセージ、読み取る受け手側の問題

篠田：彫刻家が彫刻を作る姿勢と、モニュメントを作る姿勢とではどうも違うのではないかと。私は彫刻を作っている。たまたまそれが野外のモニュメントになるという結果論であって、作るときにあまり意識したくない。普通彫刻というモニュメントになってしまうので、今は純粋彫刻という言葉を分けているんです。

他の作家の彫刻の仕事を見ていると、モニュメントというのは大きな作品で、あとは小さい作品を個展かなにかで並べるというような、モニュメント自体が1つのテーゼを持っているような気がするんですよね。

中原：篠田さんが今回出店されているこの作品は、将来的には森の中に作りたいと言っておられましたが、その時に、篠田さんにはモニュメントのつもりはないわけ

ですよね。

篠田：そうです、ありません。

中原：自己充足してしまうんですよね、そこで。だからこそメッセージ性が持ち得るのかなと。意識的にメッセージ性を持つというのは結構難しい問題ですよね。そうなると、文章を書いてしまえばメッセージ性が出来ちゃうじゃないかということになる。

篠田：そうなんですよ。モニュメントと言ったときからメッセージを持っているんですよね。そうゆう余分なものは出来るだけ排除したいというところがありましてね。メッセージはいらない。作品自体がメッセージだと考えたいんです。

中原：結局アートというのは、作り手がこういうメッセージを持つとかこう思っているというのではなくて、読み手の側が必死になって読んでいくんですよね。読み込みの深さによって、読み手として長く生き延びるかどうかみたいなところがあると思いますね。

篠田：そうですね。読んでもらいたいです。タイトルをつけないのも、タイトルそのものが、メッセージになってしまうところがありますから、番号だけで通しているんです。

中原：篠田さんの作品を一つ持っているんですが、初めてアトリエを訪ねたときに、ずらっと並んだ作品の中で訳の分からないものがあったんですよ。箱が重なっているようなもので、巨大な建築物ののイメージがあったものですから、これをスケールアップすると航空母艦だよね、なんて言いながら見ていたんです。だけどどうしてこれが作品として成り立っているんだろうとふと考え始めたんですよ。明らかに作品として成り立っているんです。それで、ずーっと見ていて、あっ、そういうことかとわかったんです。2つの箱が接しないで、上の箱が宙に浮いているんです。それがどうしても奇妙に、情報発信しているというように見えるわけですよ。それでこれがいいと。

篠田：すごくうれしかったのは、その箱を認めた最初の人が中原さんだったんです。

だれもそれを芸術とは思わないんですよ。はっきり浮いているというものから移行している時代に作った作品だったんですが、浮いていること自体も普通は気が付かないし、仮に浮いているとしても、そんなものにあまり興味を持たれなかった頃なんです。

中原：ある種アートというのは読み取る側の積極的な姿勢を必要とするところもありますよね。

篠田：そうですね。こんなことがあったんですよ。カリフォルニアのある画廊で作品を見せるときに、テーブルの上にあった、紙をくしゃくしゃに丸めたものを手で払ったんですよ。そうしたらそれはチェンバレンの作品だったんです（笑）。その作品は５００ドルぐらいしたんですが、そのときにアートというのは、置き場所という問題もありますが、それよりむしろ受け手として、彼の発信しているイメージを受信できなかったということが、後々いろんなアーチストの作品を見るときに残りますね。逆に、手で払ってもいいような作品が美術館にあるために、錯覚して受信するということもあるかもしれませんね。美術館とか、メディアが確率していなかったら本当にアートなのかなと思うような作品はたくさんあるような気がするんです。

中原：美術館という場がアートを作っている、というのもありますよね。

篠田：私の場合は、場という問題は一切関係ないですね。今回初めて画廊という場ではなくこのヤマギワ・インスピレーションで発表したわけですが、画廊と違って空間に既成概念がないので自由にリラックスして展示できますね。これからも自由な空間、固定されていない空間でやりたいですね。

現代アートに要求されるもの

篠田：たまたま昨日新聞を読んでいたら、歌舞伎の世界でものすごい酷評を書いている人がいましたね。美術でもデザインでも、評価する場面でこういう表現が出てくればいいなとかねがね思っているんです。日本では酷評が少ないですよね。酷評されたからその作品がいいかどうかは逆に言うと分からないですからね。ニューヨークタイムズに昔ジョン・キャナディという学芸欄の記者がいて、叩くことのほうが多かったんですが、酷評されることによって、作家も反発するなり、育っていくと思うんですよ。日本の場合、新聞に出たというだけでそれは褒める．ことしかないでしょう。

中原：そうですね。私もフリーのライターとして書くことがありますが、かつて書評の仕事で酷評したことがあって、その原稿を書いているときは辛かったですね。書き終って渡す直前まで、ここまでは言っちゃいけないと書き直したり。だから書くほうは、プロは分かりませんが、私は七転八倒してますね。

しかし、アートの批評は読み間違いが絶対ありますね。篠田さんはご自分の評論は必ず読むほうですか。

篠田：評論をさっきのメッセージ論で言えば、自分の作品の紹介でも、受け手としてそれをもう一回文章を読むということはありますね。逆に書くほうは苦手ですね。書けないから作っているところはありますからね。タイトルさえ決められない(笑)。後から化粧をするようでいやなんですよ。

中原：見る側からすれば一番困るのは、タイトルに文学的表現が付くものですね。文学的なものが付くと、どうしてもそれに引っ張られるでしょう。この作品はそういう表現なのかなと思うケースが随分ありますよね。ただ篠田さんの場合は、〈Tension& Compression〉が手掛かりになりますね。

篠田：〈Tension & Compression〉は一番最初のタイトルなんですが、メッセージでも何でもなくて、持っている構造、サイエンスでいうと技術に当たるようものなんです。タイトルでありながらタイトルではないく、ましてや作品の総称ではない。その後タイトルはずっとTCのナンバリングなんです。

言葉遊びのようなものはよくやりますよ〝彫刻〟という言葉を20くらい書いておいて、ほかのメディアを片方に並らべるんです。たとえば「文学的彫刻」、「演劇的彫刻」のように。そうするとそこからまた面白い発想が出てくるんですね。その逆は全く出てこない。その可逆性が全くないところが面白いんです。「彫刻的文学」とか「彫刻的建築」は何の意味も成さない。この言葉遊びをやりすぎると、じゃあ彫刻って何だということになって、矛盾といえば矛盾なんですけれどね。

中原：彫刻の定義は結構ややこしいなと、特に建築関連の人と話をすると思うんです。ドイツ人の批評家と話をしたときに、「コルビュジエのサヴォイ邸は美しいね、あれはアートだ」というので私は「あれはアートではない」と言ったんです。それでもめましてね。「サヴォイ邸とそっくりなものをブロンズで作ってそこに置いてあったら美しいと思わないか」「プロポーションから言えば美しいと思う。でも、アートではない」。アートというのはある種のメッセージ性というか、作家のメッセージ性は少なくてもあると思うんです。それがないものはアートではないと思うんです。ヨーロッパでもいまだにそうなのかなと思うんですが、一番問題なのは、美しいものはアートであるという考え方なんです。少なくてもデュシャン以降、それは変わったと思っているんですよね。美しいものは必ずしもアートではない。ところが、建築かアートかみたいな事では、一緒くたになって存在していると思うんですね。もし篠田さんの〈TC5801〉が森の中に建てられたとき、すぐフォリーと言っちゃいますね。建築的だから。だけどそれじゃあこれはフォリーかと言うとフォリーにはならないだろうし、なってほしくない。フォリーの概念が、建築家が作った用途のないもの、ある種のメッセージ性、モニュメンタルなものを持ったものと定義されているような気がするんです。もしそうだとすれば、これがそうなってしまったらつまらない。

篠田：〈TC5801〉は、作りたいという夢だけでいつ実現するか分からないですね。そういう環境の中にこういうものが必要だというのではなく、私自身がこの中を歩きたいんです。床から何から彫刻で、その中で寝転がってみたい。建築とは全く関係なくて、どこまで大きくなってもこれは彫刻なんです。建築的でもないんです、彫刻そのもの。それを今盛んに、新しい言葉で純粋彫刻、純粋彫刻といっているんですがね。

中原：ほかのことに言われるのが嫌だからでしょう。建築家とアーティストが考え直して、新しいことをしたらもっと溢路があると思うんですよね。今回の都庁の場合、彫刻に合わせて上の壁を抜いてくれたという話を聞いて、そういうことを建築がやるだけナイーブなんだなと。それがもっと根本的なところから、スタートのところから始まるといいと思うんですよね。美しくなければアートではない、だけどコンセプトも見えなければだめだと思うんです。だから今現代アートに要求される要素というのはすごく大きいから作家はくるしいでしょうね。

篠田：メディアが広がっただけ余計苦しく成ったんですよね。だから悪く言えば何でもアートいう。たた呼ぶだけでアートになってしまう。

「WAVY」No22　1991年　ヤマギワ　パンフ

「語り出す鉄たち―今日の金属彫刻から―」

東京都美術館カタログ　篠田守男（１９３１―）

テンション彫刻を始めて30年以上になる。今ではテンションが脳の隅々にいきわたっていて半自動でコントロールされている。思考から日常生活にいたるまでテンションのボリュウムが上がってきて1、2ケ月のサイクルではほとんどといって良いくらい睡眠を必要としない。この1年間で5回の個展を開催し、3時間睡眠が固定化、というより肉体化してしまった。私にとってはこの時期の緊張の連続が緊張を緩和するという、はなはだ矛盾する論理になるのだが事実ゆえに致し方ない。

かつて、テンション構造に出会ったことから出発したかにある時期思っていたのだがもともと私の魂の中にあったのだろう。そこから出ずる緊張願望がテンション彫刻を作らせているように今では思っている。やわな地球、あやふやな人間、薄い人生、等々…。すべて肯定したうえで自分の精神と肉体にテンションをかけている。日常より非常、安定より不安定、正常より異常、を好むのもそれ自体を心地よしとするより、わきでるテンションを愛するに他ならない。その結果がこれらのテンション彫刻である。最後に良く質問される題名の有無であるが、これを付さないことによって作者以上に、鑑賞者に創造を委ねたいからである。

（1982年8月21日）

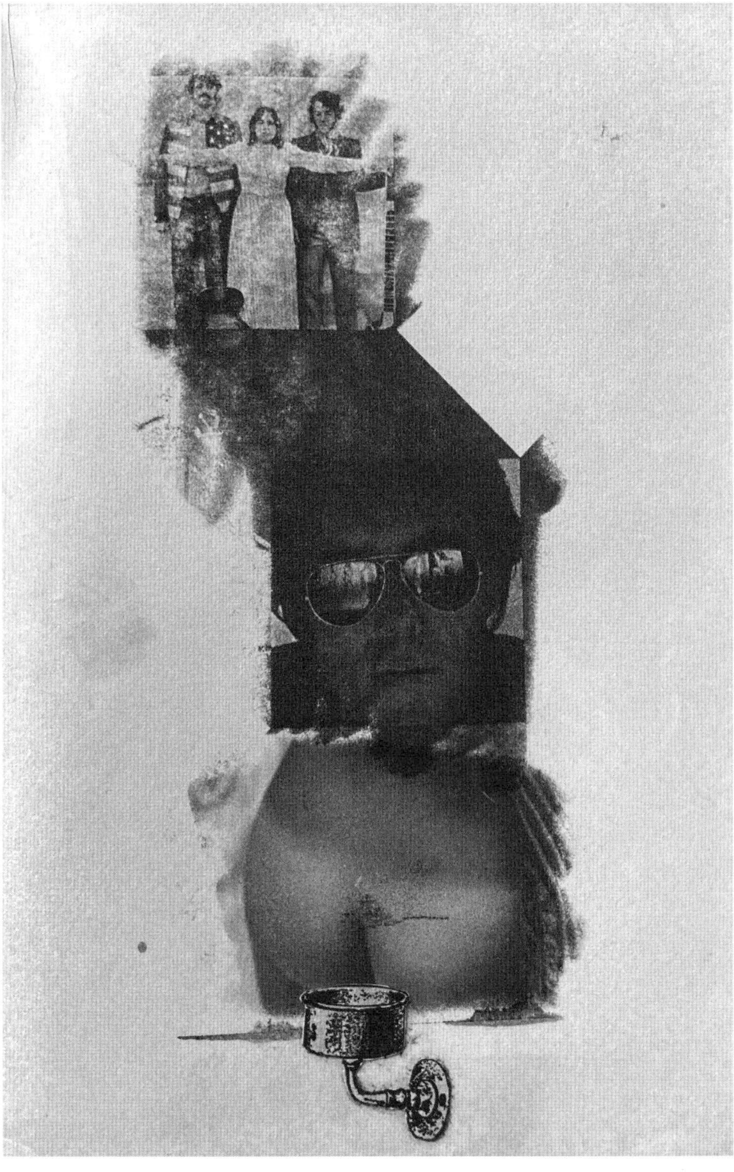

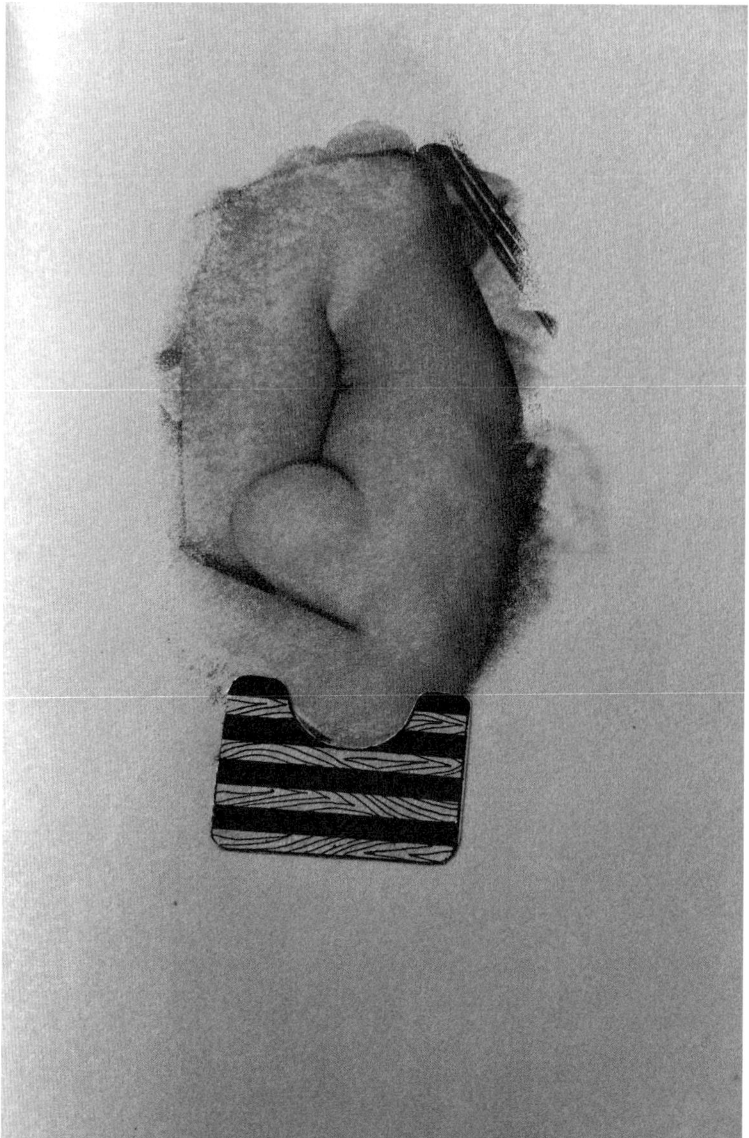

八ツ場ダム国際美術展(仮称)企画書

前原誠司国土交通大臣殿

私は約半世紀以上にわたって空間美術にたずさわってきました。1960年にはアメリカの大学の招聘を受け、カリフォルニア大学、コロラド大学、ミネソタ大学にて教授を歴任し、日本では武蔵野美術大学、筑波大学等に於て教鞭を務め、1985年にはアメリカ彫刻センターより東洋ではじめての美術教育者賞(年1名世界より選別)を受賞致しました。

1963年には師でありますバクミンスター・フラー先生(建築家・哲学者・宇宙船地球号の著者)の薫陶を受け空間造形とエコロジカルな作品を制作してまいりました。

この八ッ場ダムのニュースに触れ、中止となれば解体にするにも莫大な費用がかかると思われます。このままの設備を残し、この巨大な物体を美術、文化の場として再利用し、エコロジーとして世界を向けての発信基地にしたらと考えております。従って第1回は世界の著名な作家を招待すると同時に国際コンペを催し、展覧会を通して世界にうったえる手段としたら如何でしょうか。将来はエコロジーのコンセプトを軸とした美術館として世界に発信する。

私は10数年前の富山県入善町にある大正14年建設の北陸電力ダム発電所の建物のリニューアルにあたって発電所美術館の命名者であり、こけら落としの展覧会の作家でもあります。

発電所を再利用した美術館は英国ロンドンにあるテート・モダン美術館と富山の世界に2つしかない美術館です。以降10数年を経て世界から見学者がきております。

もしこのプロジェクトが完成したらギネス・ブックに登録されるような世界一のモニュメントを有する美術館となることは必定と思われます。

篠田守男+空間美術研究所

代表　篠田守男　筑波大学名誉教授

E C O · I · M

風呂

篠田守男

筑波大学名誉教授

彫刻家

入浴開始

ホームへ戻る

序論

論と名付けるには誠に一般性を持ち得ないが、私の長年の風呂との出会いと経験により、論とどうしても付したいのである。

従って風呂という言葉はどこに発生したのか。何故この風呂という文字をあてたのか。何処から風呂という言葉が由来したのか。風呂に入るという行動は何処の国の発明で何処からわが国に来たのか。はたまたわれわれの発明なのか。ならばいつごろであったか。一切不問とし、また調べる気も更々ない。以下に述べることとは、ただひたすらに私の個人的体験と身勝手な理論付けと、ある種の願望と誠に微少な妄想よりなるものである。ところが、わが家に尋ね来る友はこの一年で数十人に及ぶが、皆声をそろえてこの風呂と私の論を絶賛してくれるので可なりと信ずるのである。

まず妄想より述べれば、風呂は唯一この地球上で宇宙的感覚を得る、一つの手がかりではなかろうか。何故ならば最も手軽に何処の家庭でも、誰でも体験できるからである。無重力——これは私にとって妄想と同時に夢であり、それも物心ついたときからの、そして60数年たった今でも夢なのである。
更に私以外の数10人の人がすでに宇宙飛行の実体験をしており、私もと思う

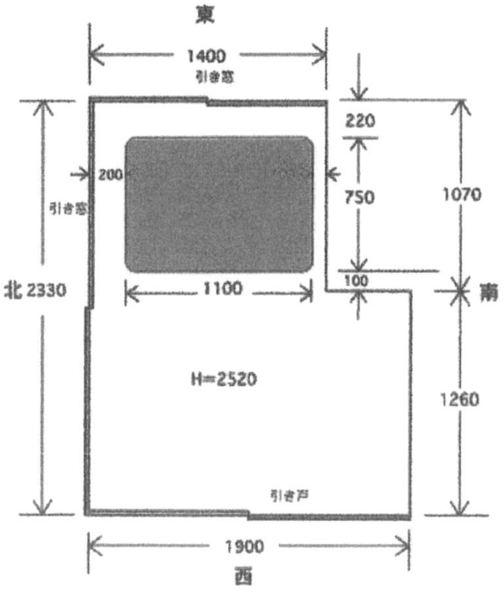

〈バスタブ〉
体積 =327,214,000・・
＜バスタブ設置状況＞
355・・床上、255・・床下
この物的空間は最小の空間であり、
望むればこれ以上が望ましい。
但しこのプロポーションで
拡大すれば良しとするものではない。
これはなかなか微妙なプロポーションで
１人で良し、２人で良し、
３人も物理的には可能であるが情緒が失われる。

のだが、この年齢と貧乏彫刻家では生存中の可能性は誠に薄いと思わざるを得ない。取り敢えずこのわずかな空間の中で疑似体験をせざるを得ない。それを読者に披露してこれを共有したいと思うのである。（南大門69号掲載）

前々号第69集において、燃えて風呂論のほんの序の口を披露したのだが、その後数年たち失念してしまった。改めて読み返して見れば、第1章風呂における物質的考察の第1節「物質的空間と量」のところで、重大なミスを発見した。寸法が異なっていたのである。小生がこの寸法にこだわるのも、後に続く風呂論が根底から崩れ去る恐れが生ずるからである。しばし読者がこの退屈な寸法に耳を傾けることを切に願う。しからば先ず風呂場と称する空間を以後御修正頂きたい。

（前ページ図参照）

第1章　風呂における物質的考察

精密主義をもって任ずる小生がこんな初歩的測量を見誤るとは情けないことであるが、実は空間とはその様に曖昧なのである。その曖昧な空間を１・２・３という様な整数で刻むこと自体が不遜なことなのだが、先ずはこの寸法に近い風呂場を読者に作ってもらわない限りこの風呂論も先へ進まないので――進まないと云うより単なる読み物とするとなんの面白みもなくなるので、この寸法的空間イメージを是非頭の中の引き出しにたたき込んで頂きたい。

さてここでやっと本論に入ることができる。

第1節　物質的空間と量

前回でも述べた如く、底部は冷たく上部は熱い。これによって下半身に極端な刺激が与えられ、当事者は屋外の景色を鑑賞するどころではない。当然目は下半身に注がれ、人によって個人差はあるが90秒も動かずにいれば冷たさと暖かさの差がなくなるはずである。余裕にたゆとう君のペニスを鑑賞できる。全ての静止の中でペニスのみがゆらゆらと。何故ならば一瞬の動きで初頭の冷水の洗礼を繰り返さなければならないからである。

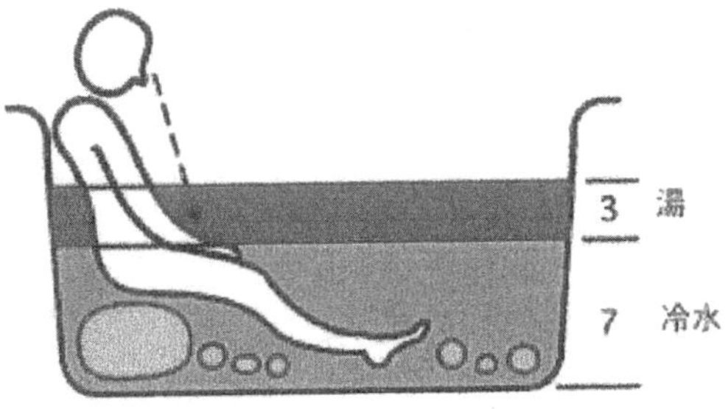

＊基準：327,214,000mm3 の冷水に対して、50℃の湯を 90 秒。

第2節　物理的考察からやや肉体と精神へ

第1節に於いて物質又は即物体というか質体というか、それは小生にもまだわからないが。まだまだ第1章であるから御許し願いたい。必ずや書きながら極めていくつもりである。ただ肉体——ここでは物体ととりあえず決めなければならない。東洋のことわざの『健全な肉体には健康な精神が宿る。』しからば健全な精神に健康な肉体が宿るのか?この可逆性はあるのか、あり得ないのか?否。小生の未熟な66年という経験では計り知れない。従ってこの第2節のタイトルは、正しくはないと思えながら、とりあえず、先ず。

第1節に於いて、風呂に入るという、ごく単純な行動をベースにして、肉体に影響する反応ということで、小生の感ずるままに記した。冷たい、熱い、痛い、かゆい、心地よい。ところがこれらは永続的か否か。更に永遠か。(永続的と永遠を同次元で理解してもらっては困る。数日か、又は数秒か、風呂の中では微かなこれらの持続性は持ち得ることは確かてしかし概念的に考えれば思考した瞬間に、厳密にはある種の過去であるこ何人も否めないであろう。ならば！！！幸はなによりも肉体保全に良し。不幸は他のすべてに超越して不幸のみにならざるはない。

風呂は幸も不幸も温度によって多少の中和を肉体及び精神に与えてくれるのである。この相反する肉体と精神の項は後述する。インドの哲学者バグワンは中国の老子を評して、ある何もしない1人の老人を見て7人の哲学者が、あれは神である、仏である、不具者であり、もしくは聖者、ひょっとしたら人類ではないかも。等等……。石か！——結局何もわからないままに数百年が過ぎてしまった。その弟子達が、ひとつもしぼらずとも先ず2つを選ぼうではないかということになり、どうせ選ぶなら反対の極を、ということで正義なら悪、平和なら戦争、但しこれは対語ではなく、何か1つの現象の直後に次の概念が生まれるという意味に於てでのこととして。従って西欧の二元論とは異なる。(例えばヘーゲル、カント、マルクス等）中国の老子は7人の合作である。イギリスのシェイクスピアが7人の作家の合作であるように。（１９４０年代にシェイクスピアは個人ではない、といった説があった。）

てなことがわが風呂に入ればフッフツと湧いてくるのである。

以下次号

〈次号予告〉

ここまで書いてきて物理編でまだ書き残したことが多々あり、次号の半分はもっと特徴的物理的考察をどうしても述べないと先に進めない。以上下図によって御認識頂きたい。

第3節　物的物から肉体へ

風呂場の中で小生にとって一番不自由を感ずるのは、わが美なる肉体を眺めるに際して、鏡がくもるのである。鏡は鏡であってほしいのである。——最近の近代ホテルの風呂の鏡の中に電気が通っていてクモラない鏡が存在している。小生も経験しているが、この鏡はどうしてもなじめないのである。と、いうより鏡のウラから誰かのぞいているのではないかという不安にかられるのであります。したがって小生にとって必要な鏡は薄っぺらい一枚の板でなければならない。ところが垂

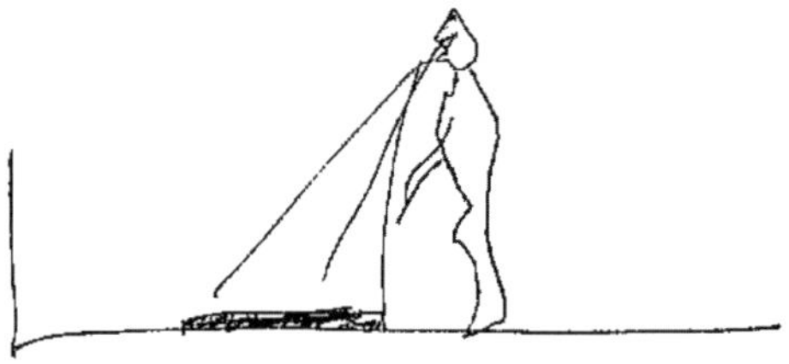

直方向では先ずくもる！　しからば垂平方向ではどうか、更に、鏡を水のなかに密閉すれば良いのではないか。床にはめ込んだ状態で曇らない方法はないか。

鏡といえば左右逆転し、何故上下は逆転しないのか。答えは否。鏡のなかでは逆転していないのである。なぜならば下図を見て頂きたい。

自分の顔を鏡で見るということは、顔の内側(脳)から顔を見ることになる。従って本人の見る鏡の中の自分の舶は左右逆転ではなく、正像を見ていることになるのである。

てなことが風呂の中で発想するのである。

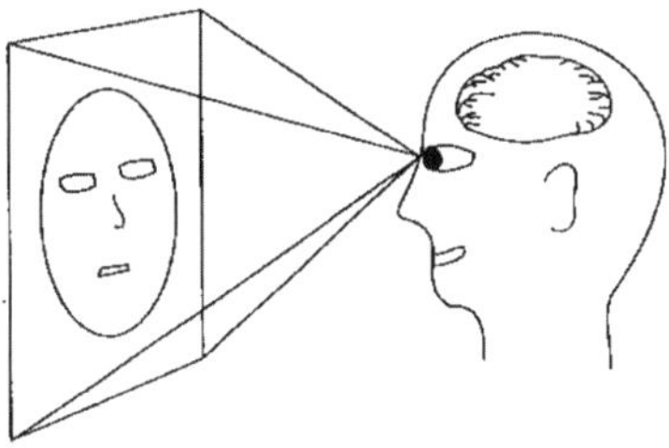

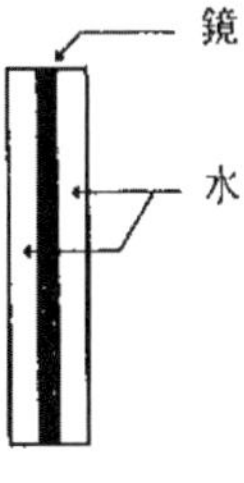

特許がとれないか。

物的にもう少し肉体を見てみよう。

小生は、この数十年石鹸というものを使川したことがない。先ず体温より2、3度上の湯に30分以上入る。よく言われる水泳選手がプールのなかで汗をビッショリかくということと同じことが言える。全身から汗が吹き出し毛穴が全開し、中から水（汗）が濁流のごとく吹き出し、毛根から汚れを押し出してしまう。後に自家製のバージン・オイルが肌を作ってくれるのである。嘘だと思うのなら66歳の小生の肌に触れてみてくれ！

第4節　更に肉体へ

21世紀に近くなるに従って、整形外科は発展し身長も伸縮自在に伸ばせるようになる。それに伴って、皮膚・内臓・筋肉も自在になろう。

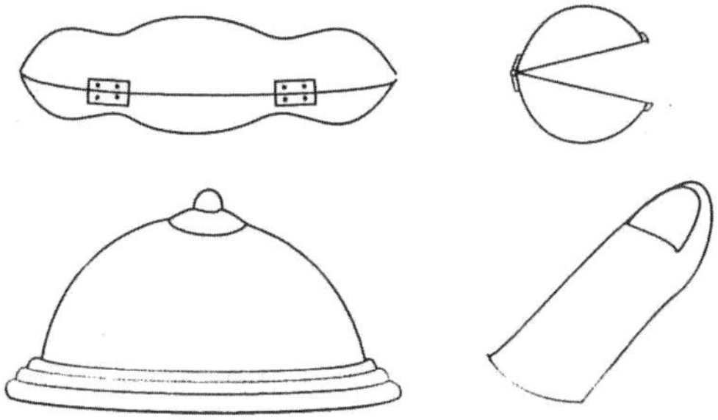

（肉体部分ケース）

この時代こそ諸君の美意識を問われることはないであろう。現代では神に与えられた肉体であるから、君の醜い肉体も神のせいにして逃げられるのだが。21世紀では君の美醜は全て君の美意識によるのである。ここで小生の肉体造形論が初めて日の目を見ることになる。

更に自己の肉体が外科の操作で分離できるようになれば、――女性が男性に「私が持っていないのに何故貴方は持っているの？」と聞かれたときに「僕も持ってないよ」と言えるのである。但し自分の肉体の一部故に欠落されては困るので、肉体のどの部品にせよ立派なケースを必要とする。これはやはり金属であるべきで、金か銀かチタンか又はアルミか。

上図のようなケースを何個も携帯し、ガール・フレンドとの大事なデートで豪華なホテルにおいて心地よい音楽を聞きながら、サアという時に君は葉巻大の銀のケースを自宅に忘れてしまった、という時代はもう目の前である。

展覧会によせて
―次なる扉を開く―

京都国立近代美術館長　柳原正樹

美術という得体の知れない世界に携わって久しいが、これほどダンディーで、人を惹きつけてやまない魅力をもった作家も稀であろう。世の人は、この作家のことを彫刻家と呼ぶが、たぶん、その範疇からは外れた所に居るのが篠田守男である。

彫刻とは元来、物のもつボリュームやフォルムが問題とされ、具象、抽象を問わず、量塊としての表現が彫刻というものの概念であった。しかし、この作家にそんな定義や理屈は無い。その作品は、物体をワイヤーで引っ張り合い、宙に浮かせるというテンション構造によって成立している。微妙なバランスを保ったための力は、緊張感のある凝縮されたエネルギーとなって空間を揺さぶる。

三次元としての立体の真髄は、作品が置かれた空間に緊張を与え、その空間を振動させ、命として空間にどのように存在するかが問題となるが、篠田のそれは、研ぎ澄まされた空間感覚が実に見事であり、さらに雄大なスケールをもつ独自の宇宙観を創出している。

そして、アルミやステンレスといった軽金属によって制作された作品は、構造物か精密機器のような幾何学的な形態を基本としている。無機的で冷たい表情を示す作品は、未来の宇宙都市の姿を連想させる。だが、それは機械仕掛の冷血な装置でなく、ところどころに有機性をもち、感受性を示す部分も備えているのだ。つまり、その両者が対立しながら不可分にからみ合って作品は成立しているのである。

さて、いささか余談となるが、1995年4月富山県の入善町の発電所美術館で、篠田は個展を開催した。この美術館のこけら落としの展覧会でもあったのだ。時を同じくして、隣の黒部市には、沈黙の彫刻家と呼ばれた毛利武士郎（1923―2004）がアトリエを構え、制作に没頭していた。寡黙で人と会うことを極力避けていた。篠田は、そんな毛利に会いたいと思ったのである。筆者が仲立ちとなって、その思いを伝えたところ、毛利は篠田と会うことを了解したのである。数日後、ふたりは対面した。簡単なあいさつを交わし、取り留めのない話から始まった。そして、「日本刀と鋳造品」について話が及んだ。それは、固く凝縮したものと、表面だけの空洞のものについての話であった。さらに、ミクロン単位の作品について、持論が交わされたのだった。

当然のように、毛利は篠田のこれまでの作品を知っていた。篠田もまた、毛利の仕事を承知していたが、それは過去の作品であり、いま現在のものではなかった。毛利は篠田をアトリエへと案内したのである。そこで見たものは、鋼鉄による作品であった。つめたい光を放つ塊は、コンピューター内臓の工作機械によって、空洞が穿たれ、溝が刻まれる。ミクロン単位に形態が形成されていく作品であった。

篠田守男もまた、精密な作品を制作していたが、毛利の作品の前で、彼はつぶやいた。「私は精密彫刻を今まで創ってきたが、今日からその言葉は使わない」と。その場に立ち会っていた筆者は、歴史的な場面に同席していると言っても過言ではなかった。後日、毛利は、篠田の仕事を高く評価していることを筆者に語ったのである。

現代日本美術を代表するふたりの作家。その出会いと会話は感動的であった。彫刻、あるいは立体造形の可能性を切り拓き、次なる扉を開けた者だけが理解できる世界。それは制作の苦悩と喜びを知っている毛利と篠田だからこそ、互いの作品を深く認めたのであろう。

このたびの個展は、初期のものから近年発表された最新作までが展示される。いわば回顧展ともいうべき展覧会となっている。この作家の過程を知るうえではまたとない企画である。

たぐいまれなる造形力、知的で構成的な作品。篠田芸術の足跡は、それ自体が、彫刻を現代の三次元的表現へと導いた、数少ない開拓者の歩みそのものである。さらに、その独創性において、篠田守男を昭和から平成を代表する象徴的作家として讃えることに異論はなかろう。

地球の開放

長年地球の解放を思考していたものが１９７９年筑波大学に教授として赴任したときから具体的な研究として、また環境支配説という持論ともあわせて授業にも還元しながら研究を重ねてきた。特に在任中筑波山国立水郷公園の環境の美しさに惹かれて、私財をなげうって購入したのが千坪の土地を手に入れたことによって様々な具体的実験が可能になった。その一部がこのNIIHARI PROJECTである。ここでいう解放とは人間からの解放である。基本的に私が生きたい環境というのは先ず地表から出来るだけはなれることを目指してる。今の試算ではひとりの人間の地球離脱は20メートルから30メートルと考えている。敷地の周辺に３００坪の土地を３年前に確保し実験が始まった。子供っぽいと言われるが正に80代にして5歳の感性を呼び戻している。誰でも抱く秘密基地！　今5歳とすると30年かかったとしても35歳の男ざかり、やっと今その緒に就いたところである。その一端を皆様とともに楽しんでみたいと思っている。

篠田守男　篠田守男研究室代表

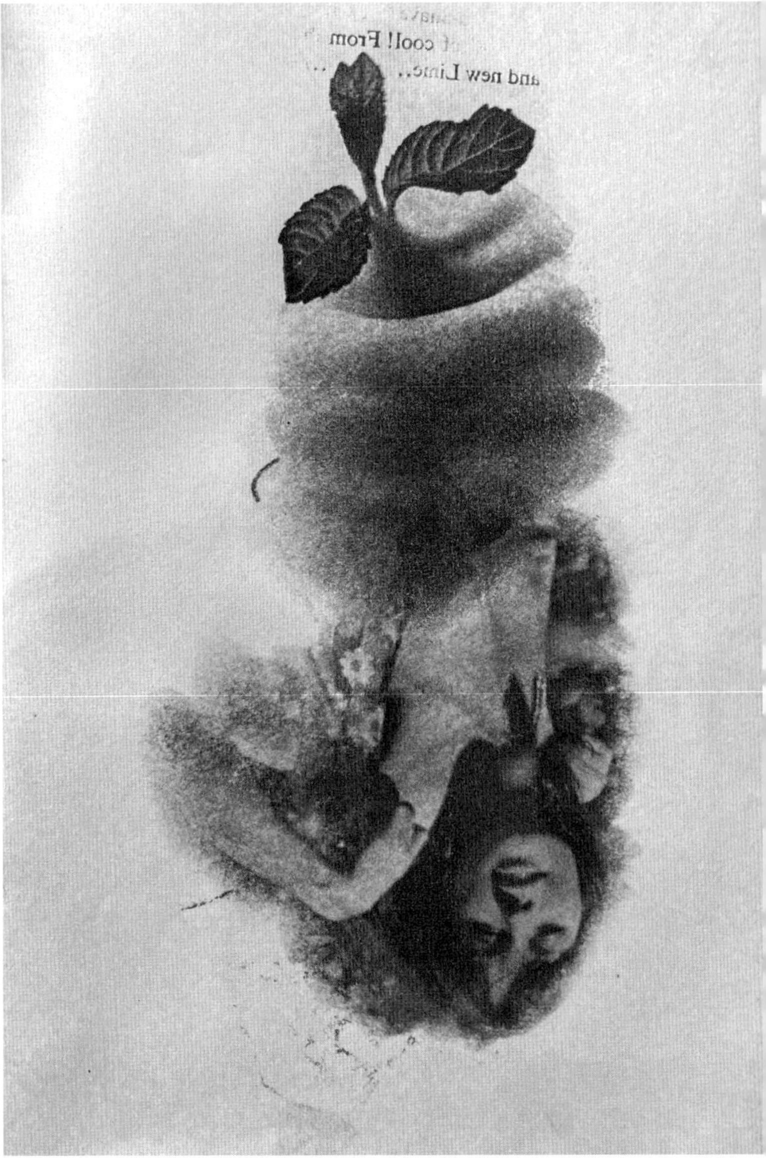

記憶と今

記憶というのはある意味でそれを認識したときにすでに過去のデーターになってしまう。私は物心ついたときから『今』にいきてる。親からは戦時中すらなにか命令された記憶がない。将来を見据えて何かを勉強するとか準備するという経験が皆無なのである。これは小、中、高と最も重要な抱卵期に植えつけられた価値観が一夜にして崩落するという今では信じられない大事件が勃発したことが私を長い浮遊の旅に旅立たせたのである。

立体作品は平面にくらべて一次元多いだけ情報量が多い。したがつてタイトルが作品の邪魔をするのでタイトルをつけずにきた。今回の個展にむけて初めて公表にふみきったのは最初のTCはテンションとコンプレッション、最初の二桁は私の年齢つぎの二桁は作品の数というようにキーワードにしてきた。とこるが80をすぎてこのかた年齢では記憶をたどれなくなりしかたなくタイトルを付することにした。しかしこれは私の記憶をたどるためのキーワードであつて作品とは無縁である。

長年制作をつずけていると一種のシステムができあがつてしまいナレで作品ができるのを恐れるのである。つねに『今』の発想で制作し、作品を進化させることを望んでいる。この持続性がとぎれたとき、引退するのみ。あとの世生を自由奔放に生きてみたい。

（2018年11月16日　篠田守男）

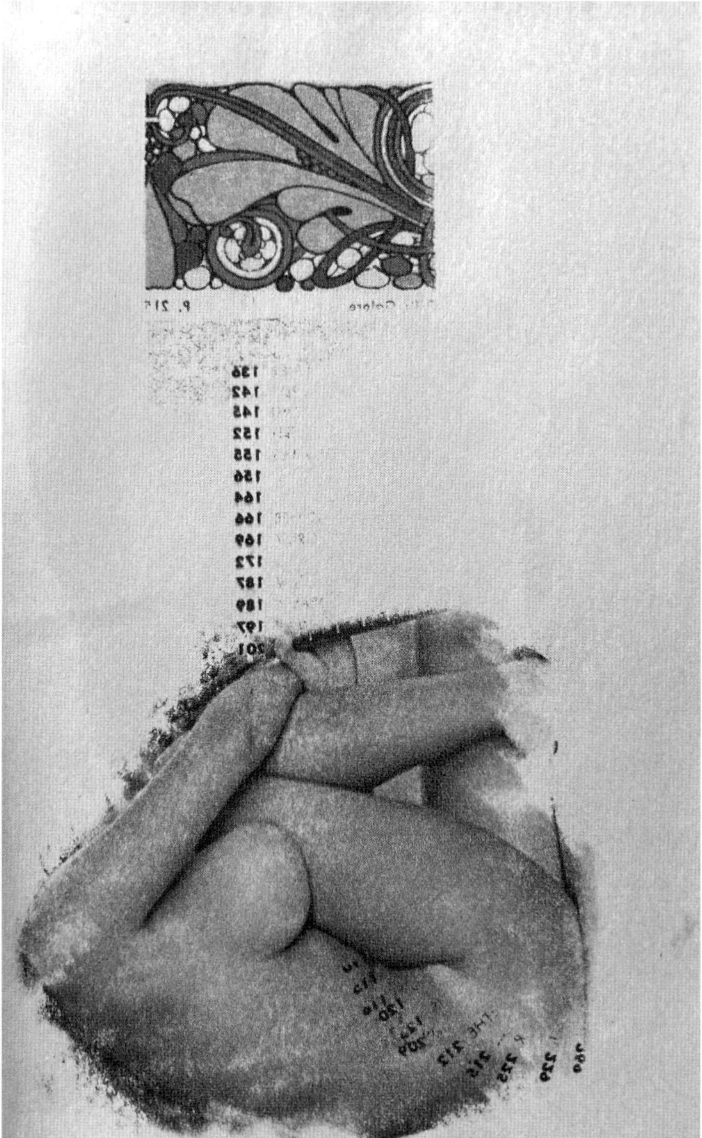

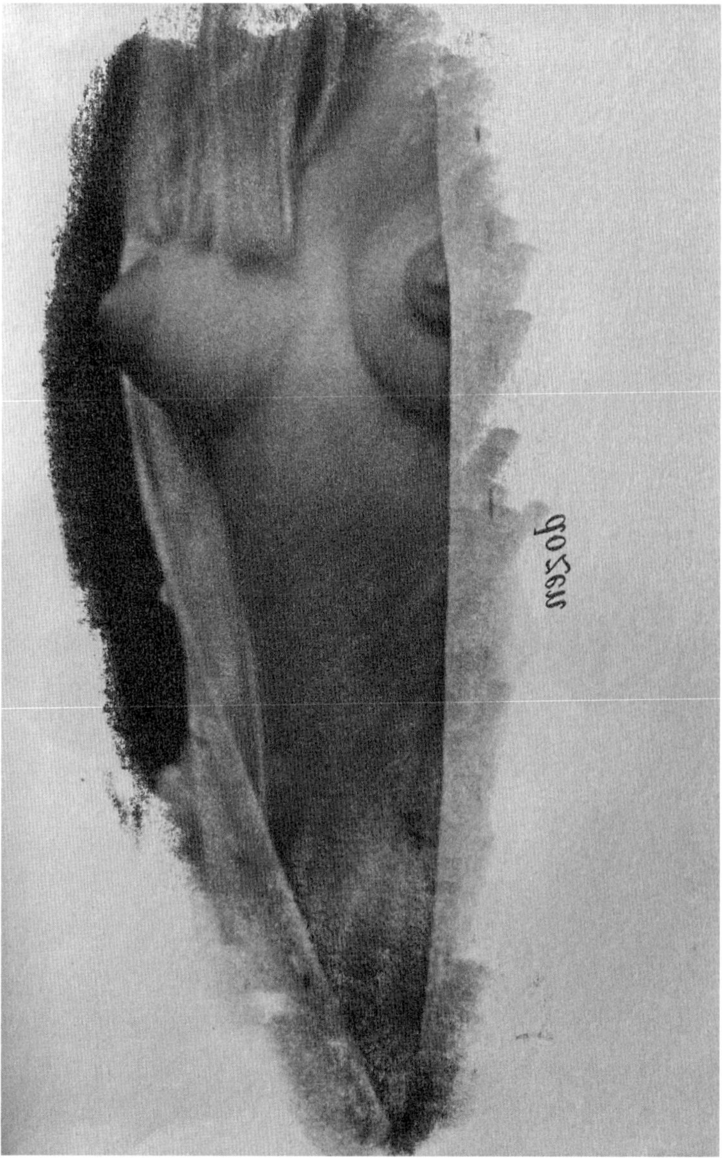

選択の芸術

選択の芸術篠田守男我々の芸術は選択より始まる。絵を描く、木や石を彫る、版を刷る。それぞれの技術を獲得したうえで造形に進む。しかしそのすべてが作品になるわけではない。むしろすべてが作品にならないことの方が多いのである。現代美術の作家達の多くがこのプロセスをふんでいる。効率のみでこのプロセスを考えてみると、先ず作りたいものがあって、必要な技術を部分的に獲得する。これで相当な時間が短縮できる。更にはすでにあるもの、別の目的で作られたものを選択する。これはマルセル・デュシャンのレデイメイドであり、ピカソの「牛」、自転車のサドルにハンドルを装着したもの等がある。昔NYである絵描きが用意した新しいキャンバスにペットとして飼っていたオームがキャンバスの上を歩いて模様をつくった。これを出品して大論争になった。即ちオームがかいたので作品ではないとするものと、作家が無作為に展示したものでなく、選択というフィルターを通過しているという二論から後者におちつき芸術作品として認められた事実がある。更には60年代の後半に入ってコンセプチュアル・アートの時代、友人でもあったLAの作家ジョン・バルデッサリ「注文絵画パット・ネルソンの絵画」（1969年作）では自分で写真をとりそのまま日曜画家に描かせたものである。ここにいたっては「芸術の一部としての選択」すら薄れてしまっている。私は作品を効率よく作り、短時間で完成させることを良とする。すでに頭の中にあるものを具体化するのであるからプロセスは早い方が良い。しかし我が国では畏く苦しむことに満足をおぼえる。いわばマゾヒスト的の理論である。具体化の悩みより頭の中で組み立てることほど試練を必要とし、苦しみ、悩み、ジレンマする。これが制作上の肉体行為よりつらいかというと自由だからである。これを論じ始めると芸術とは？　という大テーゼに関わってくるので割愛せざるをえないので、ここでは冒頭の芸術の一部をなす「選択」に基点をおくことにする。

この度の展覧会では西洋骨董を主部品として私が選び出したものである。これらは私の技術では不可能なもの、発想しないようなもの、また部品として完成していることからまず時間の短縮がえられること、思いもよらぬ、自分にとって発想の転換がはかれること等、多くのメリットがえられた。そしてなによりも、立体のコラージュともいえる奇想天外な結果が得られたことに満足している。

矢橋頌太郎

ケサランパサラン、ウドンゲの花。昭和の初めである。3000年に一度花を咲かせケサランパサランせるという。とてつもない幸せをもたらすという。逆転して不幸ももたらすともいう。80年も前のことである。植物なのか生物なのか、その存在すらも子供の好奇心を満足させること無く、未解決のまま大人になってしまった。

2010年『現代美術の新世代』展が大垣の極小美術館で開催され、20代の若い作家達が選ばれ、その審査員（青木正弘、篠田守男）の一人として立ち会うことになった。私はものを判断するとき、直感（ほとんど認識を伴わない）—直観（認識はするが判断を伴わず）—思考—分析にいたる。この段階で矢橋頌太郎の作品に興味を持った。私にとって冒頭のような幼児体験を入り口にして興味をふくらましていったのである。一般的に具象と抽象に分別すれば矢橋の作品は具象でもなく抽象でもない。しいて哲学的にいえば唯物的絵画、または純粋絵画ともいえるかもしれない。純粋絵画とは絵画以外の何者でもなく、表現すらも極力抑えて絵画という物体を存在させようと試みているのではないか。１９７０年代コンセプチュアル・アートのなかにキャンバスのフレームをおもてにして額縁にいれた作品があったが、絵画の構造をみせるにとどまって絵画の概念にまではふみこんでない。

ミッシェル・フーコーによれば絵画は二つの原理によって支配されてきた。造形表象 repre'sentation platique と言語表象 repre'sentation linquitique の分離。これが破棄されたのはクレーとカンデインスキーによると指摘する。更にマグリットの『これはパイプではない』Cecin'est pas une pipe を例に造形と言語表象との融合を論じている。しかし日本では万葉の時代よりこの二つの概念は融合されており絵画というメデイアに属している。矢橋の絵画は私の幼児体験（言語と事象の未発達期）をとうして絵画という迷宮にいざなってくれたのである。このとき独断と偏見で、彼の絵画に優秀賞を推薦し、昨年の北陸神通峡ビエンナーレ展において審査員（酒井忠康、絹谷幸二、篠田守男）の一人として優秀賞を推薦しみごとに受賞をはたし、矢橋絵画は普遍性をもつのである。

篠田守男　筑波大学名誉教授

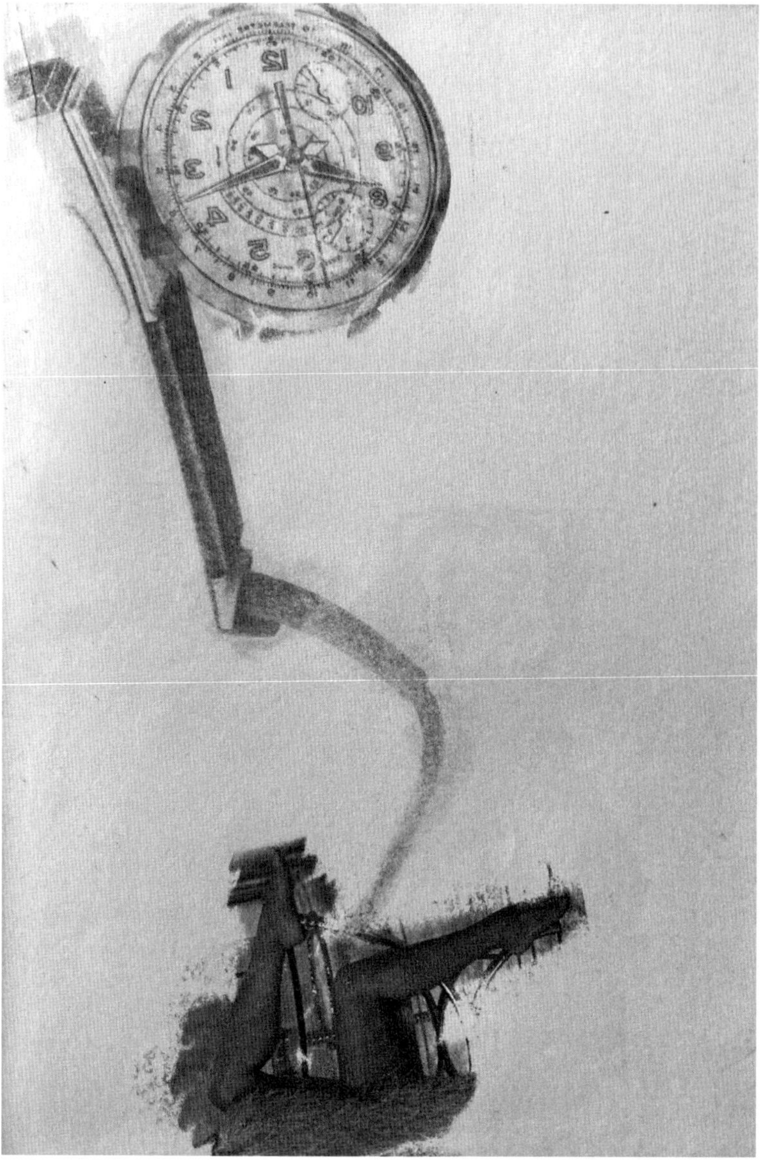

眞木雄一君へ

芸術は表現効率の高さ低さではない。マルセル・デユシャンのレデイ・メイド作品は表現すら希薄になってくる。モノ派がやったことはシンプル・ビュウテイのミニマル・アートから始まったコンセプチュアル・アートの一部である。これこそイデオロギーであって芸術ではない。その証拠に彼ら、フランチェスコ・クレメンテ、ゲオルグ・パゼリッツ、サンドロ・キア等、全員といってもいいニュウ・ペインテイングの騎手として衣替えしたのである。いまヨーロッパでモノ派がブレイクしてるのは経済の領域でアートのメディアではない。これは具体美術のそれとは誠に異なるといわざるをえない。日本の発明である俳句に勝るモノなし。これこそ貴兄のいう表現効率の高いものは無いだろう。フランスの哲学者レヴィナスの言葉に自己と他者、他者の中の芸術的鑑賞者、すなわち高度な知識をもった鑑賞者一人でいい。そのときに対等になる。鑑賞とは鑑はかがみ、賞はすぐれたものを楽しみあじあうとかく。女性に対するのと何ら異なることなし。まず芸術的存在があり、鑑賞者が直感によってとりこむ。理屈はない。プラトンとソクラテスの対話という本を思い出すがどちらがプラトンか。コメントのNawa氏にふれて一言。ロダンはぶっきちょで手跡が残るのは当たり前だ。当人はそれが不満でカミーュ・クロデールというモデルの不倫相手に手足のディテールを作らして最後にすてた男の風上にもおけぬひでえ奴。貴女もこんな男にひっかかちゃだめですよ。僕のテンションは危険が好きだから自ら飛び込む。それでひ弱な彫刻をつくっているのです。

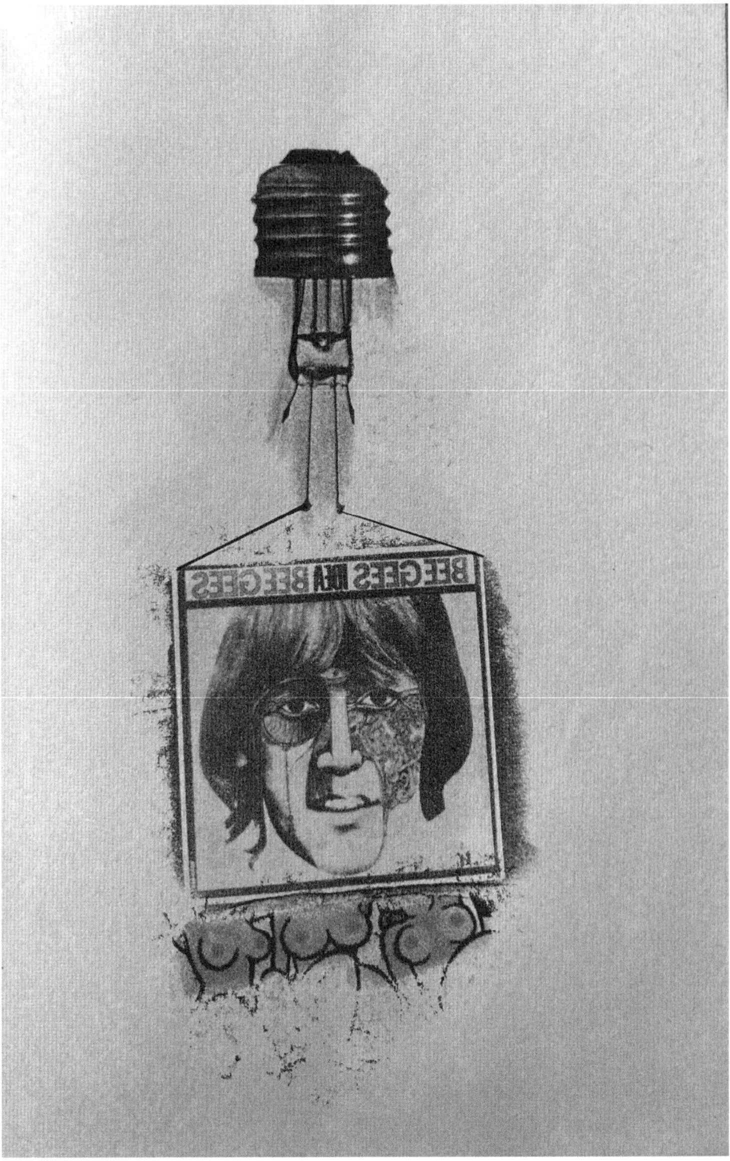
BEE GEES IDEA BEE GEES

眞木雄一君へ

ご結婚おめでとうございます。ここに御送りするのは懸案の眞木君宛のトランクと泉ちゃん宛の彫刻です。これは京都の借金の振替です。それと結婚祝いをかねております。でも作品としては誠にきにいっております。次の作品の良いエスキースと思っています。なぜならば、従来の作品がその支持母体によって吊られているのに対して自ら己を吊っていることです。これは40年前に試みています。その作品は箱根彫刻の森美術館においてグランプリを受賞した作品です。現在東京都現代美術館のパーマネント・コレクションとして収蔵されております。なんでこんなことをグダグダ記すかというと次元が異なるのです。これから説明する次元とはあなた方と大きく関わってくるからです。これを運命と言はずしてなんと申しましょう。極小美術館の長沢君に言はせると天命であると。ここからが本番です。疲れたら酒でも飲んで一休みしてください。

これは何年か前君らが結婚したときに作品とともに送ろうとした手紙です。その後作品もできず結婚とはなにか、という本論も書けずに、今日にいたってしまいました。作品とともに御送りします。本当に長い間ありがとうございました。

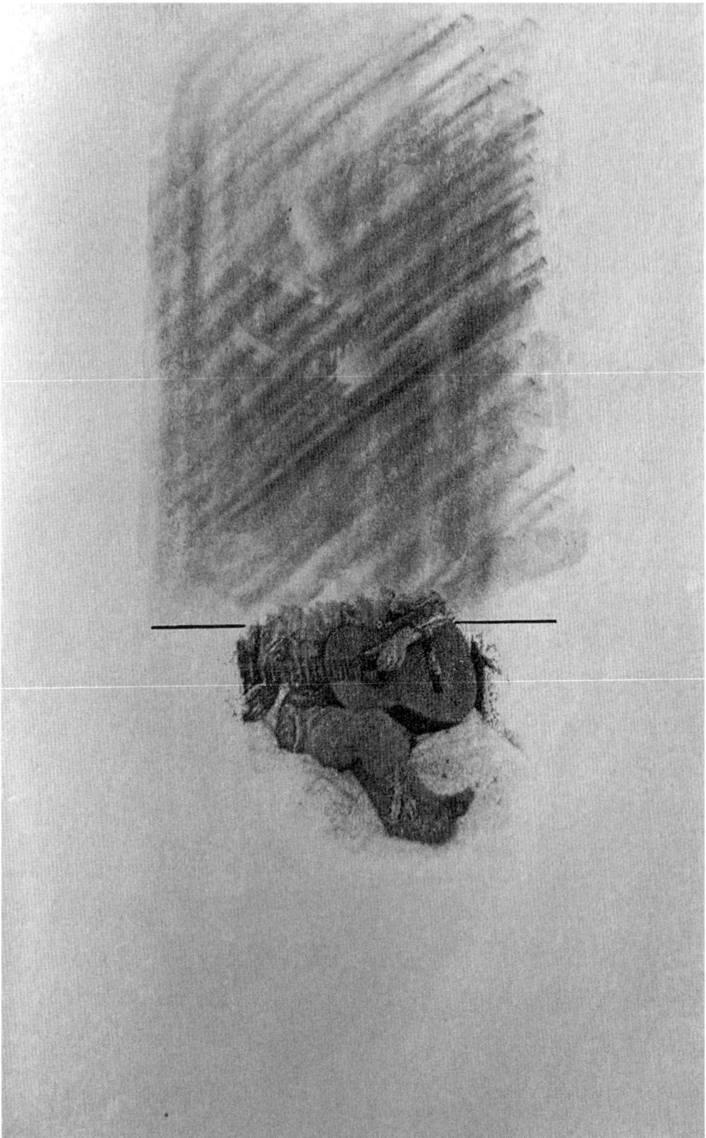

でしたが50年を経てデジタル化されたアートにたいして存在という哲学的理論を持ったレアリテーを今回の展覧会で感じました。私を含めて、星加さん然り、杉原先生しかり。これはポスト・メディア・アートと言えるのではないでしょうか。

返送ですが、IL8605～IL 8608はしばらくあずっかってください。IL8603、8604のどちらか五万のお礼に差し上げます。後はご返送ください。この前ねじが見付からなかったので同封しときます。短いネジは天板用です。領収書、その他も同封しました。

追伸：恥ずかしながら出費の件ではご面倒かけましたが、実は80歳を迎えた瞬間カードローンが停止になり約5百万の借金を年金からひたすらに返済しております。これも6年では利子だけで元金がいっこうに減りません。ここ数年、年2回は個展で売らないと生活できません。平面作品は最低値段が50万です。IL8603、8604も同額です。もし売れたら30%は星加さんがとって下さい。

篠田守男拝

星加民雄様

この度はこ苦労様でした. 僕は当初美術館企画と思っていました。そしてテンション作品を出品すればとのんびり構えていたので。しかしまてよと、思いは1968年カリフォルニア大学時代にタイムスリップして。当時アメリカではキネチックアートやオブティカルアートの時代でした。僕はそれらを200パーセント授業に取り入れて実験をしていました。丁度半世紀前です。今の人はそれを知らない。それを今の僕が作ったらどうなるか。そこで生まれたのが今度の作品です。

日本に帰ってきて俳優の一人六平直政（日下由美）が教え子の一人として育ち、キネテイツクからポケモンの石原君、岩井俊雄、パフォーマンスの授業からは土佐君（明和電気）、映像から畠山君（木村伊兵衛賞）、カリフォルニヤ大学では、ローレン・マットセン（音楽環境彫刻家）、カール・チェン（自然環境彫刻家）等を育てました。それぞれ社会で大いに活躍しています。これは教師冥利につきます。彼らに負けられません。新治にもどって今やもっと膨大な計画を進めています。半世紀前のアナログ・アートは確かにイリュージョン

金子省三様

このたび拙作お買い上げくだされ有難うございます。最近の書物
をお礼がわりと言っては何ですがお送りさせていただきます。
御買い上げくださった作品はだいぶ前になりますが、初めていった
沖縄で日本本土とは異なる文化に感動いたしました。特に首里城及
び本土とは異なる石垣に彫刻家として大いに刺激を受けました。そ
の後訪ねる機会もなくさいどゆっくり訪ねようと思っていた矢先、
残念ながら焼失してしまいました。

その思いがあってオマージュとして制作したものです。しかし著
名なコレクターである院長先生に認められたことは何よりでござい
ます。

つきましてはお願いがございます。だいぶ前から耳が遠くなり
様々の病院に診断を受けたのですが年齢といはれ諦めておりました
が、先日ラジオで耳垢を取ったら治ったという話を聞き私もとお
もっております。小さい頃小豆大の耳垢が出たことがあります。8
月10日にコロナの2度目のワクチンを打ちますのでそれ以後でし
たら、いつでも結構なのでぜひ御診断頂けたら幸いと存じます。

2021年8月25日
篠田守男

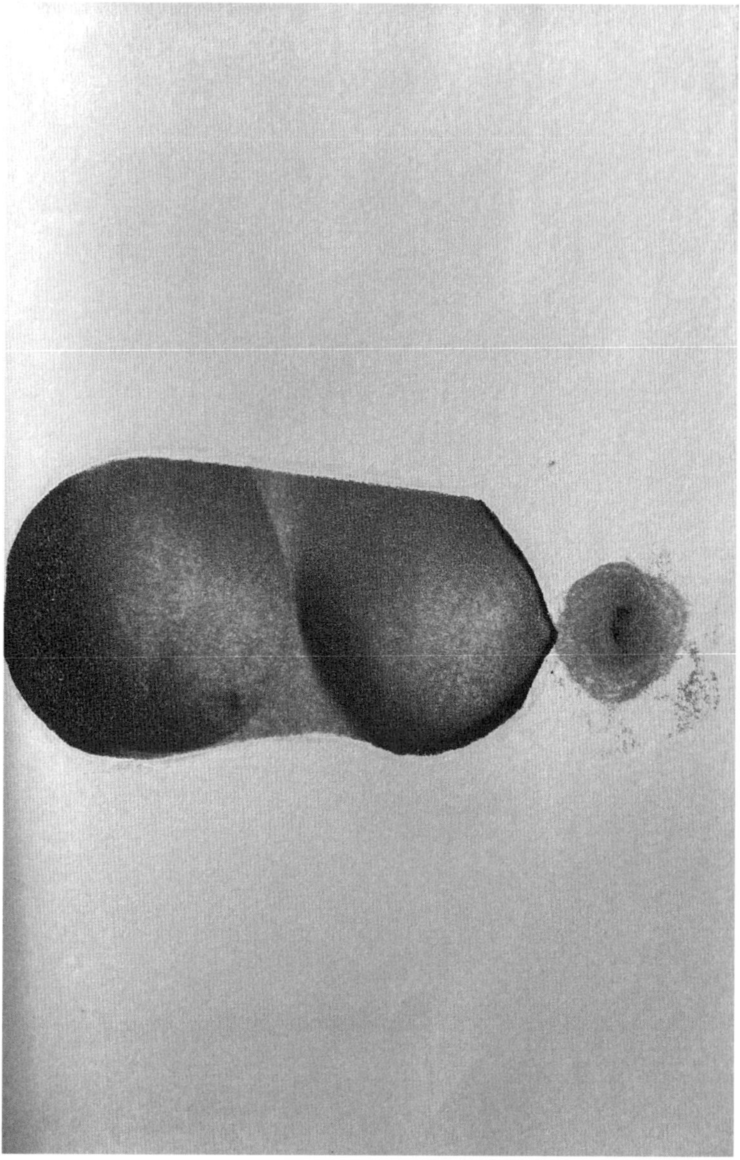

桜は蘂降る季節も楽しい

第2章

上野オサム

1995年　春

夢は愛する「ティーバック」

思いたち、ぶらり郡上へ旅もいい。
釣り人よ、四季の川風出会う旅。

出会う湧水・老舗の和菓子、抹茶の香に花が咲く。

そんな、気ままなティータイム。
―ティーバック（お茶用バッグ）あったらいいな―

岡倉天心はボストン滞在のときにも茶籠を持ち歩いたようです。北茨城の天心美術館には、その茶籠が置いてあります。多くの茶人たちも茶籠を愛し楽しんでいと聞きました。私にはお茶の心得はありませんが、飲みたいときは、自由に気軽に飲みたいものです。天心美術館から戻り、すぐに茶籠セットの制作にとりかかりました。やや茶籠とは異なりますのは、私のセットは〝抹茶〟用ではなく、その時の場所に合わせていろいろと、お茶が楽しめる〝ティーバック〟です。

お抹茶、中国茶、煎茶に珈琲、と多彩な一つのティーバックです。これをすべて入れるためのバックには迷いました。そこに現れましたのが、古道具屋さんの隅の方に朽ちていた、レザーのシルクハットケースです。

なかを開きますともちろん、ハットは跡形もなく内側はシミだらけのぼろぼろでした。一瞬、眼をそらしましたが、もう一度見直しました。ひどい、だがレザーのケースと円錐型の形は、古き良きヨーロッパを思わせます。でもかなりの手直しが必要のようです。完成すれば中の空間には、全てが入るような気がして購入しました。
その後が、やはり困難でした。ぼろぼろの内布をきれいに外して、それと同じ大きさの型紙を作りコットンチャックで黄色とブルーの柄付きの二種類の布を買い求めての制作です。
　内面の周りが黄色で上下の底と蓋はブルー。出来上がってみると見違えるほどです。20世紀末の茶籠――

湧き水を求め、古き暖簾をくぐる。
和菓子を小脇に抱え、川風を肌に感じ茶を楽しむ。
「今日の空も、また　こよなく澄んでいる」

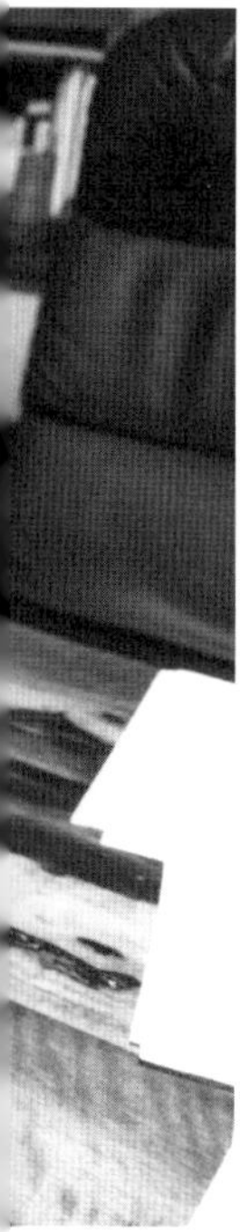

LA SOIREE（ラ ソアレ）

●篠田守男との出会い

黒柿で作られた書斎のテーブルの上に、二客のワイングラスがあります。グラスの名は〈バレリーナ〉。その脇には、グラスが縦に二客並ぶ大きさの、アルミで出来たグラスケース。女性のからだで型取られ、真鍮の取手の付いた、その器のニックネームは、ラ・ソアレ（夜会）。

〈バレリーナ〉に注がれた赤ワインの脇には、いつもラ・ソアレがたたずんでいます。なにげなく置いてあるこの二つは、思わぬことから出会ったのです。

ひとつは、ラ・ソアレを制作した、現代彫刻家の篠田守男氏との出会いでした。一九八二年ごろだったでしょうか。私は時々、仕事のあと軽く食事を済ませてから、トレーニングジムで運動をすることがあります。帰りには決まって幼馴染の寿司屋に立ち寄り、少々のお酒を飲みながら、なにげない話をするのが、なんともいえない安らぎのひと時でした。唯一、寿司屋の主人との共通の趣味は木彫をすることでした。

その日も、カウンター越しに、作りおきの木彫を眺めながら、そこそこの芸術論に花を咲かせていました。その右端のカウンターには、小柄でグレーの長めの髪に、少し白さの増した髯を生やしたお客さんが一人いました。個性的な顔で、年の頃は六十歳ぐらいでしょうか。

我々が芸術論を始めますと、なにげなくその会話に加わってきました。始めは煩わしい方かと思いましたが、話の内容は、なかなか筋が通っており、挙げ句のはてに、私も少々彫刻をするので見てほしいと言い出しました。

私たちも、ほかに予定もなく、お客さんも幸いいなかったので見てあげることにしました。私たちの許しが出ると、彼はその作品を取りに外へと出ていきました。何気なく彼の肩越しに目をやると、そこには一台のポルシェが停まっています。彼が大事そうに持ってきて見せてくれたのは一枚のポストカードでした。

カードには、金属の建物のようなものが写っていました。「この建物の何を作られたのか」と尋ねると、彼は「すべてです」と答えます。それが後になってわかる「T—Cシリーズ」の中の「新治プロジェクト」でした。篠田守男氏との最初の出会いでした。

盃を重ねていくうちに、篠田氏は筑波大学の総合造形の教授で、作品の多くは、海外の美術館にもコレクションされていることがわかりました。しかし三人の話し合いの中では、我々は自称木彫家であり、彼は金属の芸術であるから、しょせん心からわかり合うことは出来ないだろう、それなりの芸術の友でいこうということになりました。

●「BOX―3000」がなぜ「+330」になったのか?

それからは、彼が大きな作品を手がけるたびに、大学の工房に出向いては、芸術の空気に浸りながら、何とも言いようのない、新たな芸術の風の心地良さを感じていたのです。さも自分が芸術学の学生になったかのように。しかし、作品についての見解が分かれるときには、お互いに、金属と木彫だからということですぐに決着がつき、これも素敵な解決法でした。

その後、篠田氏は筑波大学を退官され、長崎大学の客員教授をされた後に、縁あってつくば市の隣の新治村に、鶏小屋だったところを改造して「とりスタジオ(とりスタ)」を持つことになりました。そこでは、彼の永遠のテーマである「空間」を主題とした作品を作り続けていたのです。

その一つとして「BOX―3000」というテーマの作品を限定五十個作る

ことになりました。それはアルミで出来た厚さ三・五センチのアタッシュケースで、中には一万円札の新札で三千万円入るという空間の演出の作品でした。そうなると、彼でなくとも、本当に入るのかどうか入れてみたくなるものです。ただ、三千万円を現金でそろえることは難しいので、紙幣と同じ厚みの紙をカットして、前面だけは本物の紙幣を使い、ケースに入れて写真を撮ることにしたというのです。その話を聞いたとき、あまりにもそれでは夢がないと思い、つい「私が用意しましょう」と言ってしまいました。しかし言っては見たものの、難しいことには違いなく、困って友人の銀行の支店長に相談しました。すると、すぐに「お貸しします」（あなたの家を抵当にして）と返事が戻ってきたのです。

しかし、そんな大きな借金を抱えることも出来ないので、支店長との相談で、銀行の外には出さず、ほんの一、二時間だけ写真を撮らせていただくことにしました。現金がそろった日は、折しも、十二月二十四日のクリスマスイブ。私のアタッシュケースに詰められた三千万円は、あたかもサンタさんからのプレゼントのようでした。
　しかし、私の気持ちとは裏腹に、撮影をする銀行内の部屋に支店長が現金を持ってくるまで、篠田氏は本当に三千万が入るのかどうか心配そうでした。なぜなら、重さは一円玉と同じ一グラム、そして一万円の新札の厚みを計測して割り出した彼の想像の空間だったからです。当然、一度も入れてみたことはありません。そんな彼の不安をよそに、私は、入らなければアタッシュケースの口を開いたまま写真撮影をすればよいのではと話していました。銀行の支店長との約束で、お札の帯封は切らないことにしていたからです。

それを聞くと篠田氏はますます不安そうでした。何にも集中できない不安とも緊張ともつかない時間が流れました。

そのときドアが開き、支店長が、前もって渡しておいた私のアタッシュケースと紙袋に入った現金を持って「あれ、ちゃんと入るね」と口ずさみながら入ってきました。その言葉で、張り詰めた緊張の糸は一瞬にしてほどけ、篠田氏の顔には、前々からさも自信があったかのような表情が現れました。

もう一度我々の前で、現金はケースの中に納まりました。その瞬間、篠田氏は、「まだ入る」と囁いたのです。残りのスペースを精密に計測すると、あと三百三十万円入ることが判明しました。そのときを境に「BOX‐3000」は、現実の空間である「BOX‐3000＋330」とサインが改められました。そのことを記念して、銀行で現金を入れた私のアタッシュケース内側に篠田氏が「1997年12月24日　BOX‐3000↓BOX‐3000＋330」とサインをしてくれたのです。

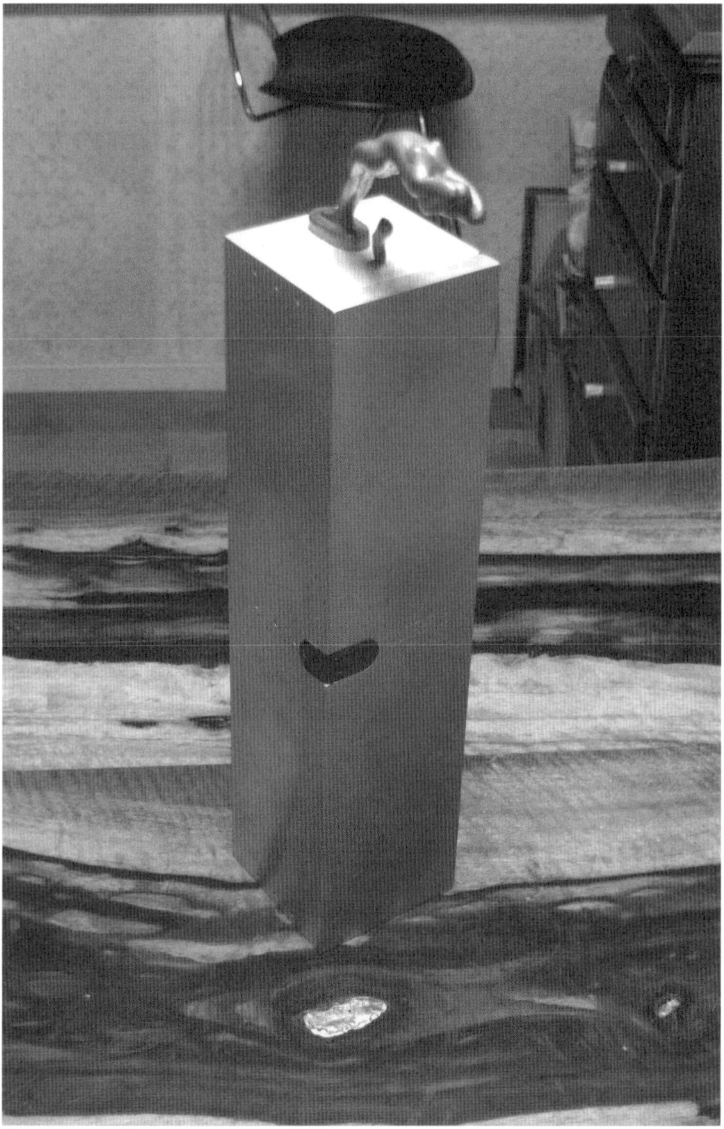

●ラ・ソワレの誕生

完成祝いの日は、一九九八年一月六日。お正月でもあり、新たな空間を祝って、レミーマルタンとアタッシュケースを持ち、「とりスタ」へと出向きました。篠田氏は私を見るよりも、レミーを見て微笑み、すぐ封を切り、埃にまみれたテーブルの湯のみにあけようとしました。

「待って!」

私は、車の中に素敵なグラスが積んであったので、そのグラスで乾杯をすることにしました。彼はレミーマルタンの入ったグラスを目の高さまで上げ、素晴らしいグラスだと感激をすると同時に、そのグラスを入れてある、私の作ったグラスケースのひどさに我慢が出来なかったようでした。

そのときのグラスがロブマイヤーのバレリーナ・シリーズの一つであり、篠田氏とそのグラスとの初めての出会いでもあったのです。

「作りたい」

私のグラスケースを見れば見るほど、彼は何とも我慢が出来なくなったようでした。彼の頭の中には素敵なグラスケースのイメージが膨らんだようです。しかし私は賛成ではありませんでした。今までの長いお付き合いの中で、往々にしてイメージが膨らんだときは、やりすぎてしまう。要注意ということもあったからです。

しかし、次の日には彼から、デザインができたから直ぐ来ないかという電話がありました。私はその日は仕事なので、とりあえず次の日の休日に会うことにしました。そのとき会ったのは、金属加工をしている彼の友達の所で、そこでは金属の厚みや重さに関する話まで具体化し、夢は膨らんでおりました。

それから二週間後、日本橋高島屋で開かれた、高島屋芸術賞の受賞式の会場で篠田氏と会い、話し合いの結果、グラスケースの作品制作を決定しました。

たまたま、その会場で受賞された方は、篠田氏が筑波大学時代に共に仕事をされた若い先生で、私にとっても共通の友人でした。

ロブマイヤーのバレリーナ・シリーズの中の一つのワイングラスとの出会いも、私にとっては素敵で不思議な出来事によるものでした。私はいつも車に、二客のワイン用のテスティング・グラスを持ち歩いています。しかし、一九九七年十二月の東京の会合のときは、なぜか車に持っていませんでした。そのとき私は、久しぶりの友との再会を祝うために、一九七八年のロバートモンタビのリゼルバを持って行っていました。これはどうしてもホテルのコップで飲む気にはなれず、つい会合を抜け出してしまったのです。たしか、渋谷東急デパートの地下にはワイン売り場があり、そこにはワインのテスティング・グラスが置いてあったはずでした。確かにそこには、記憶どおりのテスティング・グラスはありました。しかしその後ろのカウンターでテスティングをされている方のテスティング・グラスの美しさに引かれました。私はそのグラスの存在を、それまで知りませんでした。ソムリエの方に尋ねて、それがロブマイヤーのバレリーナ・シリーズの一つであることを教えていただきました。その時が私の、バレリーナのワイングラスとの初めての出会いでした。

買い求めてホテルで味わったワインの味は、また格別でした。ワインの繊細さと唇に触れるグラスの感触とのバランスは絶妙でした。次の日、自宅に戻り新しいグラスケースを一九八二年のドンペルニオンの木箱を利用して作りました。しかしそのケースが篠田氏には何とも気に入らなかったようなのです。そして、そのことがラ・ソワレを生むことにもなったのです。

●ブリティシュグリーンの偶然

夜おそく、静まり返った「とりスタ」で、完成したグラスケースからおもむろにグラスを取り出して、シングルモルトを注ぎ、それを片手に眺めていると、ほんの二、三カ月前までは想像の中にあったものが、今私たちの目の前にある。なんとも不思議な気持ちでした。想像すること、ものを作り出すことと、年代を超えた友情の素晴らしさとの出会いでした。

グラスとグラスケースを見つめているうちに、ロブマイヤーの日本総代理店の方とお会いしてみたくなりました。どんな方がこのグラスに魅了され、日本の総代理店になられたのか。

しかし篠田氏の頭の中には、次なる想像がすでに湧いておりました。グリーンを背景に置かれたグラスケース、扉は少し開かれ、グラスケースの内側に張られたグリーンのフェールトの中から、縦に向かい合って置かれたバレリーナのグラスがキラリと輝いている。そして縦長の写真の上に、大きく「LOBMEYR」と書かれているポスターがもし作られたならばなあ、などと夢を広げていたようでした。

私もそんな話を聞くと、もしポスターが作られ、どこか地下鉄の階段を登り、ふと上を向いたときに大きな縦長のロブマイヤーのポスターと出会えたらなどと考えている自分に気がつくのです。

二月のある日、私は青山通りを少し入った所にある、ロブマイヤーの総代理店ロシナンテを訪ねました。青山通りを一本入っただけですが、そこには少し前の青山の面影がありました。午後二時の待ち合わせに、志村明一氏ご夫妻で出迎えていただきました。

ワインケースを床に置き、しばらくお話をした後にテーブルの上にワインケースを置き、おもむろに扉を開きました。その時すぐに、志村氏は、なぜ内側に張ったフェールトの色がグリーンなのか尋ねられました。私たちは何色かの色を試しましたが、グリーンが一番落ち着くような気がして、ブリティシュグリーンを選んだのです。ところが、志村夫妻は、この色がまさにロブマイヤーグリーンなんですと言われました。偶然でした。私たちは、ロブマイヤーグリーンの存在を知らずに、この色を選んでいたのです。

そしてもう一つの偶然。グラスケースを持ち運ぶハンドルは、裸婦をモチーフにしたブロンズで作られています。その下に、ケースを開くための鍵を立ててあります。その形はトーシューズをデザインしたものでした。志村氏の話しによると、バレリーナというグラスの本来の名前はティプ・トゥだったのです。しかし、ティプ・トゥでは日本ではあまり馴染みが薄いので、日本での名前として、志村氏がバレリーナと命名されたというのです。私たちはこのことも知らずにグラスケースを作っていたのです。

一組のワイングラスと、それを持ち歩くためのグラスケースとの不思議な出会い。そして、人との出会い。次にどんな出会いがあるのでしょうか。グラスケースの扉が少し開かれ、中からワイングラスが少しだけ見える写真と、それにまつわる少々の物語は、志村氏のご好意で、ロブマイヤーの本社のある、オーストリアのウイーンへと旅立ちました。

猫とイチゴ

２００２年２月25日

二月だというのに、なんと暖かい日なのだろう。そんな日曜日、ゆっくりと目覚め、彫刻家・篠田守男亭を尋ねました。家は不在のように見えましたが、玄関の引き戸はかすかな錆びた音と共に開きました。でも、黙って入るのは少々ためらいます。庭にもどり野外暖炉のイスに腰を下ろし、待つことにしました。

日差しは、喉の渇きを誘います。車から愛用のティーバックを出し、一杯のコーヒーを入れました。携帯用ストーブにエスプレッソマシーンが便利です。一杯のコーヒーは、遅い朝を目覚めさせてくれます。

室内の奥から物音が。何も体にまとわずに、庭に出てきて迎えてくれました。どうやら、風呂あがりのようです。

「いいね、このままで」
「もちろん」
彫刻家はショットグラスに2／3ほどのモルトを持ち、野外暖炉の石板の上に置き話し出しました。
「直木賞は簡単に取れるね。あんなのたいしたことないよ。書こうよ、我々も」
彫刻家は以前、京都に長期間滞在をしていた折に、修行僧であった玄侑宗久氏と行きつけのバーで意気投合し、問答のような会話を楽しんだようです。その宗久氏が今回芥川賞に、その本を読んでの感想のようでした。
彫刻家は、春のような空をあおぎながら。
「食事にでも行こうか。プラスワン　カフェにでも。あそこは、いい男があつまるからな」
ブランチにはちょうどよい所です。芸術家は、いつも外出の時は身支度を整えます。ブルーと白のボーダーのシャツにグレーのハンチングを後前にブルージーンズとスニーカーです。
昼下がりのカフェは、賑わっていました。いつもの外のテラスの奥のテーブルに。私のソフトハットは、車のなかに置いていきました。
「二人でハットは、ちょっと野暮かな」
ラムとコーヒー、それにパスタ。これもいつものコースです。ここちよい風が、昼下がりを演出してくれます。テラスのスピーカーからは、今日はボサノバが流れています。室内からの騒音と共に話は続きます。
「私のこんどの直木賞小説の題名はこれでどう」。
「ただいま貸出中」
彫刻家は「いいね」。
「おれは、直木賞授賞式の挨拶の文章できたよ」
「あとは映画化だね」。
「役者は自分達で決めよう」。

「私は役所広司」。

「それじゃー私は誰にするかな。勝新、今はいないしな」

パスタが運ばれてきました。さっぱりとしたトマト味は、今日にはちょうどいいね。

脇に添えられたガーリックトーストもいい香りだ。

「こんな時間を文章に書きたい」と彫刻家は呟きます。

「また一つ、本ができる」ね。

「さあ、そろそろ笠間へでも行こうか」

日動美術館でアントワーヌ・プーペルのパリームーランルージュの舞台裏の写真展が面白そうだ。たぶん、60年代にアメリカで活躍した写真家で、権藤新也の作品にも似ているかもしれない。発表は権藤氏の方が早いはずだ。どんな作品か見てみたい。(注・権藤新也氏はアメリカ時代の篠田守男氏の写真家としてのペンネームです)

笠間までの道のりは、筑波山の東側を山並に沿って走ります。風の穏やかな光の道には、クラプトンの音楽が心地よく響きます。美術館の駐車場は閑散としております。彫刻家は車を止めた方向の奥を見て、声を上げました。

「すばらしい、見て！」

振り向きますと、そこには白いキツネ顔のねこが横たわり、ながい紐のような内臓が一筆書きの書のように、腹を突き刺すように描かれて横たわっておりました。

彫刻家は「カメラある」。

私は、ゼンザブロニカと三脚を、彫刻家は三脚を立てると何回かのシャッター音がしました。今度は三脚から外し、さらにアスファルトにひざまずきシャッターを切りました。美術館からもどる時、彫刻家は大きく天を仰ぎ、ねこに向かい合掌し車に戻りました。

「これで、あのねこも成仏できる」

車は、陽が西に傾きかけた山道を帰路に尽きました。
「エンヤの音楽がながれています」
途中道筋の、いつものイチゴ屋で少々のイチゴを求めますと、その倍のはねだしイチゴをさらに頂きました。何となくリッチな気持ちで胸が踊ります。
「エンヤのリズムのように」
野外暖炉の上のコンパクトストーブは、イチゴジャムの香りに包まれ庭に漂います。
「また夕暮れが来ました」

曲げわっぱ

2003年

「うえのさん、んだいごにはだれがごのわんづがったのが、わがんなぐなるがら、ねんごとなまげがいでおいでぐれ」

〝曲げわっぱ〟のぐい呑みの器が秋田から届きました。そのお礼に私がかけた電話口での話しででした。最初、何を話しているのか理解できませんでした。ゆっくり聞きなおしますと、

「上野さん4代後には、この器をだれが使っていたかがわからなくなる。そのために今年の年号と名前を書いておいて」ということのようでした。それは、「わたしは4代先まで使える曲げわっぱを作りました。もしその途中でも4代先でも修理ができる職人を仕立てておきます」ということでした。

ただ、その器をだれが使っていたのかは、2代目、3代目まではわかるが、その先はわからないことが多い。「そのために名を入れる」ということでした。たかが「杉の曲げわっぱ」かもしれませんが、使い込みの文化はいまもなお脈々と続いているようです。身近に、そのような文化の香を感じました。友人とともに、あるときは一人で、盃を傾けます。作り手の心意気と温もり、時間が味わいのお手伝い。さらに、あの秋田の光景も重なります。

そう、この器は頼んでから5年の歳月が過ぎておりました。さらにあの電話では、

「上野さん、なんでこんなに時間がかかったかわかるかな」

「仕事が忙しかったのか、体の具合いでも」と応えると

「いいや、待っていた、気に入った木目の杉と出会うのを。このぐい呑みの大きさ（こぶし大）は弁当箱よりもかなり小さいだろう、弁当箱と同じ木目では、小さい器には年輪の間の幅が広く、間が抜ける。一寸に60本以上の年輪でない

とだめだ。それと出会うのを待っていた。杉の丸太の太さはいつも変わらないものが届く、だが年輪間の幅はまちまちなんだ。

直径40センチぐらいの丸太で、この希望の木目は樹齢何年だと思う」

「わからない」

「300年以上だ。山のどこに立っていたと思う。沢沿いの北斜面の陽当りの悪い中腹から下。沢は尾根から栄養が流れ込み北斜面でもよく育つ、山の頂上近くの北斜面の杉は、300年たっても太くならない。その木が、ほかの材に混じってくることがある。それを待っていた。注文して探させれば、もう少し早くそろうが、値段が高すぎる」

そもそも秋田〝曲げわっぱ〟作家の柴田慶信氏との出会いは、1993年の新宿・高島屋の実演販売の会場でした。曲げわっぱの作品は、いままでも見てはいましたが、柴田氏の作品は、なめらかな杉の肌触りと流れる木の質感は、炊き立てのご飯に梅干しをいれて持ち歩きたい心地よさを連想させました。柴田

氏との会話の中で、さらにその熱き思いがつよく胸に響きました。思わず手に取った筒状の一合弱が入る、曲げわっぱの弁当箱を一つ衝動買いしました。その弁当箱は、夏のアユ釣りの河原で昼飯ごとに馴染みます。

秋田・米代川へのアユ釣りの旅のとき、柴田慶信商店を尋ねました。

「まさか、お店に来るとは」とびっくりしていました。店の奥には世界の曲げわっぱの作品群がコレクションされていました。

柴田氏は語ります。

「世界でも曲げの歴史は長く、私は、それを学び、秋田を表現したい、そのために集めた」

その話を聴きながら、私自身の曲げを見る目も秋田を離れ、世界的へと広がっていくようでした。

工房の杉の香りのなかで、ふと、また別な思いが。

「私の旅の友として、いつも持ち歩ける曲げわっぱがあれば」

柴田氏に相談をしました。
「曲げわっぱでぐい呑みはできないだろうか」
彼は、「難しい」その理由は器の径が狭すぎてうまく曲がらない。弁当箱までの径が必要だと。私があきらめかけたとき、柴田氏は秋田弁で「やってみる」と話しました。でも、いままで考えたこともなければ、やったこともない。
「でもやってみるか、だが少し時間をください」ということになりました。

私は、ひと時の別れを告げ店を後に、米代川へと戻りました。
ワクワクとした時間が流れ、それから5回目の夏が過ぎました。そして秋、一組の器が、杉の香りと秋田の山並みの空気とともに届きました。
しかし、残念なことが一つ。包みを開き二つの器をそれぞれに包んである紙を外し、内側の器と外側の器をかぶせてみました。すと、がばがばでした。初めての作品だからこの誤差はしかたないと器づくりの難しさを感じました。

「夕暮れ」

上下の器を黒柿のテーブルの上に開き、共に私の好きな日本酒〝早瀬浦〟を注ぎます。

待ち浴びた器との出会いです。感謝の一杯の酒は、喉をゆっくりと米代川の如くに流れました。空になった器を重ねて戻しますと、いままでストンと入った器が、音もなく静かに手を離すと空気のじゅうたんに沈み込むように重なっていきます。

「そうか、水分を含んでこその器」。そのことをわかっていての大きさを作っていたのでした。

「名人だ」。

内側の器の底に「2003　秋　修」と細い刀で刻みました。それから長い時が流れています。

2005年　秋

「ふと暖簾をくぐる」

古道具屋にはたまに顔を出す。
気づかなかった場所に、手の掌（たなごころ）に馴染む大きさの六面体の象牙の三味線の糸巻きが、無造作におかれていた。
糸巻きの先端は小指の頭ほどの太さで、少々小振りの三味線竿が目に浮かぶ。
つま弾くその細腕は、夢二の描く女性像をも感じさせる。
それがなぜ、道具屋の店先にあるのかは知る術（すべ）もない。

わたしの持ち物にできるなら、また別の歩みが生まれるかもしれない。
その思いとともに、わたしの書斎で眠りについた。
そして「3年のときが流れた」

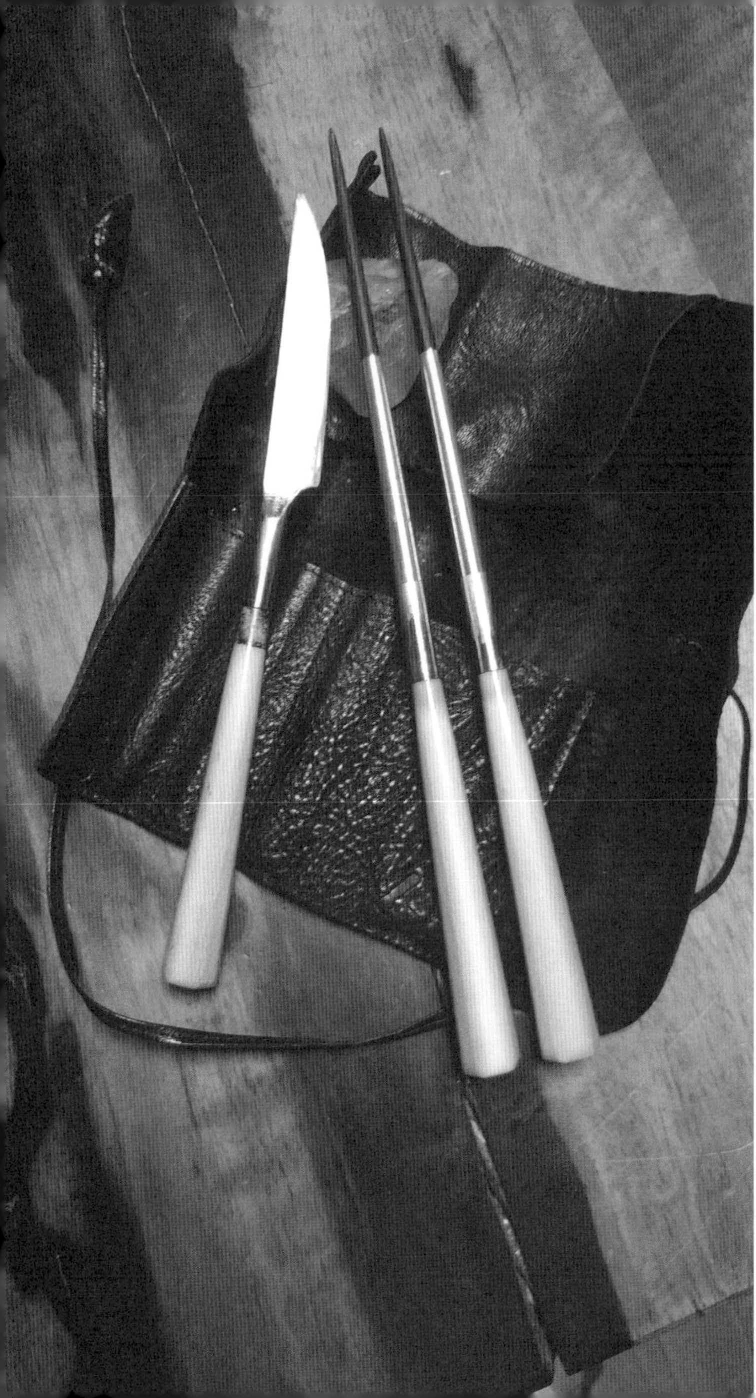

「三絃の糸を巻く。３という持物の日常」
箸は一脚。箸をホークと考えればナイフもいいかもしれない。
すべてを二つ折りにし、いつも肌のぬくもりを感じる距離感で持ち歩ける。
「エコではなく、持ちたいから持つ」
「こだわりではなく、そこにただある」その存在は、わたしの唇がいちばん親しみをもつはずだ。
旅の空、居酒屋のカウンターで、大都会の見晴らしのよい夜景を見ながら箸を休め時間を楽しむ。

ときに、
霧雨(きりさめ)の夕暮れの縁側で、剞り盆のうえの一杯の酒。そっと伽羅蕗(きゃらぶき)をつまむ。
「耳をすませば、遠く三味の音が聞こえる」

備前　盃　銘「備前稲妻」

2017年9月2日

午後1時にその盃は届きました。小さめのこぶしぐらいの、備前の盃です。色あいは、灰の中から取り出したばかりのような江戸黒をおび、内面には一点の親指大の朱色の景色が、やや中心を外した位置にありました。吸い口の一部には、縁から中心に向かって、金つぎの何本かの稲妻が走るような設えになっています。そもそも、この盃は、日々、友として持ち歩き肌のぬくもりの届くところにありました。

なぜ、私の手を離れて旅をするようになったのか。

それは、ほんのひと時の気のゆるみで、友人のすし屋さんの店先で違和感のある音とともに落としてしまいました。それから、5年の歳月の旅が始まり、

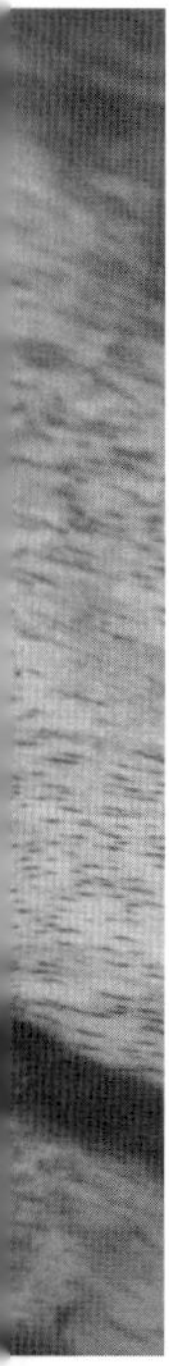

今日という日になりました。
この盃との出会いは備前への私の旅からでした。陶芸家・正宗悟（まさむねさとる）氏の窯出しに招かれ、その窯の中での出会いでした。まだ、ほんのりとあたたかい灰のなかから指先の感覚だけでさぐりあてた盃です。
落としたとき、運よく布に包まれていた盃は、すべての破片はそのなかにありました。
「どうしよう、これは、捨てられない」
と考えを巡らしながら、半年ほど書棚のなかに。ふと、千葉県在住の修復師の千鳥さんのことを思い出し、電話で相談をし、そのもとへと送ることになりました。
後日、連絡が入りました。
「私でもお直しできますが、継ぎ目の厚みで0．何ミリか器が大きくなってしまいます。でも私の友人の漆芸家の小柳さんなら、すべてが可能になると思います」との答えでした。

盃は小柳種国氏の手へと移ることになりました。友箱もなく、もちろん箱書きもありませんでした。窯出しのときのまゝで、それでも器を心よく受け入れていただきました。

「仕上がったときには、箱書きをつけてお渡しします」とのお言葉とともに。

それから時はずいぶん流れました。その間も、千鳥さんからは「できましたか」との手紙が何度もいただきました。その度に、「まだ旅をしております」とお答えいたしました。時の経過は、器と心の離別のような温度差が生まれて来ることに気付きました。待つという気持ちよりも「諦め」でした。

「できてもできなくともいい」なすがままの時間でいい。

5年が過ぎた後に、その盃は届きました。箱の前面の表書きには、「備前　盃」、内側には、「正宗悟氏　窯出に灰の内より上野修氏譲受愛玩の盃　破損　小柳

種国　修復　平成二九年九月　　朱印　　」と記されていました。

「月も雲間のなきは嫌いにて候」（村田珠光）

盃の入った箱を開き、小柳氏に電話をいたしました。
「いかがですか、お気にめしましたか」。との、第一声でした。
「器も、雲間がありて、輝く」喜びを共有させていただきました。心の底から、
時の流れの響きが聞こえました。
その夜、一人　盃に酒をそそぎ器の深き景色を眺めた。
「無言の言葉に、耳を傾け」

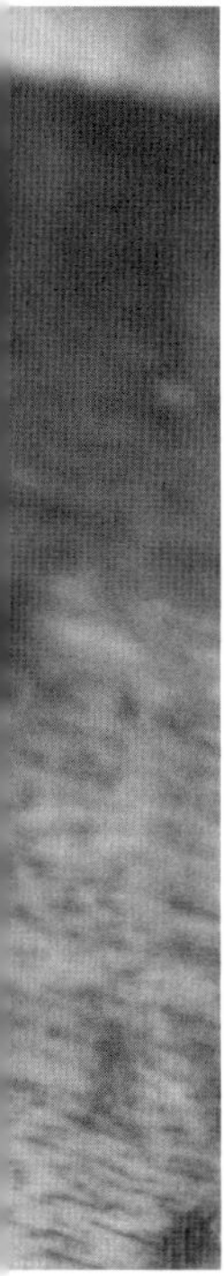

関係「のれんに腕押し」

2017年9月

人との関係は、その見えない距離のなかにあるのだと思います。エドワード・ホール著『かくれた次元』のなかにも表現されているように。さらに、人間だけでなく国家や言語、地域性の習慣のなかにも異なる距離感が存在するようです。

さて、「私と彫刻家・篠田守男氏との距離とは」。

彼は、一見しますと、常人にはとても見えないようです。「わけアリのハイカラさん」。

不思議な存在感を抱えて、茶の間の画面から出てきたような。

「あのお方はなに者ですか」と尋ねられ、「彫刻家です」と私はお答えします。

すると、「なるほど」と納得するような風貌です。「作品ではなく、自分が作品」の生きるパフォーマーなのかもしれません。

このごろ、篠田亭のアトリエ（通称・車庫スタ）の前庭でよく語ります。「思うがまま、の自然体」で。「勝手気ままに淡々」と、独り言ではなく、目を見開き熱く私に語ります。

私は、アトリエを訪ねるときは、いつものセブンイレブンの100円コーヒー2個と100円の明治チョコレートブラックを持ちます。セブンのお姉様は、二個のコーヒーカップを専用の袋に入れ、チョコを持ちますと、どこそこへの訪問なのかと、下から私をしげしげとのぞき上げます）。

「会話には、コーヒーが、ひと時には、チョコ　がかかせません。

日常の芸術論。

心は、1960年代のヒューストンが舞台となるときもあります。ある時は、

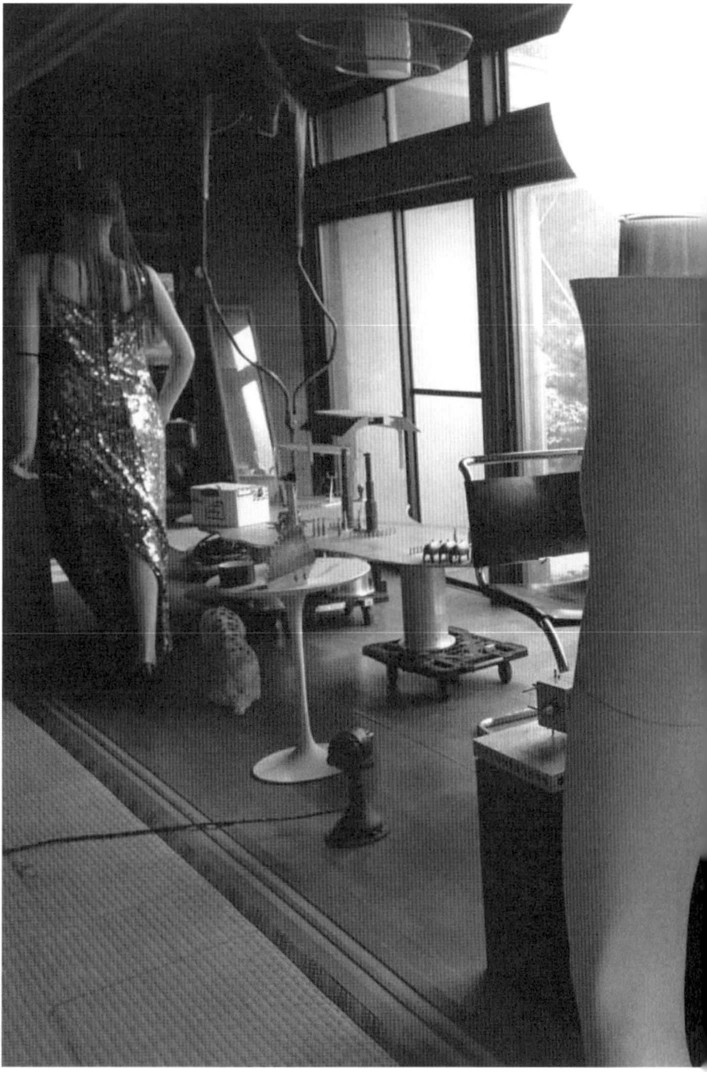

私と出会った時代。１９８０年代の筑波大・総合造形のパフォーマンスの授業のことや、工房での作品制作エピソードの記憶に花が咲きます。気がつくとそのまま家のなかに、話はつづいています。室内の廊下の南西の角には、彼のデザインで本棚がしつらえてあります。一見しますと普通の本棚にみえますが、棚の背面には、左上から右下へ、前面は右上から左下への斜めの角材の筋かいがあります。このじゃまな筋かいですが、そのじゃま感がアートです。その本棚一つ一つのなかに、彼の頭のなかの時代背景と本のページがひろがっているようでした。

しかし、来客のだれもがその世界を認識できないようです。

篠田氏特有の世界観の表現なのでしょうか。ふと一冊を手に取りますと、１９６０年代のハイパーレアリズムのアレン・ジョーンズ、ジョン・カセールが私に語りかけてきます。その右には、バーナード・ルドフスキーの The Unfashionable Human Body もあります。そこで、ハイパーリアリズムとシュー

ルレアリスムの話がまたはじまります。
セクシーとエロと芸術論。ジェントルマン・ダンディニズムと「いきの構造」論。九鬼周造と岡倉天心が語ろうとした同じＤＮＡに秘められた世界観。そこに、１９０３年のThe Book of Teeとフランクリン・ロイド・ライトが加わります。話は、１９００年代から２０００年代へと、いっきに走り抜けます。

それは、私たちにとっての、スーパーカプセルのアトリエ空間なのです。さらに、１８８９年第４回パリ万博のときのエッフェル塔の反対派の作家ギ・ド・モーパッサンとエッフェル塔との関係もよく話に上ります。
「モーパッサンはもっともエッフェル塔が嫌いだったようです」
でも出来上がってからは、ほとんどの時間を塔の上階のレストランで過ごした。
「モーパッサンへ、新聞記者たちが質問をした」
「なぜこの嫌いな場所に、長い時間滞在するのですか」

モーパッサンは答えます。

「いちばん嫌いなものを見ないですむ」。

そこから「エッフェル塔が嫌いなやつは、エッフェル塔へ行け」と。

篠田氏は「東京タワーもスカイツリーも嫌い」です。

「あれは、芸術ではない。ただの電波塔だ」

「エッフェル塔はまだ許せる」

なぜ、と尋ねますと「エッフェル塔のエレベーターは、塔脚にそってアールをえがき下から上昇している」。東京タワーは、エレベーターが塔の中心から真下に下がっている。

「あれはひどい」

篠田氏は愛車　ポルシェを所有していました。

「私は、ポルシェをこよなく愛する」
でも、お金が無くなり、愛車は売られました。
そのとき、彼は語りました。
「なかに乗っていてはつまらない、外からながめるのが一番だ」

…話はつづきます。
建築論・芸術論・絵画論。
時代の中の価値観や、真実のゆくえと美意識と。

西側の窓の向こうに、〝半熟卵のうるんだ黄身〟が、かすかに消えて行きます。
部屋は、しずかに色を失ってきました。
玄関の〝ロン・アラットのアルマジロランプ〟がぼんやりと輝きはじめます。
アルミの2〜3センチ幅のテープ状のかさなりで、生きているアルマジロを再現したランプです。光を入れると、ふしぎと七色にかがやき「美しき化け物」

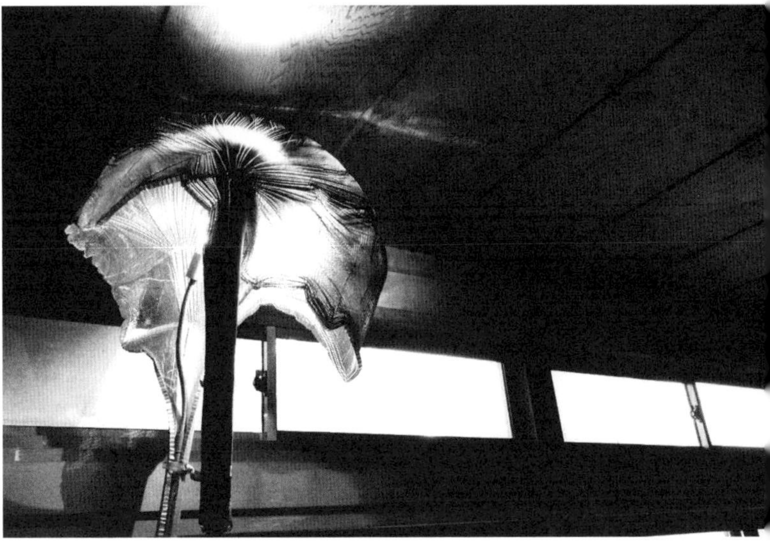

です。部屋は、不思議な国へと導かれていきました。
「ゆうぐれの酒がのどを流れます」

2017年10月11日

ガーターベルト

川は今日もとうとうと流れ、静かに海へと向かう。久慈川の流れは、やや那珂川の流れよりも優しく、柔らかさを感じる。

昼下がり、篠田氏からの携帯が胸で響いた。

「上野さん、いま、川？」。

よく川にいると鳴る。いつもなら、「帰りによらない？」とのラブコールだが、今日は違う。

「どう思う？」

いま、10月20日の二人展オープンに向けての作品選定に迷っているようだ。その一つが「女性のマネキン」の作品。等身大の裸婦の腰から下のモデル。腰の

上面には、ハンドボール大のシンプルな乳白色の円形のライトが天井を向いている。そのモデルは、目立たない存在のまま、人知れず30年間、アトリエの一階の居間の雑多のなかにあった。今年の4月にその雑多を、さっぱりとした空間へと、変貌させた。(断捨離のごとくに)。

「うん、これでいい。」

すると、マネキンライトは新たな存在感をもった。夕暮れが近づくと、腰のライトが灯る。すると室内のやわらかな空気は、みずみずしい色香を醸しだした。その作品を、今回の篠田守男、土佐信道(明和電機)の二人展に加えることを考えていたようだ。そこでの一つの問題点は単独直立ができないことだった。現在は黒いライトコードで柱に巻き、なんとか関係を保っている。これでは会場展示は難しい。

「どうやって、立たせようか。」

川の中での私の案は、「ガーターベルトでは」と告げた。腰からのガーターべルトの先の留め金受けのような、太ももに金属のベルトを片側だけつけたらという案。
「そうか。」とあっさり話は終わった。携帯を切って私は
「何のやくにもたたなかった。」と反省をした。
私のガーターベルト案は、アレン・ジョーンズ フィギアの本をイメージしての思いつきで。ハイパーアリズムにも通じるなにかを感じていた。
夕方篠田亭を尋ねた。まだ6時半だというのに、10月の日暮れは早い。室内は夜の8時ぐらいに感じる。とくに今日は釣り、朝4時には起きていた。
「一日がながい。」
篠田氏はいつものように、ニコリとして待っていてくれた。その微笑みのなかに、何かいつもとは別の輝くものがあった。彼の眼は「作品を見て！」と言っていた。アトリエに入ると、ガータベルトホルダーは、幅10センチ、厚み1・2ミリのアルミの板を左太股上部の形状にあわせて巻き、両サイドからのベルト

を固定するL字型の止め金も曲げ装着してあった。
川での話から5時間、すでにほぼ完成しそこにあった。
その金属で拘束されたスリムな足は、すずしげな魅力を醸し出していた。篠田氏も
「なぜ、これができたのかわからない。ただ気がつくとできていた。」と語る。
篠田氏は、光の消えゆく空を仰ぎ、
「夕食は近くのラーメン屋で一緒に食べようよ。」
それは、ホッとするひと時だった。
翌朝、携帯が鳴った。
「いま、ジョイフル。」（ホームセンター）残りのパーツを買いに行っているようだ。
彼の声は、朝光（あさがけ）のように聞こえた。
「夕方にまた行く。」と伝え携帯を置いた。

夕方、篠田亭を尋ねると、そこには完成した作品があった。西の空に沈みかけるあわい光のなかに、ひとときの時を止めて佇んでいた。

『新たな篠田守男ワールド』

芸術はこうして生まれるのかと実感した。

2017年10月14日

風をかいにいく　男

「そうか！　風か」ひとりごとを発しました。
「ぼく、買ってくる」とアキバへと向かう。
これが、「風」の作品のはじまりでした。

篠田亭アトリエの庭。
南を向いていた私の頬を、さきほどまでは夏風がふきぬけていました。夕暮れには秋風が北側の頬をふきぬけて行きました。
「もう秋か」
陽ざしは季節の変わり目を告げてくれます。みえない風は、それぞれ何かを伝えようとしています。篠田氏は、その風の何を捉えようとしたのだろうか。

１９２０年代のアバンギャルドの風を、60年代のアメリカでは彼なりの時流を感じていたのかもしれない。「ダダ、シュールリアリズム」

２０１７年のジェントル・ウインドを彼の心のなかにどう捉えたのだろうか。アバンギャルドの時代からほぼ１００年が過ぎた。アートはアートにあらず。数学、物理、情報工学、再生医療、哲学は、それぞれの歩みを一つの主軸へと向かわせる。

「芸術という風のなかへととけ込む」。

この風の何かを、認識のなかに表現しようとしたのだろうか。篠田守男氏と土佐信道氏（明和電機）の二人展（10月27日〜11月４日）のなかに、以前とは異なる会場の空気を表現した。それは、おおくの批評家たちには、その風を消化できなかったようだ。

しかし、これが『21世紀の「ART NOUVEAU」』の始まりかもしれません。この見えない風を、己の眼で確かめたい「証として」。

「風よ」―吹けばいい―。その認識の内にのみ、「風は吹く」。

2017年12月29日

いちにち

ある日、子供が誕生しました。
その子にとっての一日が始まります。

私の仕事の朝にも、その日の一日は回ってきます。
それぞれの一日が。

子供が言葉を覚えだしました。
「パパ、ママ」それが自分の認識の始まりのようです。
そして、自分（私）という存在認識を覚え、後に私は何者なのかと迷うかもしれません。
これが人生の始まりなのでしょうか。

ある一日を振り返って思う事があります。
「仕事をしているときの一日」
「定年後の一日」
のんびりと、一日は長いはずなのに気がつくと陽が暮れている。
「長い時間、短い時間」
認識の時間と生活の時間の関係は。
24時間は光の速度の中では平等なはずなのに。
大晦日の夜に、ふと風呂の天井を仰ぎ。
「ひさしぶりに何もしない時間の終わりに時について考えます」

スポーツマンの学生と夕食を共にすることがあります。
彼らは、3歳のときから一つのスポーツにのみ、ほとんどの時間をついやし疑問もなく今日まで来たようです。
彼らも、ふと立ち止まって、この20余年をふりかえります。
わたしも、60年余年をふりかえります。

そんな時に思うこと。
「彼らの時間（20年間）の方が長かったのではないか」と。
「それとも他人の時間は長く感じるのでしょうか」。
我々の認識は、曖昧のなかに漂う。

「一日を思う、時の不思議さを」

病み上がりの淡々

2018年1月31日

きょうの川の空気は、鋭く痛い。一週間、寒気団のいたずらで大雪も降りました。陽ざしのある日中でも6度ですが、川の中は暖かく感じられます。

久しぶりに胸の携帯が鳴りました。あまり元気なさそうな声で、「昼、イタリアン食べに行かない」。食事のお誘いの声に、ホッとしました。

篠田氏は1週間前に風邪をひき、一人新治のアトリエで寝込んでいたようです。3日間はベッドから起き上がれず、買い出しにも出られずに、ただ寝ていました。4日前に私は携帯で、「温かいスープなどをお届けしますよ」と話をしましたが、篠田氏は、「大丈夫」というだけです。さすがにこの寒波の中で、石油ストーブ一つの室内を想像しますと心配でした。

念のため共通の友人二人には、現在の状況は軽く告げておきました。
そして、本日の携帯です。我々は、イタリアンに行こうというときは、近くのサイゼリアを指します。タバコも、そして、ドリンクバーです。スタートは、カプチーノからはじまります。今日のランチメニューは、篠田氏の頭のなかでは決まっていたようです。メニューも見ないで「ぼく、コロコロポトフ」私は、「アラビアータ」。
タバコに火をつけ、いつものお気に入りのテーブル席から外を眺め、呟きます。
「私は、金沢、京都の有名店で食事をすることが時々あった。それらの店はもちろん老舗の佇まいと季節感のある食事だった」。
「いまは、この時間とこの食事」。
「あの時の感動と少しも違わないな。私にとっては、心の在り様と質感はどれも少しも変わらない、同じなんだ」と。
そしと「住む場所の感覚も同じだ」。

筑波大のときはつくばに住み、金沢の大学のときは金沢に住む。ごくあたりまえのように見えるが、住んで間もなくでも、その場所が生まれ故郷のようにすぐ街に馴染む。

「ぼく、アメリカでもそうだった。なぜか、自然体で溶けこめるんだな。自然体の空間認識に何も変わらず、楽しめるのが私の生き方の才能かもね」

私は、こんなひと時が好きです。芸術の表現と生き方の無意識のバランスが、篠田守男氏の世界観なのかもしれませんが、病み上がりにただ淡々と話すことが、病み上がりならではの食事会なのだと私には思える。

「見えないものが見える、必然の断食」なのだろうか。

病み上がりの淡々

ミーティングはサイゼリアお決まりのボックス席

2018年4月10日

風吹きぬ

春昼(しゅんちゅう)だというのに、夏が来たのかと勘違いするほど暑い、そうかと思うと夕暮れはやけに寒い日でした。消えゆく日差しとともに、冬がすぐに戻ってくるようです。篠田亭の野外炉にも、火を入れたくなるほどでした。

いつものセブンの100円コーヒーと共に話が始まります。

「先週、大塚駅のそばのバーで飲んでいたら、私が40年前にアメリカで買った透明の水差しのような形のランプがカウンターにあって驚いた。火が入っているのをはじめて見たよ。私は買ったものの、使い方がわからないままにしまってね。それを、何十年ぶりに出して眺めていいだんだ」

そこに、偶然の訪問だったようです。

「燃料は〝レイボーオイル〟」と言っていた。そんなオイルはない。火をつけたいけど、家にあるのは、ガソリンに、灯油、ホワイトガソリン。
「何がいいかな」、
「ガッソリンは危ないから、灯油かな」
筒状の透明ガラスの側面にあいた乳頭上のゴルフボール大のくぼみに注ぎ、その先の布状の沁に火をつけました。何の問題もなく火はつきましたが、煤が多く保谷はすぐに黒くすすけてしまいました。
「やはりレインボーオイルがいいんだね」
いつか…。

金魚生活

2018年5月14日

庭の入り口には、しだれ桜の枝が傘を広げている。玄関の左側には、一抱えほどの御影の石臼が水鉢として置いてあり、中には睡蓮が繁茂している。20年ほど前に石屋さんの庭先から譲っていただいたものです。睡蓮は春光に白い小柄な花をちらほら咲かせます。

「私は、ここに居ます」の如くに。

水の中をのぞくと、数匹のメダカと赤い金魚が泳いでいる。たまには、エサをあげることもあるが、いたって気ままです。魚たちもあまり期待はしていないようです。自然にボウフラや藻のようなものを食しているのかもしれない。時に、水鉢をのぞき込むと、赤い影が少ないように思われることもある。ネコがまた悪さをしたのかな、それとも静かに消えていったのか。たまには、ペットショップへ出かけ金魚を買い求めることもある。ペットショップの店員さんは、さりげなく「何にお使いですか」と尋ねる。「大型魚の餌に」、「イベントの金魚すくいに」といろいろ用途があるようです。鑑賞目的の魚種は、もともと育ちが違うのかもしれません。戸惑いながら、店員に告げます。

「観賞用です」

すると少々不思議そうでした。私も本当は、ボウフラ発生予防ですと告げたいところですが。でも、金魚たちがこの私の「観賞用」という言葉を理解できたならば、ほっとすることでしょう。「新しい時の始まりを、ありがとう」とでも。

10匹の金魚はこうして大きな水鉢の中で、新しい時間を楽しむこととなりました。たまには、猫たちのいじめから逃れるスリルを味わいながら。金魚も自覚はしていないでしょうが、食べられる運命から、楽しむ生き方へ。

見ている人間にはドラマですが、金魚はどうでしょうか。生き方の認識を持った人間からの、〝喜びと悲しみ〟のドラマとは。

「人の認識とは厄介なものなのでしょうか」

快楽宣言パート2「4人の語らい」

2018年8月9日

夕蝉どきに、街の寿司屋に入る。
17・8人が座れるL字型のカンターの客は、まだまばらだ。
店長前に座る4人の男女はまた静かに語り始める。
先程まで滞在していた、彫刻家・篠田守男氏のアトリエでの話のつづきが。
「私の今度の本はね」と熱心に語る篠田氏」
淡々と話を聞く、明和電機の土佐氏とそのスタッフ。
出版予定の「21世紀快楽宣言」は、どのような形で表現すればよいのだろうか？
それぞれの、記憶の中には、過ぎ去った時間を今という時代にどう表現し新たな創造へとつなぐことの、「この本の意味とは」
「篠田氏が描く今という時間の表現とは」
今日の文学、科学、哲学、数学、医学、情報工学、現代アート、それぞれの表現様式が一つの方向へと向かう芸術論とは。
それは、空間認識の共有の輝き、響き、の予感なのかもしれない。
それを「一つの数式として表せないだろうか」
「アインシタインのE=MC²のように」
日々の感動の瞬間を、数式でアートとして表現する試みを、この本に残せないものか？
いつもは無口の土佐氏も、穏やかに話しだした。
篠田氏と土佐氏の子弟の絆も小気味よい。
残りの二人の傍観者の存在も一味を呈しているのだろう。

21世紀の新たな本への挑戦その出発点が、このすし屋のカウンターから生まれようとしている。

好奇心のふくらみは、いつでもどこでも湧き上がる。

この、数式に当てはめれば誰でもがアーティスト。

―新鮮な本を、ここに表現したい―

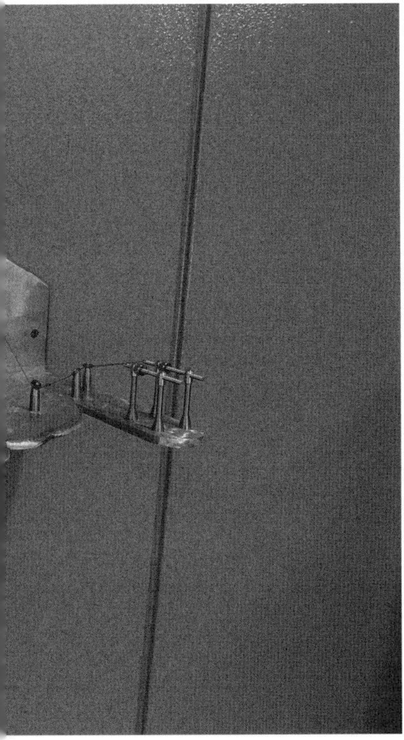

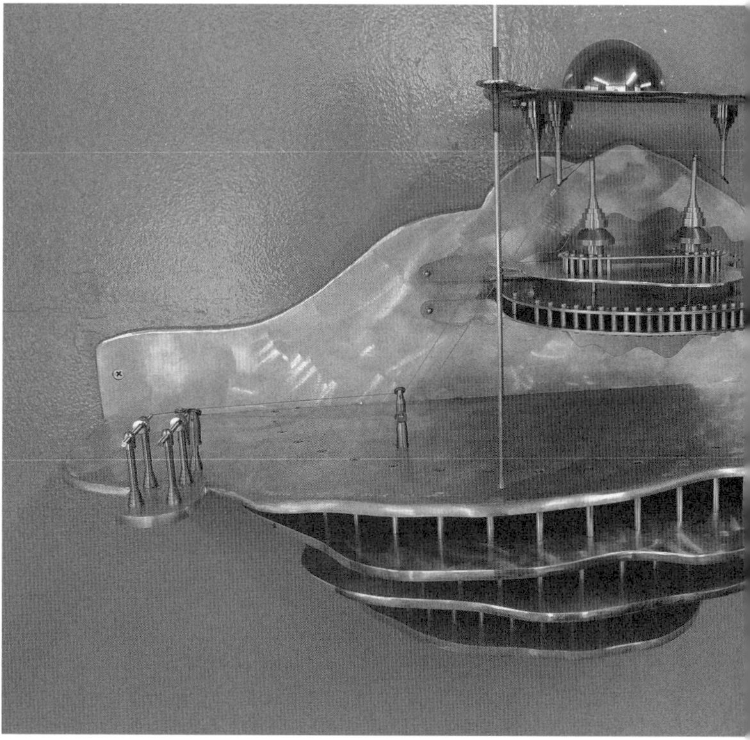

「序破急」のゆくえ

２０１８年８月25日

ある日、朝から静かに雨が落ちています。夕方にはこの雨はやむのだろうか。多くの人は気をもんでいるにちがいありません。大きな町の花火大会の日は、思い悩みます。そんな雨も昼過ぎにはあがり、日が沈む空には、息をのむような大輪の花が夜空を飾ります。このむせる様な、息をのむ花火を私はあまり好きではありません。少々へそ曲がりかもしれませんが、美しすぎて余韻が残りません。

夏には、よく奥会津・檜枝岐川の下流の伊南川に鮎を釣りに出かけた時期もありました。その宿は「民宿　与作」、「民宿　田吾作」の裏手にある常宿でした。

家の脇には、小塩橋があり、早朝の朝靄の川を眺め、水加減（水位）と透明度でその日の釣り場と戦略を描きます。

「そんな日の朝食はとくにうまい」

8月のお盆近くになりますと、伊南村の花火大会があります。夕暮れ、日焼けした身体が心地よい疲労感と共に漂います。そっと橋の欄干に寄りかかり川面を眺めますと、朝の川とはまた異なる柔らかさの流れがぼんやりと輝きます。しばらく待ちますが、町の空には、何も変化もありません。

「日にち間違えたかな」

でも、村人がまばらにいるところから、やはり今日だろうか。さらに待ちますと、村の有線が何か話しております。すると、ヒュー…、夜空に響いたと思ったら、パと菊の花が一輪。

すぐ後で「ド～ン」と川の両脇に迫る山肌が叫びます。それとともに、いや同時に私のハラワタが「ズシー」と響きます。急なことで、驚きのなかにその一輪の花にヘソも痺れます。また、しばらくの後に　一輪。
　これが、故郷を離れた人々が懐かしさをもって、戻ってくる花火大会なのかもしれません。
　ふと気が付きますと、村人は誰もいません。阿吽の呼吸で、終わっていたようです。でも、私の五臓六腑はまだどよめいているようです。

●夏の終わり

　裏庭にバケツを置き、一本の「スボ手牡丹の線香花火」に火をともす。
「パッ・パッと花が咲き」
　終わったかなと思いフーと息を吹くと、パッと輝きます。
「線香花火の一本の燃え方には、『序破急』があり、『起承転結』があると、寺田寅彦氏が語った」と、日本経済新聞にありました。
　おこがましいですが、―私はそれが好きです―

2018年9月6日

楠見貞男の世界「絵画のある風景」

――秋――

旅から戻り、玄関の赤い扉を開きますと、「夕焼けのパリの街角」の50号の油絵が「おかえり」と迎えてくれます。オフィスの扉を開くときは、正面には大きな「二輪の枯れたひまわり」の油絵が。リビングには、1960年代のパリの街角・1980年代のバラの絵たちが静かに、ときに鋭く研ぎ澄まされた声で語りかけてくれます。

「これが、私の空間表現の志です」と語るかのように。

深夜のリビングで、一人ワイングラフを片手に、好きな音楽とともに過ごすこともあります。そんなときは「別な声が聞こえます」

１９８７年ごろの楠見宅二階のアトリエに、二人きりで日が沈むことも忘れ、キャンパスの描きかけの絵を眺めながら語ります。〈あの時の声が〉ほんの昨日のことのように。

「そんな夜が私は好きです」

―冬―

冷え切った室内の絵の前に立ち、思います。

あの時に、もう少し私に絵を理解する能力があったならば、「アトリエでの語らいをより深く理解できたかもしれない」、と反省と後悔をいたします。ですが、あの時には、私は気付きませんでした。今は、楠見氏はこの世を去り語りあうことは出来ません。ですが、絵というものは不思議なものなのです。

「あのね……」といまも語りかけてくれる。

今の自分はといいますと、あの時より少しは、彼が描こうとした何かを感じられるようになったかもしれません。すると「う〜ん、少々理解するのが遅いよ」と絵が微笑みます。

なぜあの時（１９８７年）、１９６７年に描いた、このブルーの背景にクリスタルの花瓶と椿の表現を理解できなかったのだろう。絵はずっと発信しつづけていたのに、私は気付きませんでした。今という時に「この美しい響きの時間と向き合う」共有の物語の楽しみとして。

―春―

川に立つ。

サクラマスを追い続ける私にとっては、待ちにまった季節です。ぬるみゆく水の流れは、足もとを心地よく流れていきます。
「今年の遡上は、どうかな」
昼過ぎ、胸の携帯が鳴ります。篠田守男氏からのようです。
「帰りに、お茶しない」
よく、川の帰りには、篠田氏のアトリエを訪ねます。
アトリエでの話は多岐にわたります。ある時はシュールリアリズムについて、ある時は、なぜデュシャンは、ひとつの時代の地位を確立したのかと。モーパッサンとエッフェル塔の話もよくします。
「好むことと好まざること」との意味について。
篠田氏は最初に楠見氏の油絵「二輪の枯れたひまわり」(30号)と私の自宅で出会いました。そのときは、ほとんど関心を示しませんでした。
20年後、私たちの話のなかには楠見氏の表現の原点、「地球軸のテンション、書家としての筆の線と油絵の表現」、篠田氏の「テンションとコンプレッション

（T／Cシリーズ）」の空間認識の共有の喜びに花を咲かせます。

―夏―

旅。

「ねー、あなた、今日も暑いわね。北海道はさぞ涼しいでしょうね。旅に出ません」

楠見氏の奥様、智保子さんはご主人に話しかけます。

「じゃ、旅に出ようか」と楠見夫妻は旅立ようです。楠見氏83歳のときです。

楠見氏の運転で野宿生活をしながら。時

には喧嘩をし、楠見氏は小さなテントで車外にというときも、多々あったようです。奥様は車内。

旅は、いつも、10日前後で益子にもどっていたようです。夏が来ると北海道へというスタイルで、何年か続きました。

北海道からは、ときどき私のもとにハガキが届きます。滞在場所の風景を水彩で、脇には短い詩が添えられています。一枚のはがきは、私も旅の友として誘われる思いでした。

蜩（ぐらし）の声とともに、秋めくころにも、「二人の心の旅は、まだ続いているようです」

2018年12月29日

欲望という名の好奇心

ある時、宇宙空間で他の惑星からの来客に出会いました。
「あなたの星（地球）の年齢は何歳ですか」と尋ねられた。
「46億歳」と私は答えますと。
「まだ若い星ですね」と言葉が戻ってきました。

今、地球では2018年が終わろうとしています。ふと、地球時間で考えますと、人類誕生は4億年前ぐらいでしょうか。平均寿命100歳という響きに、違和感を感じない時代です。75歳は現役で、という時代に地球の年齢46億歳を指標として物事を考えるとするならば、人間の年齢は何歳であろうと取るに足らない時間なのかもしれません。
類人猿で生き残れたのは、力強いネアンデルタール人なのか弱々しいホモサピエンスなのか。そのカギとなったのは、人間関係の協調と宗教観が文化を創り上げたことなのでしょうか。欲望という名の好奇心が、そのカギを握っているとも語られています。
ダーウィンの進化論は、進化は進歩ではなく、適応力とも。やはり、欲望の中に潜む適応力、好奇心が文明を生んだのでしょうか。なぜ、ネアンデルタール人は、滅びの方向へと向かったのでしょう。
人は「一切皆空」という空間認識のなかに秘められた「輝き」を、人間の生き方としてどうとらえるのでしょうか。スピノザの「エチカ」には、「自分がいまいる場所でどのように住み、どのように生きていくか」という問いがあると國分功一郎氏は語ります。

2019年1月15日

酒は景色となった

また、正月を迎えました。大きな区切りのイベントもなく、ただ淡々とですが、今年は少々いつもとは異なることもありました。友人から頂戴致しました紹興酒の瓶の存在です。

頂戴した時には、すでに10年ものの紹興酒でした。その後、地下のセラに置かれて30年が過ぎました。

「のんびりと、眠りについていたようです」

ここで問題なのは、いつ誰と飲むかが難しいのです。

「一斗の瓶」

そのことを考えながら、5年の月日が流れました。

「今日　飲もう」と、私が感じた時に飲む、と心には刻んではいたもののなかなか難しいものです。株を買う時と同じように、買うことは簡単ですが、売るタイミングが難しいものです。早すぎても遅すぎても悔いが残ります。

いつもと変わらない年末気分でしたが、ふと「今日飲もう」と何の気なしに思い立ちました。5～6人といつもよりは少々友人の数は多いですが、特別なパーティーでもありませんでした。「思い立って」、ある意味、お酒はこれでよいのかもしれません。

1961年代のワインを飲むときも2人ぐらいで、このタイミングで。呑むための肩書などは必要ないようです。どんな時でも、私の持ち物ですから、私はいつもそこに居ます。

それで十分なのです。偶然そこに居合わせた方は、降ってわいた事故のようなものかもしれません。ただこの事故は少々後遺症が心地よいようです。

「しかし、今回の後遺症はいつもとは違う」ようです。

紹興酒の瓶の頭の竹籠を外し、石膏をノミで割りますと、瓶の中蓋はこぶし大の素朴な皿が朴葉でくるまれ湿り気をもち、みずみずしく覆われておりました。なかをのぞきますと、琥珀色の澄んだ酒は、龍泉洞の深い地下水のように湧き上がってくるようでした。

「味は、どうだろう」

みなさんも中をのぞき込みながら、ごくりと生唾を飲み込みました」。柄杓で透明なグラスに注ぎ、「出会い」に軽く乾杯をしました。まろやかな舌触りと鼻に抜ける香りは、時の経過を感じさせます。でも、酒の旨さは感じられません。ただ、「美しき水が」あっただけでした。

ただ一つ、粋な贈り物がありました。それは、瓶の外側に表現された「雨だれの如く、牡丹雪の如く」。長い時間の景色が、李朝の壺にも勝る作風が表現されておりました。

「無言の芸術の誕生です」

2019年6月19日

「小屋という名のアトリエ」

銘『命のさけび』

ここに、作品〝ウォール〟を超えた空間が、
その瞬間、"The Book of Tee"の認識も消えた。

● October　2018

夕暮れに、新治のアトリエ篠田亭に小屋が届きました。それは、4ントントラックの保冷庫の使い古しを、骨董屋で買い求めたものでしだ。見た目には、トラックの荷台にあった古びた箱ですが、篠田氏にとっては輝く幼年期の誕生日プレゼントのようです。80歳をゆうにこえていますが、うれしさは隠し切れません。
「ぼく、こんな空間が欲しかったんだ」
このなかに作品を展示し、そして新作ができるたびに変化していく。この空間（ミニミュージアム）と共に、世界中旅できたら、会場を借りるお金も節約できるし、私の宿泊費もたすかる。
「いいだろう」
箱の底部の中央には、荷を奥へと移動するためのローラーをはめ込んだ跡の、幅40センチの長方形の溝が奥の壁面まで彫り込まれています。同時に買い求めました長火鉢を、入り口のその溝のなかに納めますと、箱の内部は、茶室へと変容いたしました。篠田氏のさらなる夢は、膨らみます。
「この長火鉢の童虎で、燗も楽しみたい」
「雲間の月も、喉がなるだろう」
その日から、夕暮れになると、火鉢に炭を入れ人肌燗で楽しんだ、と氏の舌が

第一の小屋

語ります。私も時折訪ねては、長火鉢の鉄瓶の湯を使い抹茶を振る舞っていただきました。長火鉢の引き出しのなかの落雁もそっと添えて。

●Winter 〝ある日〟

ミニミュージアム構想はさらに続きます。
「上野さん、もうひとつ小屋が欲しいなー」
「それは無理です。庭に置くスペースも、金銭的にも」
「そうだね」
2日後の昼過ぎに、篠田氏から電話がありました。
「庭に小屋を置くためのレイアウトの図面ができたから、夕方見に来て」
彼の創造の世界は、消すことができないようです。夕暮れにアトリエを尋ねますと、彼の眼はさらに輝いておりました。
「どう思う、このレイアウト」
まだ、どこで小屋を調達するのかの見通しもありません。しかしレイアウトの発想は面白いものでした。この庭のスペースと二つの小屋の配置と母屋とのバランス、お隣の友人の土地ですが、うっそうと茂る杜の全てが篠田氏の脳のなかで一つのアトリエとして広がっていました。
これが、篠田氏の新しい作品の幕開けであり、表現なのだと直感いたしました。その後、時を同じくして偶然にも私の友人の産廃業者の廃材置き場のなかから新たな小屋を発見いたしました。
「ぼく、これがいい」
「その小屋は明日にでもスクラップにしようと思っていた」と友人。
それは、工事現場用の移送式事務所の箱のようでしだ。すぐに自分の持っていたメジャーで測り、一人つぶやきます。

第二の小屋

「大丈夫、ピッタリ」
でも移動方法も、金額もまだ決めていないのです。ちょっと心配。
後日、その箱の重さを量り、その鉄の重量の相場で分けていただけることになりましたが、輸送にはまだ多くの問題が残っております。

●March

二つ目の小屋がトラックの荷台に乗せられ届きました。今日は暖かい日です。篠田亭の庭に、一つの箱が空を飛びました。大きなトラックの荷台に乗せられ、篠田亭の入口近くに止まりました。夢の小箱か、アリスの密箱のように、二坪の白い鉄の小屋は大きなクレーンに釣られて、まさに宙を。これで篠田氏の頭の中で描く創造の空間と、現実の箱の空間が一つとなりました。

「人間の存在認識は虚構のアートとなる」

小屋は無事、スポッと居場所におさまりました。もうすでに、10年前からその場所にあったかのように、空間は新たな広がりをかもし出しました。

その日から、小屋と小屋を屋根の上でもう一つ重ね、立体的空間構想を描き始まっておりました。

新しい今の小屋の内部には腰高の高さに三畳ほどの座敷を新たなアトリエとしたいと考えていました。

「畳の下の部分は、収納用の引き出しを二つ作る。そうすれば作品も収納できる」。

大工さんにベニヤ板で床も張ってもらい、自分で床は茶色に塗りたい。

「この茶色にはイミがあるんだ」

作業用の部品は0・何ミリという精密部品が多い。床に落ちると二度と見つからない。

「そのためにはこの色が必要なのだ」と。
まさに、この小屋はスイスの時計工房のようです。壁面はターコイズブルー、天井は白くマスキングテープを使い自分で塗りました。何日も何日も、全て思い道理になるまで。それは、何かにとり憑かれたかのように、ただ黙々とやりとげました。気が付けば、身体はへとへとに干し大根のようでした。
「さあ明日完成祝いを昼にやろう」と篠田氏。
朝、いつもの休日のように私は川へ。釣りをしていた時に、携帯が鳴りました。時計を見ますと10時、少々約束の時間には早いようです。電話の向こうで、篠田氏は苦しそうに話します。
「上野さん、息できない、どうしたらいいかな」
すぐに、私は救急車を呼ぶように話し、三分後に掛け直しました。
「あと8分で来る」。
その後、行先の病院名を告げる電話をもらいました。無事に、病院に入院することができたようです。
昼過ぎに病院を尋ね看護婦さんとの話では、かなりの重症のようでした。
「あと5分遅れていたら」と…。
詳しくは、検査結果が2、3時間後にはわかるとのことで、次の日の夕方に病院を訪ねることにしました。一か月の入院が必要のようですが、命の問題はとりあえず軽減したとのことでした。
病室での最初の一言。
「ここいいよ。室温も一定で、黙って三食でるよ」
看護婦さんは、
「救急車での入院の患者さんで、だれも家族の方が来ないのは初めてです」
それぞれの、サポートの感じ方の表現は違うものです。感じ方の理由を私なりには話せますが、説明の必要はなさそうです。見たままの現実が全てです。
日々、篠田氏の容態は改善に向かっていくのが、感じ取れました。すると、

ニックネーム"金のウンコ"

7月末の個展が気になりだしたようです。

「早く新しい作品が作りたい」意欲は十分のようです。

二週間後には、やや強引に退院いたしました。退院時、支払のお金を持っていなかったために、少々もめたようでしたが無事に。

篠田氏は語ります。

「私は個展をふくめ、やりたいことが山ほどある。寝てはいられない」

彼は、病院の天井は嫌いなようです。

「上野さん、これ見て」

その時すでに個展の材料の注文は済み、病室で描いていたデッサンが現実の図面となり、そこにはありました。アトリエの畳の上には何十年間にわたり趣味で集めた、西欧骨董の銀製の道具の数々が並べてあります。これを個々の壁面に並べて、絵巻物を表現したい。これが「不思議の国のアリス」の誕生へと。

「どう思う」

もう頭のなかでは完成している。ただ、確認のために問い掛けるのです。
「そだね、それで、いいと思う」
「あーよかった」
これが、いつもの流れです。篠田氏の頭の中は、もうすでに別の世界を走っていることでしょう。それにしても、脳はぜんぜん病んでないようです。

●July　20th

ニックネーム〝金のウンコ〟、作品名「不思議な国のアリス」。
病院のベッドで薬袋の裏に書かれたスケッチは、今日　作品となり、7月29日からの銀座の個展への準備は、一つの方向を指しました。ですが、この作品では本来のイメージの途上のようです。10月の別の個展までには、さらなる進化を遂げる、成長する作品群の第一段階のようです。

7月の個展前だというのに、今年は長雨が続きます。アトリエのスペースでは、スケールのある作品制作場所としては、困難をきたしていました。

彫刻家菅野氏（かんちゃん）のいつものような大きな働きのお陰で、退院からこの短い期間になんとか形となりました。流石、弟子と師匠の連携プレーも見事でした。何かが生まれるときは、母親の気持ちのように数々のドラマはつきものなのでしょうが、今回はまさに〝ドラマの連続〟でした。退院から2週間の出来事でした。「雨と、湿気と、疲労」の戦いが続きました。そんななかでも、飛びぬけて持続し続けたものは、「湧き上がる想像力」のようでした。

我々は、夕暮れにこの作品と向かいあいます。黄金色のウンコは、沈みゆく太陽に反射し横たわるティラノサウルスの頭部と見違える迫力を醸し出しております。悠久の大地に眠る化石の存在感と同じように、今という時代にアリスの壁面もまた語りかけてくれます。

「虚構の空間への継承」なのか、「ウォールという作品空間の存在価値への叫び」なのか。

人は静けさを、無音とは表現しないだろう。作品ではなく、私自身のなかに語らいを感じ取る意義性の思いとは。篠田氏の頭の中の「無言の調和」とは。見てみたい、完成された彫刻「不思議な国のアリス」を。そこには、それぞれの胸の内に何を語ってくれるのか。

●July 29th 月曜日 銀座

個展の日を迎えました。

夕暮れのオープニングの会場、羅針盤のフロワーは今までには経験しえなかった、ふしぎな輝きを発しておりました。多くの困難を通過したからこその響き

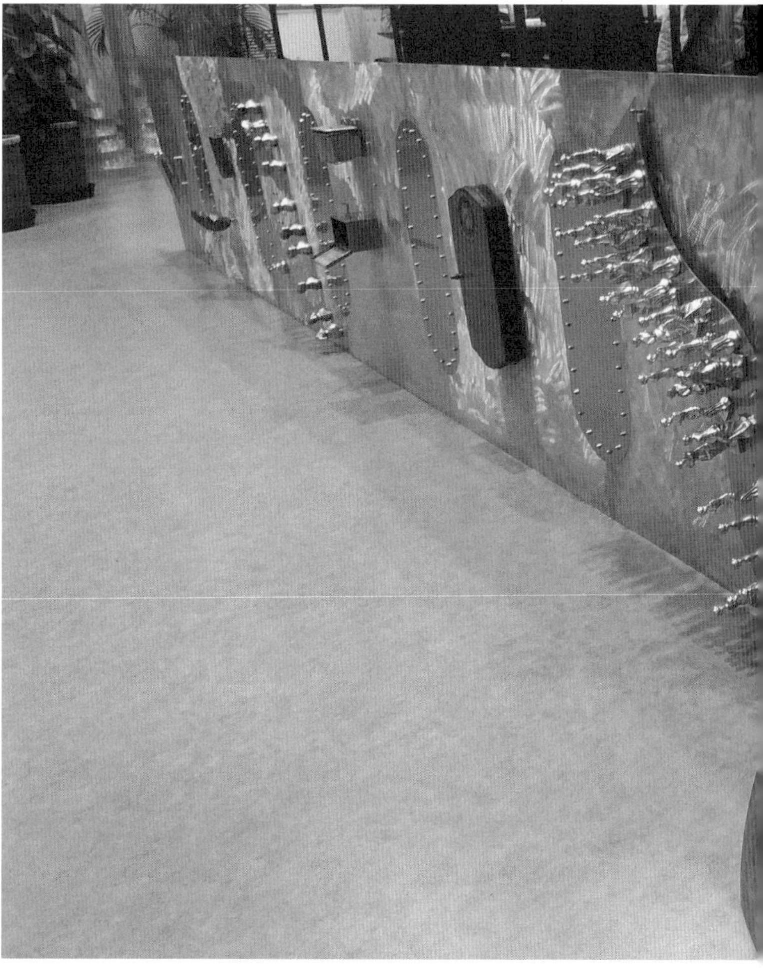

不思議の国のアリス

なのか、それとも篠田氏の生きた証の表現の鋭い方向性なのか。かんちゃんの運命共同体の証なのか。

私は近い距離で語れるこの時期に、さらに新鮮に見えることとは。それが個展という、表現方法の区切りの面白さなのでしょうか。オープニングに参加された、それぞれの方々には、その作品との距離感の感動と出会いの共有なのでしょうか。

アメリカ合衆国ヨセミテ公園を歩いていますと、46億年間のこの場所の歴史や苦しみはわかりません。ただ、今を楽しむ人がいます。

「篠田守男ワールドは、テンション（T＆C）のバランス、ウォールでの空間へと誘い」、そして「過去からつづく時間の物語〝不思議な国のアリス〟の空間」それぞれが融合し一つのアートとして羅針盤のフロワーに広がります。

「友人は、そこに集う」

白い本ケース

プロフィール

篠田守男（しのだもりお）

１９３１年東京生まれ　１９５２年 通産省大臣官房渉外課勤務（〜54）　１９５３年 青山学院大学第２文学部英米文学科中退　１９５４年 通産省工業技術院産業工芸試験所（ＩＡＩ）勤務（〜67）　１９５６年モダンアート展新人賞　１９６３年アート・インスティテュート・オブ・シカゴに留学（〜64）　１９６４年 京都近代美術館「現代美術の動向」　１９６６年 第９回高村光太郎賞を受賞　第33回ベネチア・ビエンナーレ展に日本代表で出品　１９６８年 カリフォルニア大学ロスアンゼルス校の客員教授（ＵＣＬＡ）（〜70）　１９７６年 コロラド州立大学およびミネソタ大学客員教授として渡米（〜77）　１９７３年「戦後日本美術の展開」国立近代美術館　第４回中原悌二朗賞優秀賞　１９７４年「日本伝統と現代」デュッセルドルフ市立近代美術館　１９７５年 彫刻の森美術館彫刻大賞展大賞　１９７９年 筑波大学芸術学系教授（〜94）　１９８１年「１９６０年代‐現代美術の転換期」国立近代美術館　１９８３年「現代美術の動向 Ⅱ」東京都美術館　１９８４年「20世紀彫刻の展望」滋賀県立近代美術館　１９８８年「現代美術の展開と表現の多様性」広島市現代美術館　１９８９年「抽象彫刻の旗手たち」福島県立美術館　１９９１年「現代日本美術の動勢—立体造形」富山県立近代美術館　１９９４年 長崎大学大学院専任教授（〜96）、「篠田守男個展」つくば美術館　１９９５年「篠田守男水力発電所展」入善町下山発電所美術館　２０００年 国際彫刻センター（ＩＳＣ）優秀彫刻教育者賞をアジア人として初受賞　２００１年 International Sculpture Conference at Pittsburgh,U.S.A　２００３年 金沢美術工芸大学大学院専任教授（〜２００９）　２００５年「SPACE WALKING」開館10周年記念発電所美術館　2013年 篠田守男個展　西脇市岡之山美術館　2018年「メタルフェティッシュ〈金属造形〉」日本橋タカシマヤ美術画廊　2019年 篠田守男現代アートギャラリーオープン
現在　筑波大学名誉教授

上野オサム（うえのおさむ）

1950年生まれ。1975年 日本大学歯学部卒業。1981年 つくば市に歯科医院を開業。画家・楠見貞男氏とつくばの個展にて出会い、時折、益子のアトリエに通う。1982年 寿司屋のカウンターにて篠田氏と出会う。それ以降、筑波大学総合造形講座を時々受講。1987年 自宅にアトリエ兼リビングルームを増築。1991年7・8月家族と共にキャンピングカーにてボストン〜オレゴンのアメリカ12000キロ横断の旅を行う。フライフィッシングにて、食事を調達。1994年 篠田守男氏、筑波大学退官後、茨城県土浦市新治（当時、新治村）の塚田陽威氏紹介にて住まいとして新治アトリエを開く。1995年　アメリカ ウィスコンシン州 レイク・ジェニーバにて Outdoor Education AEE Workshop を開く。2015年〜2019年　ラケットボール　アジア連盟会長就任。2003年　篠田守男氏、金沢美術工芸大学大学院専任教授時代に金沢で友好を築く。2009年 篠田守男氏、金沢美術工芸大学大学院を退官後、新治アトリエに戻り、さらに交流を深める。2019年（令和元年）12月　株式会社アルテック社長（現会長）野澤俊夫氏の好意にて、株式会社アルテックに「篠田守男現代アートギャラリー」を立ち上げ。2020年（令和2年）1月　一般社団法人　篠田守男現代アート研究会を設立。1982年〜　アラスカ、ニューメキシコ、カナダ、ニュージーランド、アイルランド、日本（北海道）にてフライフィッシング（ツーハンド）釣り旅。

Art, Graduate School (-2009) 2005 "SPACE WALKING" 10th Anniversary of the Power Plant Museum 2013 Morio Shinoda Solo Exhibition at Oka-no-yama Museum of Art, Nishiwaki City 2018 "Metal Fetish" Nihonbashi Takashimaya Art Gull 2019 Morio Shinoda Contemporary Art Gallery open
Professor Emeritus, University of Tsukuba

Osamu Ueno

Born in 1950 Graduated from Nihon University School of Dentistry in 1975. Opened a dental clinic in Tsukuba City in 1981. Met painter Sadao Kusumi at a solo exhibition in Tsukuba, and occasionally went to his studio in Mashiko. 1982: Met Shinoda at the counter of a sushi restaurant. Since then, she has occasionally attended a general art course at Tsukuba University. 1987 Built an additional studio and living room in his house. 1991 Traveled 12,000 km across the U.S. from Boston to Oregon in a campervan with his family in July and August. Procured food by fly fishing. 1994 After Mr. Morio Shinoda retired from Tsukuba University, he opened the Shinji Atelier as a residence with Mr. Hirotake Tsukada in Shinji, Tsuchiura City, Ibaraki Prefecture (Shinji Village at that time). 1995 Opened the Outdoor Education AEE Workshop in Lake Geneva, Wisconsin, USA. 2015-2019 Appointed President of Asian Racquetball Federation. 2003 Established a friendship with Morio Shinoda in Kanazawa when he was a full-time professor at Kanazawa College of Art. 2009 After Morio Shinoda retired from the graduate school of Kanazawa College of Art, he returned to the Shinji Atelier to further deepen the relationship. December 2019: With the kind support of Toshio Nozawa, President (now Chairman) of Altec Corporation, the "Morio Shinoda Contemporary Art Gallery" was established at Altec Corporation. January 2020: Established the Morio Shinoda Contemporary Art Study Group as a general incorporated association. 1982- Fly-fishing (two-handed) in Alaska, New Mexico, Canada, New Zealand, Ireland, and Japan (Hokkaido).

profile

Morio Shinoda

1931 Born in Tokyo 1952 Worked at the External Relations Division, Minister's Secretariat, Ministry of International Trade and Industry (-54) 1953 Withdrew from the Department of English Literature, Faculty of Letters, Aoyama Gakuin University (-54) 1954 Worked at the Industrial Arts Research Institute (IAI), Industrial Technology Agency, Ministry of International Trade and Industry (-67) 1956 Awarded the Modern Art Exhibition Newcomer Prize 1963 Studied at the Art Institute of Chicago (-64) 1964 Awarded the 9th Kotaro Takamura Prize for Contemporary Art at the Museum of Modern Art, Kyoto 1966 Represented Japan at the 33rd Venice Biennale 1968 Visiting Professor at the University of California, Los Angeles (U.C.L.A.) (-70) 1976 Visiting Professor at Colorado State University and the University of Minnesota 1973 "The Development of Postwar Japanese Art" The National Museum of Modern Art, Tokyo 1974 "Japanese Tradition and Modernity" The Museum of Modern Art, Dusseldorf, Germany 1975 Grand Prize, Sculpture Grand Prize Exhibition, The Hakone Open-Air Museum, Tokyo 1979 Professor of Art and Design, University of Tsukuba, Tsukuba, Japan (-94) 1981 "The 1960s: A Turning Point in Contemporary Art" The National Museum of Modern Art, Tokyo The National Museum of Modern Art, Tokyo 1984 "Prospect of 20th Century Sculpture" The Museum of Modern Art, Shiga 1988 "Development of Contemporary Art and Diversity of Expression" Hiroshima City Museum of Contemporary Art 1989 "Standard Bearers of Abstract Sculpture" Fukushima Prefectural Museum of Art 1991 "Movement of Contemporary Japanese Art" The Museum of Modern Art, Toyama 1994 Professor, Nagasaki University Graduate School (-96) 1995 "Morio Shinoda Hydroelectric Power Plant Exhibition" Tsukuba Museum of Art 1995 "Morio Shinoda Hydroelectric Power Plant Exhibition" Nyuzen Town Shimoyama Power Plant Art Museum 2000 First Asian to receive the International Sculpture Center (ISC) Outstanding Sculpture Educator Award 2001 International Sculpture Conference at Pittsburgh,U.S.A. 2003 Full-time Professor at Kanazawa College of

Alice in Wonderland

I would like to see the completed sculpture "Alice in Wonderland". I would like to see the completed sculpture "Alice in Wonderland" and wonder what it will say to each of us.

Monday, July 29th, Ginza

The day of my solo exhibition arrived.

At the opening at dusk, the floor of Rashinban was radiant with a strange glow that I had never experienced before. Was it the sound of having passed through so many difficulties, or was it the sharp direction of Shinoda's expression of living proof? Is it a sign of Kan-chan's shared destiny?

What is it that seems even fresher at this time when I can talk about it from a close distance? Is that the fun of a solo exhibition, a break in the method of expression? Is it the sharing of impressions and encounters of distance with the works for each of the people who attended the opening?

As I walk through

Yosemite Park in the United States, I don't know the 4.6 billion years of history and suffering of this place. However, there are people who enjoy the present.

"Morio Shinoda's world is a balance of tension (T&C), an invitation to the space of the wall, and a space of "Alice in Wonderland," a story of time that continues from the past.

Each of these is fused together to form a single piece of art that spreads across the floor of the compass.

"Friends gather there.

hospital bed became a work of art today, and the preparations for my solo exhibition in Ginza starting July 29th have taken a turn. It seems to be the first stage of a growing body of work that will evolve further before another exhibition in October.

It has been raining a long time this year, even though it is before my solo exhibition in July. The space of my studio has been difficult to use as a place to create works of scale.

Thanks to the great work of sculptor Kan-chan, I managed to get it into shape in this short period of time since his release from the hospital. The collaboration between apprentice and master was superb. When something is born, there are always many dramas, just like a mother's feelings, but this time it was truly a "series of dramas. It was two weeks after I left the hospital. "It was two weeks after I left the hospital, and I was battling with rain, humidity, and fatigue. The one thing that kept me going through all of this was my "bubbling imagination.

We face this work at dusk. The golden poop reflects the setting sun, creating a powerful image of the head of a Tyrannosaurus lying on its side. In the same way as the presence of fossils lying in the eternal earth, Alice's wall also speaks to us in the present time.

"Is it an "inheritance to the space of fiction" or a "cry for the value of the existence of the wall space?

One would not describe silence as silence. What are the thoughts of significance that I can perceive the words not in the work but in myself? What is the "silent harmony" in Mr. Shinoda's mind?

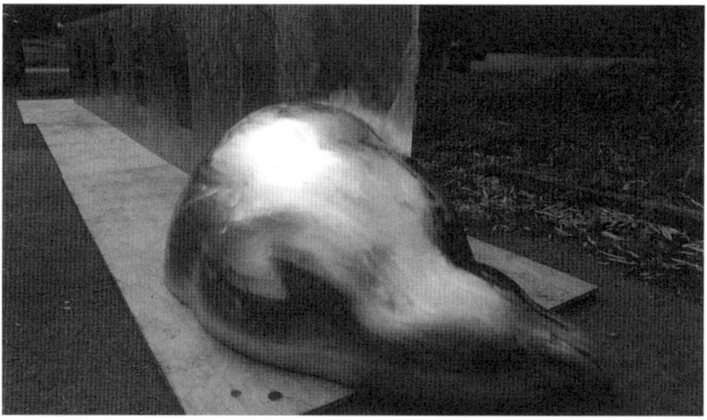

Nickname "Golden Poop"

individual walls to create a picture scroll. This is how Alice in Wonderland was born.

"What do you think?

I have already completed the work in my mind. But I ask her to confirm it.

"Yes, I think it's fine."

"Oh, good."

This is the usual flow. Shinoda's mind must already be running in a different world. But his brain doesn't seem to be sick at all.

July 20th

Nickname "Golden Poop", work name "Alice in Wonderland". The sketch that was written on the back of a medicine bag in a

"I like it here. The room temperature is constant, and you get three meals a day in silence.

The nurse said.

"The nurse said, "This is the first time we have had a patient admitted by ambulance without any family members present. Each of us has a different way of expressing our feelings of support. I can tell you why I feel the way I do, but I don't think I need to explain it. Reality as I see it is all that matters.

Day by day, I could sense that Shinoda's condition was improving. Then he started to worry about his solo exhibition at the end of July.

"He seemed to be fully motivated, "I want to make new works as soon as possible.

Two weeks later, I was somewhat forcibly discharged from the hospital. There seemed to be a little trouble because he didn't have the money to pay when he left the hospital, but he made it safely.

Shinoda said.

"I have a lot of things I want to do, including a solo exhibition. I can't stay in bed.

He didn't like the ceiling of the hospital.

"Ueno-san, look at this.

At that time, the materials for the exhibition had already been ordered, and the sketches he had drawn in the hospital room had become real drawings. On the tatami mats of his studio, he had collected a number of Western antique silver tools as a hobby for decades. I wanted to arrange them on three minutes later.

He'll be here in eight minutes.

Then I got a call telling me the name of the hospital to go to. I was admitted to the hospital without any problems.

I visited the hospital in the early afternoon and talked to the nurse, who told me that his condition was quite serious.

She said, "If I had been five minutes later....

We decided to visit the hospital the next evening, as we were told that the test results would be available in a couple of hours. I was told that I would need to stay in the hospital for a month, but that the life-threatening problem had been alleviated for the time being.

The first words in the hospital room were.

The second hut

"That's why we need this color."

This shed is exactly like a Swiss watch workshop. I painted the walls turquoise blue and the ceiling white by myself using masking tape. I painted the walls turquoise and the ceiling white, using masking tape, for days and days, until everything was exactly as I wanted it. It was as if I was possessed by something, and I just kept at it. Before I knew it, my body was exhausted like a dried radish.

"Let's celebrate the completion tomorrow at noon," said Shinoda.

In the morning, I went to the river as I usually do on holidays. While I was fishing, my cell phone rang. I looked at the clock and saw that it was 10:00 a.m., a little early for the appointed time. On the other end of the phone, Mr. Shinoda was talking in a distressed tone.

"Mr. Ueno, I can't breathe, what should I do?

Immediately, I told him to call an ambulance and called back

The first hut

The hut is now safely in its place. The space took on a new dimension, as if it had already been there for ten years.

From that day on, I began to draw a three-dimensional spatial concept, stacking one hut on top of another on the roof. Inside the new hut, I wanted to create a new studio with a waist-high tatami mat room of about three tatami mats.

"In the lower part of the tatami, I would make two drawers for storage. I'll make two drawers for storage under the tatami, so I can store my works.

I want to have a carpenter put up a plywood floor and paint the floor brown myself.

I want to paint the floor brown myself. "This brown color has an imprint.

Many of the parts used for the work are precision parts with a diameter of 0.1mm. If they fall on the floor, you'll never find them again.

company.

I like this one.

I was going to scrap that shed tomorrow," my friend said.

It looked like a transportable office box for a construction site. I quickly measured it with my measuring tape and muttered to myself.

It's okay, it fits.

But we haven't decided how to move it yet, nor how much to pay. I was a little worried.

Later, we will weigh the box and share it with the market price of the weight of the iron, but there are still many problems in transportation.

March

The second hut arrived on the back of the truck. Today is a warm day. A box flew through the air in the garden of Shinoda-tei. It was placed on the back of a large truck and stopped near the entrance of Shinoda-tei. Like a small box of dreams or Alice's secret box, the white iron hut of 2,000 square meters was suspended in midair by a large crane. The space of creation in Shinoda's mind and the space of the box in reality became one.

The perception of human existence becomes the art of fiction.

on, his tongue told me, he enjoyed heating charcoal in a brazier and heating tea in human skin. The tea was served with some rakugan in the drawer of the brazier.

The mini-museum project continues.

Winter - "One day"

"Mr. Ueno, I want another hut..."

"That's impossible. "That's not possible, not in terms of space in the garden, and not financially.

"I guess so."

Two days later, in the afternoon, Mr. Shinoda called me.

"Two days later, Mr. Shinoda called me in the afternoon and said, "I've made a drawing of the layout for the shed in the garden, so please come and see it in the evening.
It seems that his creative world cannot be erased. When I visited him in his studio at dusk, his eyes were even brighter.

"What do you think of the layout?

We still have no idea where to get a shed. But the idea of the layout was interesting. The balance between the garden space, the two huts, and the main house, as well as the dense forest on his friend's land next door, all came together in Shinoda's mind as a single studio.

I had a hunch that this was the beginning of Shinoda's new work and expression. Later, at the same time, I happened to find a new hut in the scrap yard of my friend's industrial waste

A Studio Named "Hut"

Name: "The Scream of Life

Here was a space beyond the "wall" of my work.

At that moment, the recognition of "The Book of Tee" also disappeared.

At dusk, a hut arrived at Shinohar's studio Shinoda-tei. It was a used four-ton truck cold storage unit that I had purchased at an antique store. Although he is well over 80 years old, he can't hide his joy.

"I've always wanted a space like this," he said.

I've always wanted a space like this," he said, "where I can exhibit my works and change them as I create new works. If I can travel around the world with this space (mini-museum), I can save money on renting venues and my accommodation costs.

"It would be nice."

In the center of the bottom of the box, there is a 40cm wide rectangular groove carved into the back wall, where the rollers used to move the load to the back were installed. When a long brazier, which I bought at the same time, was placed in the groove at the entrance, the inside of the box was transformed into a tea room. Shinoda's dream continues to grow.

"I want to enjoy heating sake with this long brazier," he said. "The moon in the clouds will also make me thirsty.

From that day on, Shinoda's tongue tells me, he enjoyed heating sake with charcoal in the brazier at dusk. From that day

January 15, 2019

When I removed the bamboo basket from the head of the Shaoxing wine bottle and broke the plaster with a chisel, I found that the inside of the bottle was covered with a simple fist-sized plate wrapped in magnolia leaves, moist and fresh. When I looked inside, the clear, amber-colored sake seemed to be bubbling up like the deep underground water of Ryusen Cave.

"How does it taste?

Everyone gulped down their saliva as they peered inside. We poured it into a clear glass with a ladle and lightly toasted the encounter. The mellow texture and aroma on the nose reminded me of the passage of time. However, I couldn't feel the flavor of the sake.

There was just "beautiful water".

There was only one chic gift. On the outside of the bottle, there was an expression that said, "Like a rain shower, like peony snow. The long time view was expressed in a style that surpassed even that of Yi Dynasty vases.

"The birth of mute art.

Liquor Became the View

It's New Year's again. There is no major event to mark the occasion, just a blandness, but there was something a little different this year. I received a bottle of Shaoxing wine from a friend.

When I received it, it was already 10 years old. It has been sitting in the cellar for 30 years now.

"It seems to have been sleeping peacefully.

The problem here is that it is difficult to know when to drink it and with whom.

"A dart bottle."

Five years went by as I thought about this.

"I had made a mental note to drink when I felt like it, but it was not easy. Just like when you buy stocks, it is easy to buy, but difficult to know when to sell. If you buy too early or too late, you will regret it.

There were five or six of us, a little more friends than usual, but it was not a special party. "Five or six people, a bit more friends than usual, but nothing special, just a spur of the moment thing.

This is also a good time to drink wine from the 1961s, with about two people. There seems to be no need for a title to drink. No matter what time of day it is, it is mine, and I am always there.

That's enough for me. If you happen to be there, it may be like an accident that just happened. However, this accident seems to have a slightly comfortable aftereffect.

"But this time, the aftereffects are different from usual.

Curiosity in the Name of Desire

September 6, 2018

One day, in outer space, I met a visitor from another planet.
He asked, "What is the age of your planet (Earth)?"
I reply, "Forty-six million years old."
"He replied, "It's still a young planet.

Now, on Earth, the year 2018 is coming to an end. When I think about it in terms of global time, the birth of the human race was about 400 million years ago. If we consider the age of the earth, 4.6 billion years old, as a benchmark in an age where 75 years old is still active, the age of human beings may be insignificant no matter how old we are.

Who survived among the apes, the powerful Neanderthals or the weak Homo sapiens? Was it the cooperation of human relationships and religious beliefs that created the culture that was the key? It has also been said that curiosity in the name of desire is the key.

Darwin's theory of evolution says that evolution is not progress, but adaptability. After all, was it the adaptability and curiosity lurking in our desires that gave birth to civilization? Why did the Neanderthals head in the direction of extinction?

How do we perceive the "brilliance" hidden in the spatial perception of "all is empty" as a way of human life? Koichiro Kokubu says that Spinoza's "Ethica" contains the question of "how to live and how to live in the place where we are now.

From Hokkaido, I sometimes received postcards. They were watercolors of the scenery of the place where I was staying, with a short poem on the side. One of the postcards invited me to be a friend on the trip.

With the sound of evening cicadas, it seems that the journey of our hearts is still going on.

established himself in a certain era. We often talk about Maupassant and the Eiffel Tower.

On the meaning of "like it or not".

Mr. Shinoda first met Mr. Kusumi's oil painting "Two Withered Sunflowers" (No. 30) at my home. At that time, he showed little interest in it.

Twenty years later, our conversation blossomed into the joy of sharing the origin of Kusumi's expression, "tension of the earth axis, brush line as a calligrapher and oil painting expression", and Shinoda's "tension and compression (T/C series)" spatial recognition.

-Summer

Travel.

It's hot again today, isn't it? It must be so cool in Hokkaido. Let's go on a trip.

Mr. Kusumi's wife, Chihoko, spoke to her husband.

So, let's go on a trip," said Mr. and Mrs. Kusumi. Mr. Kusumi was 83 years old.

Mr. Kusumi was 83 years old, and he drove them around, living in the field. Sometimes they had quarrels and Mr. Kusumi had to stay outside the car in a small tent. His wife stayed in the car.

The trip always took around 10 days to return to Mashiko. When summer came, they went to Hokkaido, and this continued for several years.

at that time. Now, Mr. Kusumi has passed away and we cannot talk to each other. However, pictures are a mysterious thing. "It still speaks to me, "You know, ...

As for myself now, I may be able to feel something of what he was trying to draw a little more than I did then. Then the painting smiles at me and says, "Hmm, you're a little slow to understand.

Why didn't I understand then (1987) the expression of the crystal vase and camellia on the blue background that I painted in 1967? The painting had been transmitting for a long time, but I hadn't noticed it. It was a pleasure to share the story of "facing this beautiful sounding time" in the present moment.

-Spring

Standing in the river.

It is the season I have been waiting for, as I continue to chase cherry salmon. The flow of the warm water is flowing comfortably under my feet.

I wonder how the run will go this year.

In the early afternoon, my cell phone rings in my chest. It seemed to be from Morio Shinoda.

Let's have tea on the way back.

I often visit Mr. Shinoda's studio on my way back from the river.

We talk about a wide range of topics in his studio. Sometimes it is about surrealism, other times about why Duchamp has

The World of Sadao Kusumi "Landscape with Paintings"

-

Autumn

When I return from my trip and open the red door of my front office, a No. 50 oil painting of "Paris Street Corner at Sunset" greets me with a "welcome home". When I open the door to my office, there is a large oil painting of "Two Withered Sunflowers" in front. In the living room, a painting of a Parisian street corner from the 1960s and a rose from the 1980s speak to you quietly, sometimes sharply and with a clear voice.

It's as if to say, "This is my aspiration for spatial expression.

I sometimes spend time alone in my living room late at night with a winegraph in my hand and my favorite music. At such times, I hear a different voice.

In the studio on the second floor of Kusumi's house around 1987, the two of us alone, forgetting the setting of the sun, talk over the freshly painted pictures on the campus. They talk about the voices of that time as if it were only yesterday.

I like those nights.

-Winter.

I stand in front of my painting in the cold room and think.

As I stand in front of the painting in the cold room, I reflect and regret that if I had had a little more ability to understand the painting, I might have been able to understand the conversation in the studio more deeply. But I didn't realize it of villagers suggests that it is today. As I waited for more time, I heard the village wired talking about something. As I waited further, I heard something on the village wire, and then a whoosh echoed in the night sky, followed by a single chrysanthemum flower.

Soon after, the mountainside on either side of the river shouted,Boom! At the same time, I felt my heart skip a beat. It was sudden, and in the midst of my surprise, I felt my belly button go numb at the sight of the single flower. After a while, there was another flower.

Perhaps this is the kind of fireworks display that brings people who have left their hometowns back with a sense of nostalgia.

Suddenly, I noticed that there was no one in the village. It seemed to be all over with the "A-Un" breathing. But my five organs are still throbbing.

The end of summer

I set up a bucket in the backyard and lit one of the "Subote Peony Sparklers".

Poof, poof, the flower blooms.

You think it's done, you blow on it, and suddenly it shines.

I read in the Nihon Keizai Shimbun, "Mr. Torahiko Terada said that the way a sparkler burns has a 'beginning, middle, end and conclusion'.

I'm sorry to be rude, but - I like it.

The Fate of "The Beginning and the End"

One day, the rain is falling quietly in the morning. Will it stop raining in the evening? Many people must be wondering. On the day of a fireworks display in a large town, I worry about it. The rain stops by midday, and as the sun sets, the night sky is decorated with breathtakingly large flowers. I am not a big fan of these breathtaking fireworks. I may be a bit of a navel-gazer, but I find them too beautiful to leave a lasting impression.

There was a time when I used to go fishing for sweetfish in the Inan River, downstream from the Hieki River in Okuaizu in the summer. The inn was "Minshuku Yosaku", a regular inn located behind "Minshuku Tagosaku". There was a koshio bridge beside the house, and I would look at the river in the early morning mist and draw my fishing spot and strategy for the day based on the water level and clarity.

Breakfast is especially good on such days.

Near the Bon Festival in August, there is a fireworks display in Inan Village. In August, near the Bon Festival, there is a fireworks display in Inan Village. At dusk, my tanned body drifts with a pleasant sense of fatigue. I gently lean on the parapet of the bridge and look at the surface of the river, the softness of the current shining dimly, different from the morning river. I wait for a while, but there is no change in the sky over the city.

Maybe I picked the wrong day.

I wonder if I've got the date wrong, but the sparse presence

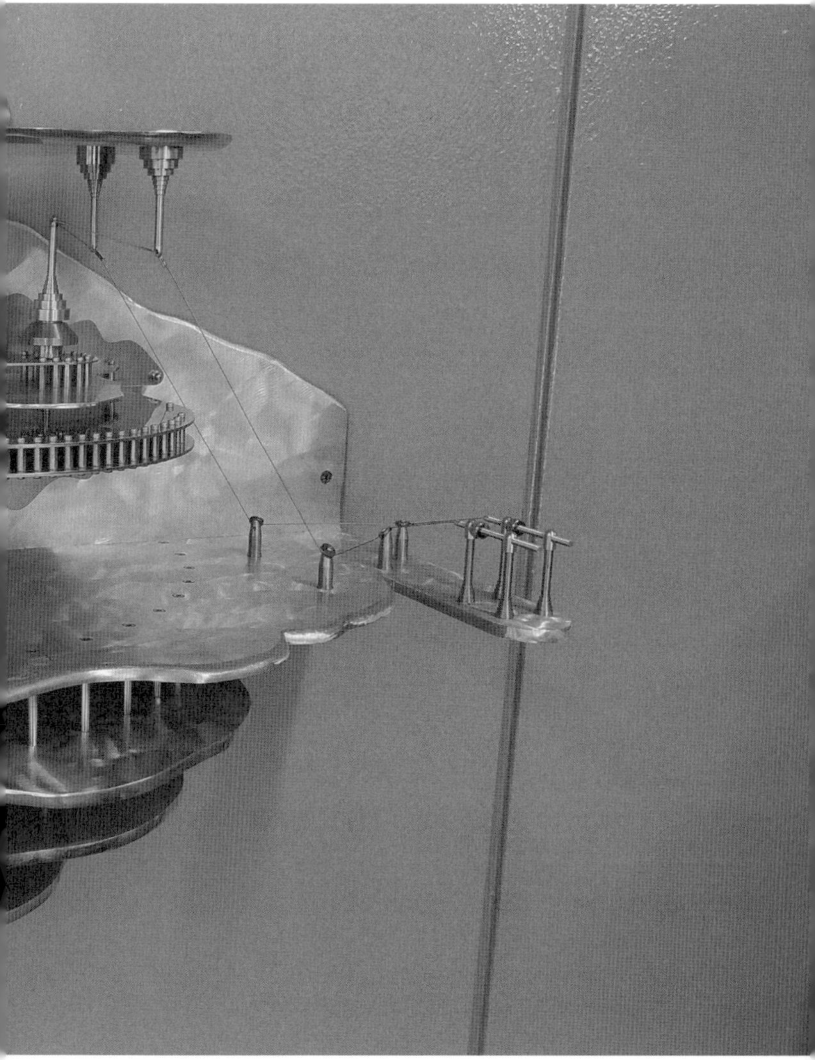

direction?

It may be the glow, the resonance, the anticipation of a shared spatial awareness.

Can't we express it as a formula?

Like Einshteyn's $E=MC^2$.

Can't we leave behind in this book an attempt to express the moments of our daily impressions as art using mathematical formulas?

The usually quiet Mr. Tosa began to speak calmly.

The bond between Mr. Shinoda and Mr. Tosa's children was also very pleasant.

The presence of the other two bystanders also added to the flavor.

The starting point for the challenge of a new book in the 21st century is about to be born at the counter of this sushi restaurant.

The swelling of curiosity springs up anytime, anywhere.

If you apply this formula, everyone is an artist.

I would like to express a fresh book here.

Declaration of Pleasure Part 2

"A Talk with Four"

It's evening cicada time and I walk into a sushi restaurant in town.

The customers in the L-shaped canter, which can seat 17.8 people, are still sparse.

The four men and women sitting in front of the manager start talking quietly again.

They are talking about their time at the studio of the sculptor Morio Shinoda, where they had just stayed.

"My next book," Shinoda says enthusiastically.

Mr. Tosa of Meiwa Denki and his staff listen to the story without hesitation.

In what form should we describe the "Declaration of Pleasures for the 21st Century" to be published?

In each of our memories, there was a question about the meaning of this book, about how to express the past in the present and connect it to a new creation.

"What is Shinoda's expression of the present time?"

What is the theory of art that moves today's modes of expression in literature, science, philosophy, mathematics, medicine, information technology, and contemporary art in one goldfish at events. Perhaps the fish species that are intended for appreciation grow up differently by nature. Puzzled, I told the clerk.

It's an ornamental fish.

The clerk looked a little puzzled. I would have liked to tell him that I was trying to prevent the spread of fungus. But if the goldfish understood my word "ornamental," they would be relieved. "Thank you for the beginning of a new era.

The ten goldfish are now enjoying their new time in the big water bowl. Every once in a while, they enjoy the thrill of escaping the bullying of the cats. The goldfish may not be aware of it, but they have gone from being destined to be eaten to enjoying life.

It's a drama for the humans watching, but what about the goldfish? What about the goldfish? What is the drama of "joy and sorrow" from a person who is aware of their way of life?

Is it possible that human perception is a tricky thing?

Goldfish Life

At the entrance to the garden, a weeping cherry blossom branch is spreading its umbrella. To the left of the entrance, a two-tiered granite mortar sits as a water bowl, with water lilies mooring inside.

The water lilies moored inside. The water lilies bloom here and there in the spring light with small white flowers.

As if to say, "I am here."

When I look into the water, I see a few killifish and red goldfish swimming around. I feed them once in a while, but they are quite unconcerned. The fish don't seem to expect much from me. They may be naturally eating something like bowfin or algae. Sometimes, when I look into the water bowl, there seems to be less red shadows. I wonder if the cat has misbehaved again, or if it has quietly disappeared. Sometimes, I go to a pet store to buy goldfish. The clerk at the pet store casually asks, "What are you using them for? The clerk at the pet shop casually asks, "What do you use them for?" They seem to have a variety of uses, from "feeding large fish" to "scooping

April 10, 2018

The fuel is 'Raybow oil,'" he said. There is no such oil. I want to light it, but I have gasoline, kerosene, and white gasoline at home.

"What would you like?"

"Gasoline is dangerous, so kerosene would be better."

I poured the gasoline into a golf-ball-sized hole in the side of a transparent glass tube, and lit the cloth-like sink at the end of the glass. The fire went off without a hitch, but there was so much soot that Hoya soon turned black.

I guess rainbow oil is the way to go.

Someday....

The wind blows Nomore

It was a spring day, but it was so hot that I thought summer had come, but the evening was very cold. With the fading sunlight, it seems that winter will soon return. It was so hot that I wanted to light the outdoor fireplace at Shinoda-tei.

The story begins with the usual 100 yen coffee from Seven.

Last week, while drinking at a bar near Otsuka station, I was surprised to see a lamp on the counter, shaped like a transparent jug that I bought in America 40 years ago. It was the first time I saw it lit. I bought it, but put it away without knowing how to use it. It's been decades since I've seen it.

It was a chance visit.

January 31, 2018

Kyoto, which of course had a long-established atmosphere and seasonal food.

Now it's this time and this meal.

Now it's this time and this meal," he said, "and it's not all that different from how it was back then. For me, the state of mind and the textures are all the same.

I also feel the same about where I live.

When I was at Tsukuba University, I lived in Tsukuba, and when I was at Kanazawa University, I lived in Kanazawa. It may seem quite natural, but even after living in a place for a short time, you immediately become familiar with it as if it were your birthplace.

I was the same way in America. I don't know why, but I can blend in naturally. Maybe it's a talent of my way of life that I can enjoy my natural perception of space without changing anything.

I love moments like this. The balance between artistic expression and the unconsciousness of the way of life may be Morio Shinoda's view of the world, but it seems to me that just talking plainly after being sick is a dinner party that can only be held after being sick.

I wonder if it is a "fast of necessity, where the invisible can be seen.

After illness

convalescence

The air in the river today is sharp and painful. For a week, the cold air mass has been playing tricks on us, and we've had some heavy snowfall. It's six degrees even during the day when the sun is shining, but it feels warm in the river.

For the first time in a long time, the cell phone in my chest rang. It didn't sound very cheerful.

Let's go eat Italian food for lunch. I was relieved to hear the invitation to eat.

Mr. Shinoda had caught a cold a week ago and had been sleeping alone in his atelier in Shinji, unable to get out of bed or go shopping for three days. But Mr. Shinoda only said, "Don't worry." As I imagined the room with only an oil heater in this cold wave, I was worried.

Just to be safe, I told our two mutual friends about the current situation.

And here is today's cell phone. When we want to go to an Italian restaurant, we point to the nearby Saizeriya. Cigarettes, too, and a drink bar. We start with a cappuccino. It seems that Mr. Shinoda had already decided on today's lunch menu in his mind. Without even looking at the menu, he said, "I'll have corocoro pot-au-feu," and I had "arrabbiata.

He lit a cigarette, looked out from his favorite table, and muttered.

I had occasionally eaten at famous restaurants in Kanazawa and Kyoto. I used to eat at famous restaurants in Kanazawa and

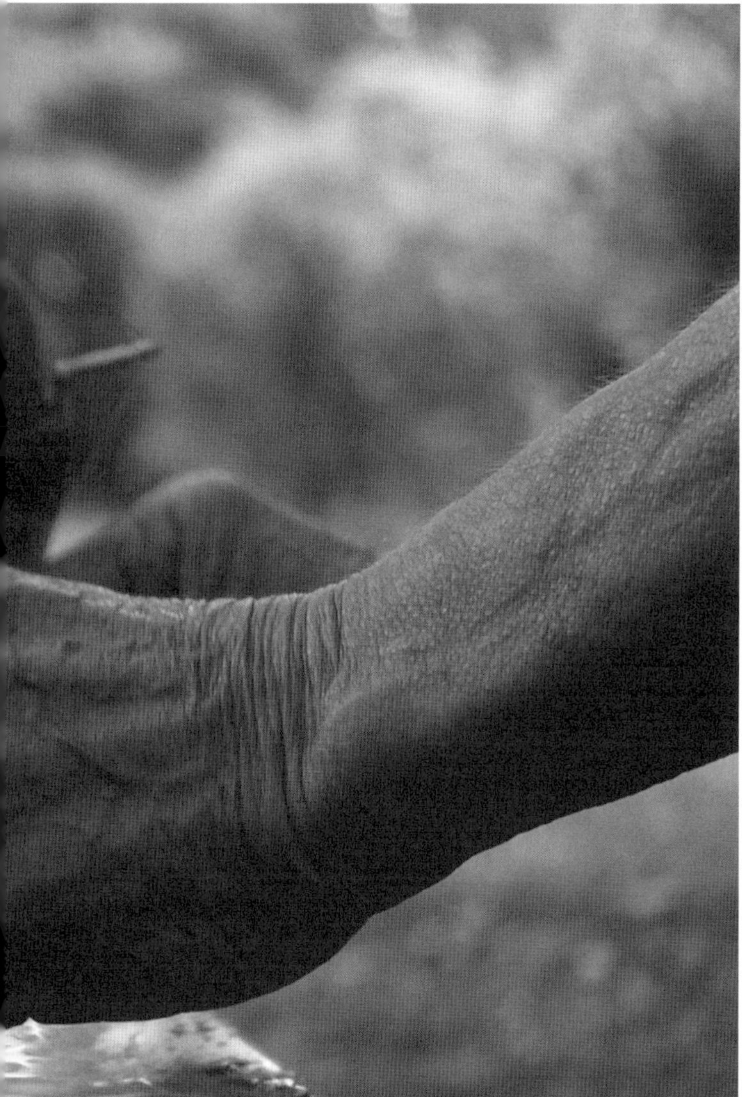

the time of life?

Twenty-four hours are supposed to be equal in the speed of light.

On the night of New Year's Eve, I looked up at the ceiling of the bath.

"For the first time in a long time, I think about time at the end of a day when I have nothing to do.

I sometimes have dinner with sports students.

They have spent most of their time since they were three years old playing only one sport.

They seem to have come to this day without question.

They also stop to reflect on the past 20 plus years.

I, too, look back over the past 60 years or so.

When I do, I think.

"Wasn't their time (20 years) longer than mine?

"Or does someone else's time seem longer?

Our perceptions drift in and out of ambiguity.

"We think of a day, and the wonder of time."

One day

One day, a child was born.
A day begins for that child.

On my work mornings, the day also comes around.
A day for each of us.

The child begins to learn words.
"Papa, mama", that seems to be the beginning of my own recognition.
Then they learn to recognize themselves (me), and later they may wonder who I am.
Is this the beginning of life?

I look back on a day and think, "When I was at work, I had no idea what I was doing.
"A day in the life of my job.
"A day in retirement."
A day at work, a day in retirement, a day at leisure, a day that should have been a long day, but before I knew it, the sun was setting.
"Long time, short time."
What is the relationship between the time of perception and

October 14, 2017

How did he see the Gentle Wind of 2017 in his mind? Almost a century has passed since the age of the avant-garde. Art is not art. Mathematics, physics, information technology, regenerative medicine, and philosophy are all moving towards one main axis.

"The wind of art.

I wonder if he was trying to express something of this wind in his perception. In the two-person exhibition by Morio Shinoda and Nobumichi Tosa (Maywa Denki) (October 27-November 4), I expressed a different atmosphere in the venue. It seems that most of the critics could not digest the wind.

However, this may be the beginning of "ART NOUVEAU" in the 21st century. I want to see this invisible wind with my own eyes "as a proof".

"O wind" - let it blow. Only in this awareness will the "wind" blow.

A man going to bay the wind

"I see! I'll go buy some," he said to himself.
"I'm going to buy some," he said, heading for Akiba.
This was the beginning of the work "Wind.

The garden of Shinoda-tei's studio.

A summer breeze had just blown across my cheeks as I faced south. At dusk, an autumn breeze blew across my cheeks on the north side.

"Is it autumn already?

The sunshine tells us that the seasons are changing. Each invisible wind is trying to tell us something. I wonder what Shinoda was trying to capture in the wind.

Perhaps he felt the wind of the avant-garde in the 1920s, or the current in his own way in America in the 1960s. "Dada, surrealism."

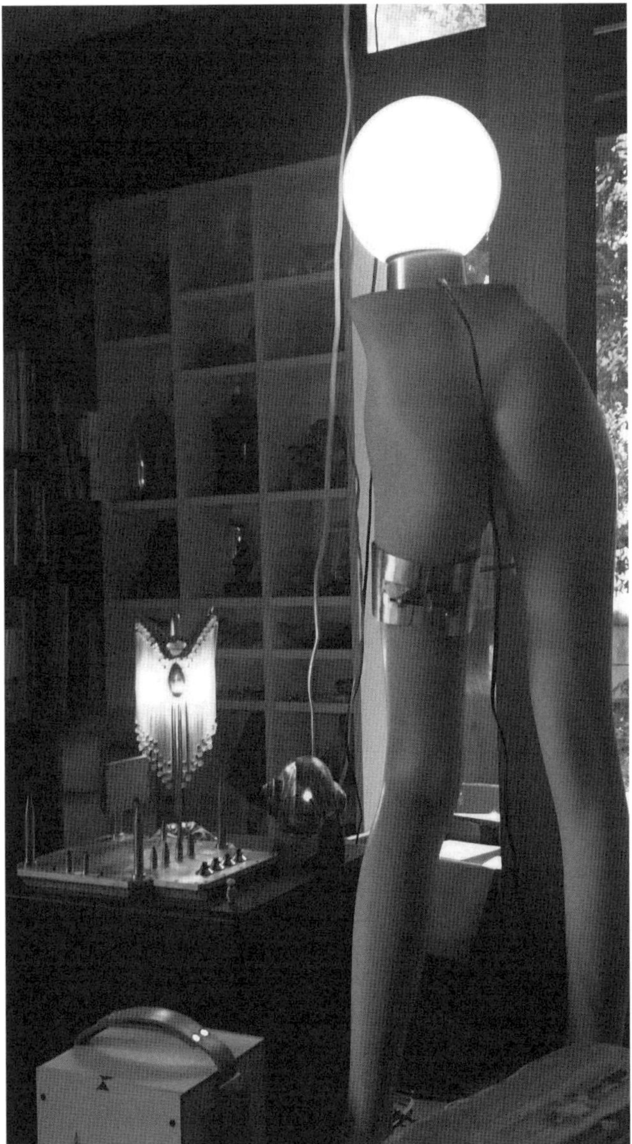

Mr. Shinoda looked up at the sky where the light was fading.

Shinoda looked up at the fading sky and said, "Let's have dinner together at a nearby noodle shop.

It was a relieving moment.

The next morning, my cell phone rang.

I'm at Joyful." He seems to have gone to buy the rest of the parts.

His voice sounded like morning light.

"I'll see you in the evening," I told him. I told him, "I'll see you in the evening," and put the phone down.

In the evening, I went to Shinoda-tei and found the finished work there. In the faint light of the setting sun in the western sky, the work stood still for a moment.

A new Morio Shinoda world.

I realized that this is how art is born.

"How can I make it stand?"

My idea in the river was to use a garter belt," I said. In the river, I told her that my idea was to use a garter belt, a metal belt attached to one side of her thigh, like a clasp at the end of a garter belt.

"I see." The conversation ended easily. I hung up my phone.

"That didn't do any good. I felt sorry for myself.

My garter belt idea was inspired by the Allen Jones Figurines book. I felt that it had something to do with hyperallism.

In the evening, I went to Shinoda-tei. Even though it was only 6:30 pm, nightfall was early in October. It felt like eight o'clock at night indoors. Especially today, I was up at four in the morning, fishing.

"It's a long day."

Mr. Shinoda was waiting for me, smiling as usual. There was something different and radiant in his smile. His eyes were saying, "Look at my work! His eyes were saying, "Look at my work! When I entered his studio, I saw that the garter belt holder was a 10 cm wide, 1.2 mm thick aluminum plate wrapped around the upper part of his left thigh, with an L-shaped stopper bent to secure the belt from both sides.

Five hours after our conversation at the river, it was already almost finished and there it was.

His slim legs, bound with metal, exuded an air of effortless charm. Mr. Shinoda also asked

I don't know how it came to be. I just found myself doing it. Shinoda said.

Garter belts

The river finally flows today, quietly heading towards the ocean. The flow of the Kuji River is somewhat gentler and softer than the flow of the Naka River.

In the late afternoon, Shinoda's cell phone rang in my chest.

"Ueno-san, are you at the river? It often rings when I am at the river.

It often rings when I am at the river. Normally, it's a love call, "Do you want to come by on your way home? But not today.

"What do you think?"

At the moment, she seems to be having a hard time choosing works for the opening of the two-person exhibition on October 20. One of them is a work of "female mannequin. It is a life-sized model of a nude woman from the waist down. On the upper surface of the waist is a simple milky white circular light, the size of a handball, facing the ceiling. The model had been sitting unnoticed in the clutter of the living room on the first floor of my studio for 30 years. In April of this year, I transformed the clutter into a clean space. (As in decluttering).

"Yes, this is good."

Then, the mannequin light took on a new presence. As dusk approached, the lights on the hips were turned on. The soft air in the room became fresh and fragrant. He was thinking of adding the work to the two-man exhibition by Morio Shinoda and Nobumichi Tosa (Meiwa Denki). One problem there was that the work could not stand alone. At present, I have managed to maintain the relationship by wrapping it around a pillar with a black light cord. This makes it difficult to display it in a venue.

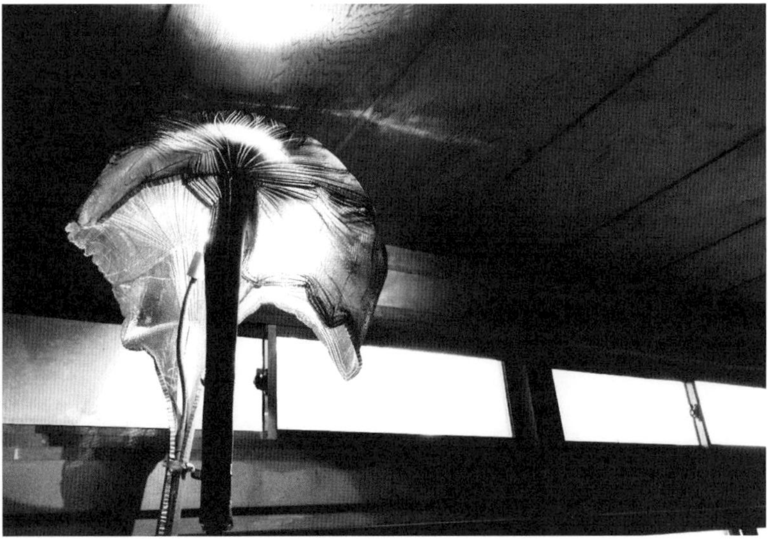

Mr. Shinoda had a Porsche, his favorite car.

I love Porsches so much.

But when he ran out of money, his car was sold.

At that time, he told me.

He said, "It's boring to drive inside, it's best to look at it from the outside.

...The story continues.

Architecture, art, and painting.

The values of the times, the future of truth and aesthetics.

Beyond the west window, the "wet yolk of a half-boiled egg" faintly fades away.

The room is slowly losing its color.

The "Ron Arat Armadillo Lamp" in the doorway begins to glow dimly. The lamp is made of 2-3 cm wide tapes of aluminum, and is a reproduction of a living armadillo. When the light is turned on, the lamp glows in seven different colors, creating a "beautiful monster. The room was led to a magical land.

"The wine of Yugure flows down my throat.

It's a super capsule studio space for us. In addition, we often talk about the relationship between the Eiffel Tower and Guy de Maupassant, who was an opponent of the Eiffel Tower at the 4th Paris Exposition in 1889.

It seems that Maupassant hated the Eiffel Tower the most. But once it was finished, he spent most of his time in the restaurant at the top of the tower.

The newspaper reporters asked Maupassant questions.

"Why do you spend so much time in this place you hate?" Maupassant replied.

Maupassant replied, So I don't have to see the thing I hate the most.

From there, he said, "If you don't like the Eiffel Tower, go to the Eiffel Tower.

Shinoda dislikes both the Tokyo Tower and the Sky Tree.

Shinoda dislikes Tokyo Tower and Sky Tree. It's just a radio tower.

"I can still forgive the Eiffel Tower."

When I asked him why, he said, "The Eiffel Tower's elevators are curved along the tower legs and rise from the bottom. In the Tokyo Tower, the elevator goes straight down from the center of the tower.

That's terrible.

were in the house, and the conversation continued. In the southwest corner of the hallway, there is a bookshelf designed by him. At first glance, it looks like an ordinary bookshelf, but on the back of the shelf, there are diagonal stripes of square wood running from upper left to lower right and from upper right to lower left on the front. The back of the shelf has diagonal stripes running from upper left to lower right, and the front from upper right to lower left. In each of the bookshelves, the historical background and the pages of the books in his mind seemed to spread out.

However, none of the visitors seemed to be able to recognize that world.

I wondered if this was an expression of Shinoda's unique view of the world. When I picked up a book, Allen Jones and John Cassell of the 1960s hyperrealism spoke to me. To the right is Bernard Rudofsky's The Unfashionable Human Body. So the talk of hyperrealism and surrealism begins again.

Sexy, eroticism and art theory. Gentleman Dandinism and the Theory of the Structure of Iki. Shuzo Kuki and Tenshin Okakura tried to talk about the world view hidden in the same DNA. Add to that The Book of Tee from 1903 and Franklin Lloyd Wright. The story runs from the 1900s to the 2000s in a flash.

from Seven-Eleven and a 100-yen Meiji Chocolate Black. (The lady at Seven-Eleven puts the two cups of coffee in a special bag and holds the chocolates, then looks up at me from below to see if I am visiting somewhere.

Coffee is a must for conversation, and chocolate is a must for a moment.

The art of the everyday.

Sometimes my mind takes me to Houston in the 1960s. At other times, my mind wanders back to the time when we first met, to the 1980s, when I was in a performance class at Tsukuba University's School of Art and Design, and to the episodes of making art in the studio. Before we knew it, we

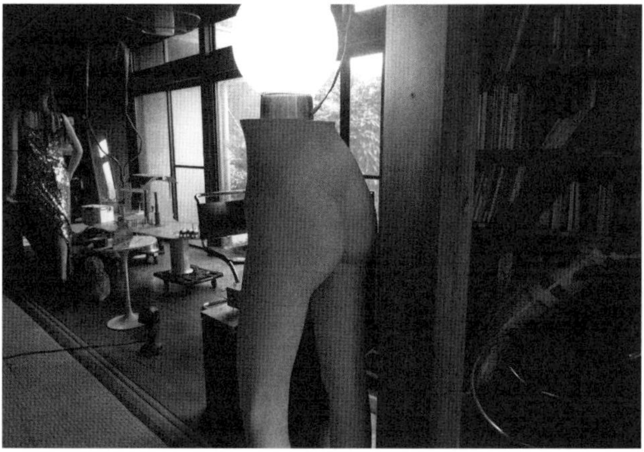

Relationships
"Arm push on Goodwill"
Morio Shinoda, Sculptor

I believe that relationships with people are found in that invisible distance. As expressed in Edward Hall's "The Hidden Dimension". Furthermore, there seems to be a different sense of distance not only among people, but also among nations, languages, and local customs.

Now, "What is the distance between me and the sculptor Morio Shinoda?

At first glance, he does not look like a normal person. "He is a "high-collared person with a reason.

He seems to have emerged from the screen of the tea room with a mysterious presence.

"When asked, "Who is that man?" I answered, "He is a sculptor. I am a sculptor," he says, and I am convinced that he is. "He may be a living performer who says, "I am the work, not the work.

These days, I often talk with him in the front yard of Shinoda-tei's studio (known as "garage stairs"). "I often talk in the front yard of Shinoda-tei's studio (a.k.a. Garage Star). "He is not talking to himself, but he is talking to me passionately with his eyes wide open.

When I visit her studio, I always bring two 100-yen coffees

Tanekuni, September 2009, red seal.

I hate the moon when there is nothing between the clouds.

I opened the box containing the sake cup and called Mr. Koyanagi.

How do you like it? How do you like it?" was his first words.

I was able to share the joy of seeing the vessel shine through the clouds. From the bottom of my heart, I could hear the echoes of the passage of time.

That night, I poured sake into a cup and looked at the deep scenery of the vessel.

I listened to the mute words.

Saturday, September 2, 2017

Later, I received a call from him.

I could fix it myself, but the thickness of the seam would make the vessel larger by a few millimeters. But I think my friend, Mr. Koyanagi, a lacquer artist, will be able to do everything.

The sake cup was now in the hands of Mr. Tanekuni Koyanagi. There was no friend's box, and of course there was no note on the box. Even so, he accepted the pottery with open arms, just as it was when it was fired.

He said, "When it is finished, I will give it to you with a box.

A long time has passed since then. During that time, I received many letters from Mr. Chidori asking if it was ready. Each time, I replied, "I am still traveling. I realized that the passage of time creates a temperature difference between the vessel and the heart, like a separation. Rather than waiting, I gave up.

It doesn't matter if I can do it or not, it's time to be at the mercy of others.

Five years later, the cup arrived. The inscription on the front of the box read, "Bizen Cup," and on the inside it read, "A cup of appreciation given to Mr. Ueno Osamu by Mr. Masamune Satoru from ashes in the kiln, damaged, restored by Koyanagi

Bizen Cup signed "Bizen Inazuma"

The sake cup arrived at 1pm. It is a Bizen sake cup, about the size of a small fist. The color was Edo black, as if it had just been taken out of the ashes, and there was a thumb-sized vermilion landscape on the inside, slightly off-center. On the inside, there is a thumb-sized vermilion landscape slightly off-center. A portion of the mouthpiece is decorated with several lightning bolts of gold from the rim to the center. To begin with, this sake cup was a friend that I carried around with me every day, where it could reach the warmth of my skin.

How did it come to travel away from my hands?

In a moment of carelessness, I dropped it with an uncomfortable sound at a friend's sushi restaurant. Since then, a journey of five years has begun, and today is the day.

My first encounter with this sake cup came from my trip to Bizen. I was invited to a kiln opening by the potter Masamune Satoru, and it was in the kiln that I met this cup. I picked up the sake cup from the still warm ashes using only my fingertips.

Luckily, it was wrapped in a cloth when I dropped it, and all the pieces were inside.

What should I do? I can't throw it away.

I thought to myself, "What should I do? Suddenly, I remembered Mr. Chidori, a restorer living in Chiba Prefecture, so I called him for advice and decided to send it to him.

Autumn, 2005

At the counter of an izakaya (Japanese style pub) in the sky of a trip, I rest my chopsticks and enjoy the time while looking at the beautiful night view of the metropolis.

Sometimes

A glass of sake on a wooden tray at the edge of a drizzling evening. Gently picking up a butterbur.

"If you listen carefully, you can hear the sound of shamisen in the distance.

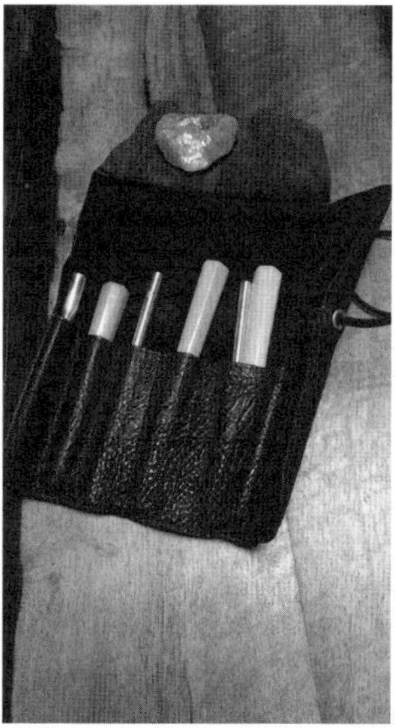

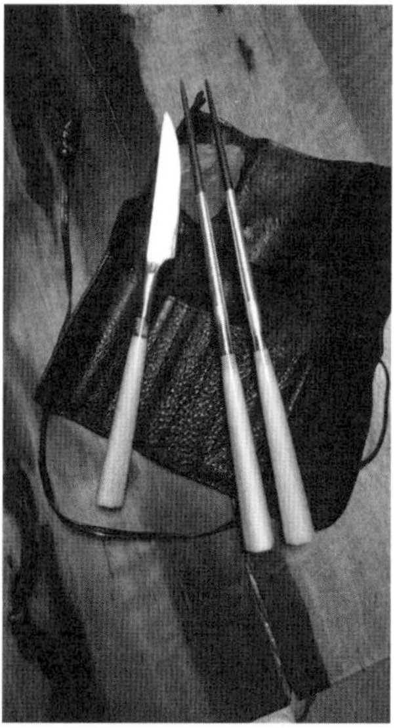

Passing through the curtain

I visit an antique shop from time to time.
In a place I hadn't noticed before, I found a hexahedron ivory shamisen spool that fit comfortably in the palm of my hand, haphazardly placed.
The tip of the spool was as thick as the head of my little finger, and I could see a slightly smaller shamisen rod in my mind's eye.
The slender arms playing the strings reminded me of the female figure Yumeji had drawn.
I have no way of knowing why it is in the store of a toolmaker.

If I can make it my own, I may be able to make another progress.
With this thought, I fell asleep in my study.

Three years have passed.

Winding the strings of a three-stringed instrument, the daily life of a three-stringed instrument.
A pair of chopsticks. If you think of chopsticks as a hawk, a knife might be a good idea.
I can fold everything in half and carry it with me, always feeling the warmth of my skin.
I carry because I want to, not because I am eco-conscious.
My lips will be most familiar with the existence of "not being particular, but just being there.

making a vessel.

"Dusk.

I opened the top and bottom bowls on the black persimmon table and poured my favorite sake, Hayaseura, into them.

This is the encounter with the vessel I have been waiting for. The grateful cup of sake slowly flowed down my throat like the Yomishiro River. When I put the empty vessels back on top of each other, the ones that had previously been placed on top of each other noiselessly and quietly sank into the carpet of air when I removed my hand.

"I knew that the vessel had to contain moisture. He knew this, and had made the size of the bowl.

"He was a master.

On the bottom of the inner bowl, I inscribed "2003 Autumn, Osamu" with a thin knife. A long time has passed since then.

with me as a travel companion.

I asked Mr. Shibata about it.

"I asked Mr. Shibata if it would be possible to make a glass bottoms from bent-wappa.

He replied, "It's difficult, because the diameter of the vessel is too narrow to bend well. He said, "It's difficult. When I was about to give up, Mr. Shibata said in his Akita dialect, "I will try. But I had never thought about it before, and I had never done it before.

"He said, "But I'll give it a try, but please give me some time.

I said my goodbyes and left the store, heading back to the Yondai River.

An exciting time passed, and then the fifth summer passed. In the fall, a pair of vessels arrived with the scent of cedar and the air of the Akita mountains.

However, there was one regret. I opened the package, removed the paper wrapping each of the two vessels, and put the inner vessel on top of the outer vessel. When I put the inner and outer vessels together, I found that the inner vessel was too big and the outer vessel was too small. It was my first work, so this error was unavoidable, but I felt the difficulty of around a bowl of freshly cooked rice with pickled plums. During my conversation with Mr. Shibata, his passion resonated even more strongly in my heart. I couldn't help but pick up a cylindrical bent-wappa lunch box that could hold a little less than one cup of rice, and bought it on impulse. I bought one of these lunch boxes on impulse.

During an ayu fishing trip to the Yoneshiro River in Akita, I asked about the Keishin Shibata Shop.

"I was surprised to see him at the store. In the back of the store, there was a collection of bent-wappa pieces from around the world.

In the back of the shop there was a collection of kawarewappa pieces from around the world," Shibata said.

Mr. Shibata said, "Bending has a long history in the world, and I wanted to learn about it and express Akita, so that's why I collected them."

As I listened to his story, my own view of bending seemed to expand beyond Akita to include the rest of the world.

In the scent of the cedar in the workshop, another thought occurred to me.

"If only there was a curved paper bag that I could always carry logs is always the same, but the width between the annual rings varies.

The log is about 40 centimeters in diameter, and the desired grain is how old do you think it is?

"I don't know.

"It's over three hundred years old. Where do you think it was standing on the mountain? On the north slope along the stream, in the middle to the bottom of the mountain, where the sun was not shining. The cedar trees on the north slope near the top of the mountain do not get thicker even after 300 years, because the stream is fed by the ridge and grows well on the north slope. The cedar trees on the north slope near the top of the mountain do not grow thick even after 300 years. That's what I was waiting for. If we had to order the wood and have them find it, we could have it a little faster, but the price would be too high.

The first time I met Akita "bent-wappa" artist Yoshinobu Shibata was at a demonstration and sale at Takashimaya in Shinjuku in 1993. I had seen bent-wappa products before, but the smooth texture of the cedar and the flowing wood of Mr. Shibata's products reminded me of the comfort of carrying help the taste. The scene in Akita also comes to mind.

Yes, five years had passed since I had ordered this bowl. And that phone call.

"Mr. Ueno, do you know why it took so long?

"I replied, "Maybe I was busy with work, or maybe it was my health.

I said, "No, I've been waiting to find a cedar with a grain I like. The size of this cup (fist-sized) would be much smaller than a lunch box, and with the same grain as a lunch box, the width between the annual rings would be too wide for a small bowl. The same grain as a bento box would be too wide for a small bowl, so it would have to have more than 60 annual rings per inch. I was waiting to meet it. The thickness of the cedar

Magewappa

"Ue-no-san, UNDAIGO NIWA DAREGA KONO WAN ZUGATTANO GA WAGANNAKU NAREAR...?"

A drinking cup made of "bent-wappa" has arrived from Akita. It was a phone call I made to thank him. At first, I could not understand what he was saying. I slowly listened again.

"Mr. Ueno, in four generations, we won't know who used this vessel. So, please write down the year and name of this year. It was as if he was saying, "I have made a curved wappas that can be used for four generations to come. I have made a curved wappas that can be used for four generations to come, and even if it is in the middle of that time, I will have a craftsman who can repair it for four generations to come.

However, it is often the case that we can tell who used the vessel up to the second or third generation, but not beyond that. "That's why we put the name on it.

It may only be a "cedar bent-wappa", but it seems that the culture of using it is still alive and well. I felt the fragrance of such a culture close at hand. I sipped my cup with friends, or sometimes alone. The spirit, warmth, and time of the creator shouts, "Great, look!

"Look at this!

The sculptor turned around and saw a white fox-faced cat lying on its side, its long cord-like internal organs drawn like a stroke of calligraphy, piercing its belly.

The sculptor "has a camera.

I got my Zenza Bronica and tripod, the sculptor set up the tripod and heard several shutter clicks. The sculptor set up his tripod and heard several shutter clicks, this time he took it off and knelt down on the asphalt to release the shutter. When he returned from the museum, the sculptor looked up at the sky, faced the cat, and returned to his car.

"He returned to the car and said, "Now the cat can go to heaven.

The car returned to the mountain road as the sun began to set in the west.

"Enya's music was playing in the background.

I asked for a few strawberries at the usual strawberry shop on the way, and was given more strawberries, twice as many as I had expected. My heart danced with a sense of richness.

"Like the rhythm of Enya.

The compact stove above the outdoor fireplace fills the garden with the scent of strawberry jam.

"Dusk has come again.

ceremony.

"Now we have to make a movie.

"We'll choose the actors ourselves.

"I'm Koji Yakusho."

"Then, who should I choose? Katsuhito, he's not here now.

The pasta was brought in. The refreshing tomato flavor was just right for today.

The garlic toast on the side also smelled good.

"I want to write about this time," the sculptor mutters.

"Another book in the works.

"Now, let's go to Kasama.

The exhibition of Antoine Poupel's behind-the-scenes photos of the Paris Moulin Rouge at the Nichido Museum looks interesting. It's probably similar to the work of Shinya Gondo, an American photographer who was active in the 1960s. Gondo's work was published earlier than mine, I believe. I would like to see what kind of work he has done. (Note: "Shinya Gondo" is a pseudonym for Morio Shinoda, who was a photographer in the United States.

The road to Kasama runs along the east side of Mount Tsukuba along the mountain range. Clapton's music echoes pleasantly on the light road where the wind is gentle. The parking lot of the museum is deserted. The sculptor looks towards the end of the road where he parked his car and

February 25, 2002

favorite bar and enjoyed a question-and-answer session. He was awarded the Akutagawa Prize this time, and this is what he had to say after reading the book.

The sculptor fanned the spring-like sky.

"Shall we go out to eat? Let's go to the Plus One Cafe. There are a lot of nice guys there.

It's a good place for brunch. The artist always prepares himself when he goes out. He wears a blue-and-white bordered shirt with a gray hunting cap in the back, blue jeans and sneakers in the front.

The café was crowded in the late afternoon. I took my usual table at the back of the outside terrace. I left my soft hat in the car.

"My soft hat was left in the car. "Two hats is a bit outrageous.

Lamb, coffee, and pasta. This is also the usual course. A nice breeze was blowing in the afternoon. The speakers on the terrace are playing bossa nova today. The conversation continues with noise from inside the room.

"How about this for the title of my next Naoki Prize-winning novel?

"It's on loan.

The sculptor said, "Good idea.

"I've already written the address for the Naoki Prize

Cats and Strawberries

What a warm day it was, even though it was February. On such a Sunday, I woke up slowly and asked for the sculptor Morio Shinoda Tei. The house appeared to be empty, but the sliding door of the entrance opened with a faint rusty sound. But I was a little hesitant to enter without saying a word. I went back to the garden, sat down on a chair by the outdoor fireplace, and waited.

The sunshine made me thirsty. I took out my favorite tea bag from the car and made a cup of coffee. My portable stove and espresso machine came in handy. A cup of coffee wakes me up in the late morning.

I hear a noise from the back of the room. Without any clothes on my body, I came out to the garden and was welcomed. It seems that he has just finished taking a bath.

"I'll leave it like this.

"Of course."

The sculptor took a shot glass with about two-thirds malt, placed it on the stone slab of the outdoor fireplace and began to speak.

It's easy to win the Naoki Prize," he said. It's not that big a deal. Let's write, too.

When the sculptor was in Kyoto for a long period of time, he and his monk friend, Gen'yu Munehisa, hit it off at their

Toe Shoes. According to Mr. Shimura, the original name of the glass, Ballerina, was Tipu-Tu. The original name of the glass was Tipu Toe, but Tipu Toe is not very familiar in Japan, so Mr. Shimura named it Ballerina as a Japanese name. We didn't even know this when we were making the glass cases.

It was a strange encounter between a pair of wine glasses and a glass case to carry them around. And an encounter with a person. What will be the next encounter? With the kind permission of Mr. Shimura, this photo of a glass case with its door slightly opened to reveal a few wine glasses inside, and a little story about it, traveled to Vienna, Austria, where Robmeier's headquarters is located.

he would become the exclusive distributor in Japan?

However, Mr. Shinoda already had the next idea in his mind. A glass case set against a green background, the door slightly opened, a glass of ballerina placed vertically facing each other glittering through the green felt on the inside of the glass case. He seemed to be dreaming of a poster with the word "LOBMEYR" written in large letters above the vertical photo.

As I listened to him, I found myself thinking that if a poster were to be made, and when I climbed the stairs of a subway somewhere and looked up, I would see a large vertical Lobmeyer poster.

One day in February, I visited Lobmeyer's exclusive distributor, Rocinante, located just off Aoyama-dori. It was only one street away from Aoyama Dori, but there was a hint of the Aoyama of a while ago. We were met at 2:00 p.m. by Mr. Akikazu Shimura and his wife.

They placed the wine case on the floor, and after a short conversation, they placed the case on the table and opened the door. Immediately, Mr. Shimura asked us why the inner felt was green. We had tried several colors, but chose british green because it seemed to be the most relaxing. However, Mr. and Mrs. Shimura told us that this color was exactly Lobmeyer green. It was a coincidence. We had chosen this color without knowing that Lobmeyer green existed.

Another coincidence. The handle to carry the glass case is made of bronze with a motif of a naked woman. Underneath it stands a key to open the case. Its shape was designed by wine tasting glasses there. There was indeed a tasting glass there, just as I remembered it. However, I was drawn to the beauty of the tasting glass of the person tasting at the counter behind me. I had never heard of the glass before. I asked the sommelier and he told me that it was one of the Ballerina series by Lobmeyer. That was my first encounter with the Ballerina wine glass.

The taste of the wine I bought and tasted at the hotel was exceptional. The balance between the delicacy of the wine and the feel of the glass against my lips was exquisite. The next day, I returned home and made a new glass case out of a wooden box of Dom Pernion from 1982. The next day, I went home and made a new glass case out of a wooden box of Dom Pernion from 1982, but Shinoda didn't like the case at all. And that is how La Soiree came to be.

A Coincidence of Brittish Green

It was late at night, and in the quiet of Torista, I took a glass out of the finished glass case, poured a single malt into it, and looked at it with one hand... What had been in my imagination just a few months before was now right in front of my eyes. It was a very strange feeling. It was a wonderful encounter of imagination, creation, and friendship across the ages.

As I gazed at the glass and glass case, I wanted to meet the person who is the exclusive distributor of Lobmeyer in Japan. What kind of person would be so fascinated by this glass that

The more he looked at my glass case, the more he couldn't stand it anymore. The more he looked at my glass case, the more he couldn't resist. I, however, did not agree. In our long relationship, we often overdid it when the image swelled up. It was because I had to be careful.

However, the next day he called me and asked me to come over immediately because he had finished the design. I had to work that day, so we decided to meet the next day, on my day off. At that time, we met at a friend's place who worked in metal processing, where we talked about the thickness and weight of the metal, and my dream was expanding.

Two weeks later, I met Mr. Shinoda at the Takashimaya Art Award ceremony held at the Nihombashi Takashimaya Department Store, and as a result of our discussion, we decided to create a glass case. The recipient of the award happened to be a young professor that Mr. Shinoda had worked with when he was at Tsukuba University, and we were mutual friends.

The encounter with one of the wine glasses from the Robmeier Ballerina series was also a wonderful and magical event for me. I always carry two wine tasting glasses with me in my car. But for some reason, I didn't have them in my car when I went to a meeting in Tokyo in December 1997. I had brought along a bottle of the 1978 Robert Montavi Riserva to celebrate a reunion with a friend I hadn't seen in years. I couldn't bring myself to drink it out of a hotel cup, so I left the meeting. There was a wine section in the basement of the Shibuya Tokyu Department Store, and I thought there were

Once again in front of us, the cash was placed inside the case. At that moment, Mr. Shinoda whispered, "It's still in there. A precise measurement of the remaining space revealed that we could fit another 330,000 yen. After that moment, the "BOX-3000" was signed as "BOX-3000+330", the real space. To commemorate this, Mr. Shinoda signed the inside of my attache case with cash in it at the bank, "December 24, 1997 BOX-3000 -> BOX-3000+330.

The Birth of La Soiree

The day of the completion celebration was January 6, 1998. It was also New Year's Day, and to celebrate the new space, I went to Torista with Remy Martin and an attache case. Rather than look at me, Mr. Shinoda looked at Remy, smiled, immediately cut the seal, and was about to open it into a cup of hot water on the dusty table.

"Wait!"

I had a nice glass in the car and decided to make a toast with it. He raised the glass of Remy Martin to his eye level and was impressed with the wonderful glass, but at the same time he couldn't stand the awful glass case I had made for it.

At the same time, he couldn't bear to see how badly I had made the glass case that held the glass. That glass was one of the Robmeier Ballerina series, and it was the first encounter between Mr. Shinoda and that glass.

"I want to make it."

million yen in my attache case looked as if it was a present from Santa Claus.

However, despite my feelings, Mr. Shinoda seemed to be worried about whether the 30 million yen would actually fit in the case until the manager brought the cash to the room in the bank where we were going to take pictures. This was because it weighed one gram, the same as a one yen coin, and it was a space he had imagined by measuring the thickness of a new 10,000 yen bill. Naturally, he had never tried to insert it. Despite his uneasiness, I told him that if it didn't fit, he could just leave the mouth of the attache case open and take a picture. This was because I had promised the bank manager that I would not cut the bandage of the bills. Mr. Shinoda looked even more anxious when he heard this. I could not concentrate on anything for a long time, neither anxious nor nervous.

Just then, the door opened and the branch manager walked in with my attaché case and a paper bag of cash that I had given him beforehand. With these words, the tense thread of tension was instantly released, and Mr. Shinoda's face showed a look of confidence as if he had always had it.

art. However, when we had a disagreement about a piece of work, we quickly settled on the fact that it was metal and wood sculpture, which was also a nice solution.

Later, after retiring from Tsukuba University and working as a visiting professor at Nagasaki University, Shinoda was fortunate enough to open a "Tori Studio (Torista)" in a converted chicken coop in Niiharu Village, next to Tsukuba City. There, he continued to create works on the theme of "space," his eternal theme.

As one of them, he decided to make a limited edition of fifty pieces on the theme of "BOX-3000". It was a 3.5 cm thick attache case made of aluminum, and it could hold 30 million yen in new 10,000 yen bills. Even if you were not him, you would want to try it to see if it would really fit. However, it was difficult to get 30 million yen in cash, so he decided to cut a piece of paper with the same thickness as the bills and use real bills for the front, then put it in the case and take a picture. When I heard this story, I thought it was too much of a dream, so I said, "I'll get it for you. However, although I said that, it must be a difficult task, so I consulted the manager of the bank of my friend. He immediately replied, "I'll lend you the money" (with your house as the mortgage).
He replied, "I will lend you the money.

However, I couldn't afford such a big debt, so in consultation with the manager, I decided to stay out of the bank and let him take my picture for just an hour or two. It was Christmas Eve, the 24th of December, when the cash was ready. The 30 conversation was quite reasonable, and to top it off, he asked to see some of my sculptures.

Fortunately, we didn't have any other plans, and there were no customers, so we decided to give him a look. After our permission was granted, he went outside to pick up his work. I casually looked over his shoulder and saw a Porsche parked there. He brought out a postcard, which he showed me with great care.

The card showed what looked like a metal building. "When I asked him what was made of this building, he replied, "Everything. This was the "Shinji Project" in the "T-C Series" that I would later learn about. It was my first encounter with Mr. Morio Shinoda.

As we drank more and more cups, we found out that Shinoda was a professor of general plastic arts at Tsukuba University, and that many of his works were also collected by museums overseas. However, in our discussions, we decided that since we were both self-proclaimed woodcarvers and he was a metal artist, we would never be able to truly understand each other, so we decided to be friends in our own way.

Why did "BOX-3000" become "+330"?

After that, every time he worked on a large piece of art, I would go to his studio at the university and soak up the atmosphere of art, feeling the comfort of a new wind of art that I can't describe. It was as if I had become a student of

LA SOIREE

An encounter with Morio Shinoda

On a table in my study made of black persimmon, there are two wine glasses. The name of the glasses is "Ballerina. Next to them is a glass case made of aluminum, the size of two glasses lined up vertically. The nickname of the vessel, which is molded in the shape of a woman's body and has a brass handle, is La Soiree.

La Soiree always stands beside the red wine poured into the Ballerina. These two pieces, which are placed casually, came together unexpectedly.

The first was an encounter with Morio Shinoda, a contemporary sculptor who created La Soiree. It must have been around 1987. Sometimes after work, I would go to the gym to exercise after a light meal. On my way home, I would stop by the sushi restaurant of a childhood friend, drink a little sake, and talk about casual things, which was a moment of peace. The only hobby I shared with the owner of the sushi bar was wood carving.

That day, we were chatting over the counter, looking at the wood carvings we had made, and discussing about art. At the counter on the right side of the room, there was a small customer with long gray hair and beard that had turned a little white. He had a unique face and was probably about sixty years old.

When we started discussing art, he casually joined the conversation. At first I thought he was a bit annoying, but his

Spring, 1995

Matcha, Chinese tea, Sencha, and coffee are all available in one tea bag. I had a hard time finding a bag to hold all of them. Then I came across a leather silk hat case that was rotting in the corner of a secondhand store.

When I opened it, of course, there was no trace of the hat and the inside was tattered and stained. I averted my eyes for a moment, but then took another look. It was terrible, but the leather case and the conical shape reminded me of good old Europe. But it looks like it needs a lot of work. I bought it because I felt that once completed, everything would fit in the space inside.

After that, it was still difficult. I had to remove the tattered inner fabric, make a paper pattern of the same size, and buy two kinds of fabric from Cotton Chuck, one with a yellow pattern and the other with a blue pattern.

I bought two types of cotton chucks with yellow and blue patterns. The inside is yellow and the top and bottom are blue. A tea basket from the end of the 20th century.

Seeking spring water, I pass through an old curtain.
A tea basket from the end of the 20th century.
The sky is clearer today than ever.

My dream is beloved "tea bag"

A trip to Gujo is a good idea.
For anglers, a trip to encounter the seasonal river breeze.

Spring water, Japanese sweets from a long-established shop, and the fragrance of matcha bloom.

This is the time to enjoy tea at your leisure.
I wish I had a tea bag.

It seems that Okakura Tenshin carried a tea basket with him when he stayed in Boston. There is a tea basket in the Tenshin Museum of Art in Kitaibaraki. I heard that many tea masters also loved and enjoyed tea baskets. I don't know anything about tea, but when I want to drink it, I want to do so freely and easily. After returning from the Tenshin Art Museum, I immediately started work on the tea basket set. Slightly different from the tea baskets, my set is not for "matcha," but for "tea bags," which can be used to enjoy a variety of teas depending on where you are at the time.

Chapter 2

Osamu Ueno

Cherry blossoms are also fun in the pistil-falling season.

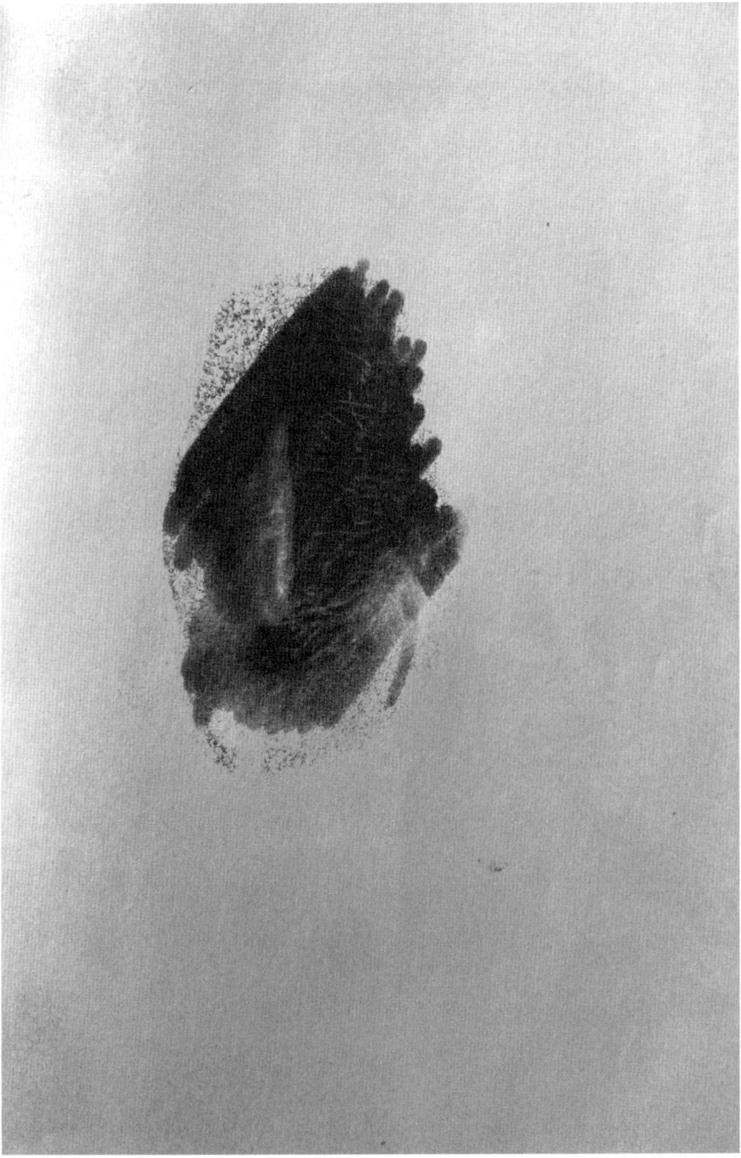

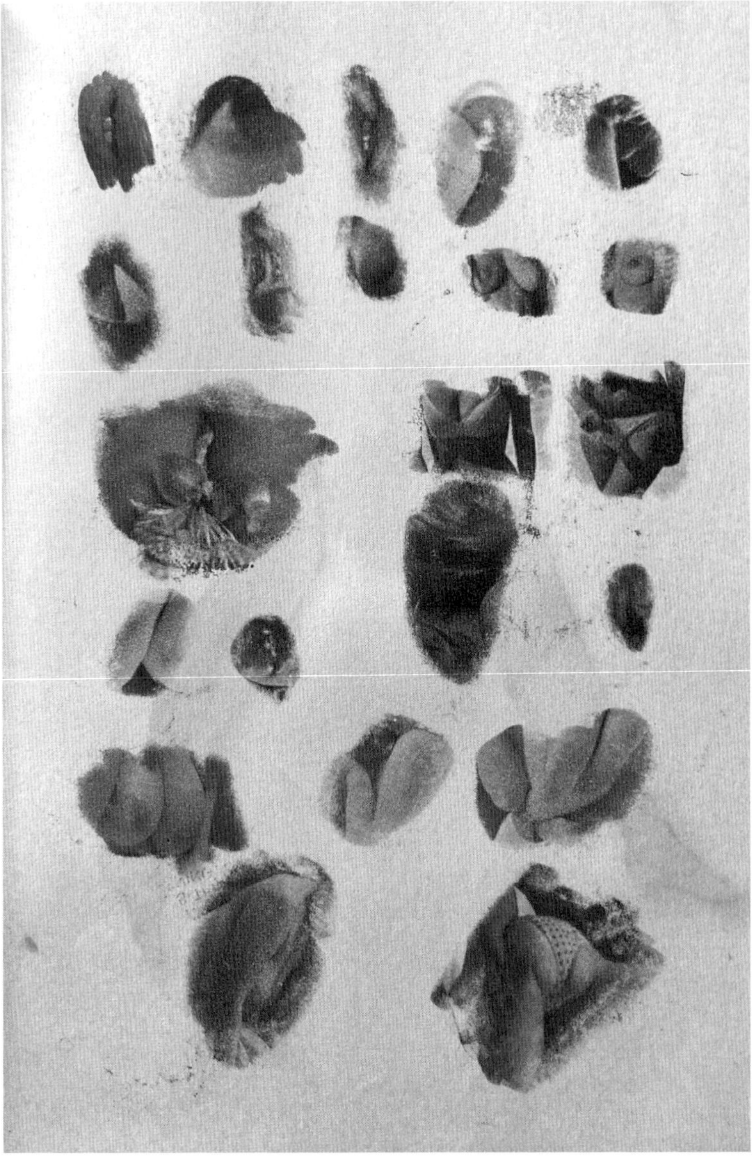

Mr. Shozo Kaneko

Thank you very much for your purchase of my work. I would like to send you a recent book as a token of my appreciation.

It has been a long time since you purchased my work, but it was my first visit to Okinawa, and I was impressed by the different culture from mainland Japan. As a sculptor, I was especially inspired by Shuri Castle and its stone walls, which are different from those of the mainland. I did not have a chance to visit the castle after that, and unfortunately it was destroyed by fire just as I was thinking of visiting it again.

It was with this in mind that I created this piece as a tribute. However, I am very happy that it was recognized by the Director, who is a famous collector.

I would like to ask you for a favor. I've been deaf for a long time, and I've been diagnosed by various hospitals, but they said it was my age and I gave up. I had earwax the size of a pea when I was a child, and I will be getting my second corona vaccine on August 10, so I would be very grateful if you could diagnose me any time after that.

August 25, 2021 Morio Shinoda

alf a century ago, analog art was certainly an illusion, but 50 years ater, I felt a real sense of reality with a philosophical theory of xistence in relation to digitalized art. Including myself, Ms. Hoshika, and Dr. Sugihara. I think this can be called post-media art.
As for returns, please keep IL8605 to IL8608 for a while, and I will give you either IL8603 or IL8604 for 50,000 yen. Please return the rest to me. I couldn't find the screws last time, so I'll enclose them here. The short screws are for the top panel. I've also enclosed the receipt and other information.

P.S. I'm embarrassed to say that I've given you a lot of trouble about my expenses, but actually, the moment I turned 80, my credit card loans were suspended, and I've been paying off about 5 million in debt from my pension. In the past six years, I have only been able to pay the interest and the principal has not decreased at all. For the past few years, I have had to sell my work at least twice a year at solo exhibitions to make ends meet. The minimum price for two-dimensional works is 500,000, and the same for IL8603 and 8604. If you sell them, please give me 30% of the proceeds.

Dear Morio Shinoda

Mr. Tamio Hoshika

Thank you very much for your hard work on this project. At first I thought it would be a museum project. I thought it would be a museum project, and I was prepared to exhibit my tension works. But then, my thoughts slipped back to my time at the University of California in 1968. It was the era of kinetic art and obtuse art in the United States. I was experimenting with kinetic art and obtuse art, incorporating them into my classes 200% of the time. That was exactly half a century ago. People nowadays don't know about it. What would happen if I made it now? That's how this work was born. When I came back to Japan, one of the actors, Naomasa Rokudaira (Yumi Kusaka), grew up as one of my students, Mr. Ishihara (Pokémon) and Toshio Iwai from the Kinetic Institute, Mr. Tosa (Meiwa Denki) from the performance class, Mr. Hatakeyama (Kimura Ihei Award) from the video class, Lauren Matthesen (music environment sculptor) and Carl Chen (nature environment sculptor) from the University of California, Los Angeles. At the University of California, we trained Lauren Matthesen (music environment sculptor), Carl Cheng (nature environment sculptor), and others. Each of them is very active in society. This is a great honor for me as a teacher. I can't lose to them. Now I am back in Xinji, and I am working on a much bigger project.

To Yuichi Maki

Congratulations on your marriage. I am sending you a trunk for Mr. Maki and a sculpture for Izumi. This is a transfer of money owed by Kyoto. It is also a wedding gift. But I really like the work. I think it is a good sketch for my next work. I think it is a good esquisse for my next work, because it hangs itself, whereas my previous works were hung by their supporting bodies. I attempted this 40 years ago. That work won the Grand Prix at the Hakone Open-Air Museum. It is now in the permanent collection of the Museum of Contemporary Art Tokyo. The reason why I'm dwelling on this is that there are different dimensions. The dimension I am about to explain has a lot to do with you. What can I say if I don't call this fate? In the words of Mr. Nagasawa of the Micro Art Museum, it is your destiny. This is where the real work begins. If you are tired, please take a break and have a drink.

This is a letter that I tried to send you along with my work when you got married a few years ago. Since then, I have not been able to produce any work, nor have I been able to write my main thesis on what marriage is, and here we are today. I am sending it to you with my work. Thank you very much for your support over the years.

To Yuichi Maki

Art is not a matter of high or low efficiency of expression. Even the expression of Marcel Desjuchamps' ready-made works becomes diluted. What the Mono-ha did was part of conceptual art, which started with the minimalist art of Simple Beauty. This is ideology, not art. As proof of this, they, Francesco Clemente, Georg Baselitz, Sandro Chia, etc., have all changed their clothes as riders of nu painting. The breakthrough of Mono-ha in Europe is in the realm of economy, not in the medium of art. This is truly different from that of Gutai art. There is nothing better than Haiku, a Japanese invention. There is nothing more efficient in expression than haiku. In the words of the French philosopher Levinas, there is only one self and one other, one artistic viewer among others, i.e., one viewer with a high level of knowledge. At that point, we become equals. The word "appreciation" is used to describe the appreciation of a work of art, while the word "prize" is used to describe the enjoyment and appreciation of an excellent work. There is no difference between appreciation and appreciation of women. First of all, there is artistic existence, and the viewer takes it in through intuition. There is no logic. This reminds me of a book called "Dialogue between Plato and Socrates", which one is Plato? I would like to say a few words in response to Mr. Nawa's comment. It is natural that Rodin left some marks on his work. He was so unhappy with it that he had Camille Claudel, a model with whom he had an affair, make the details of his hands and feet, and finally discarded him. Don't fall for this guy, either. My tension is that I like danger, so I jump in. That's why I make weak sculptures.

the structure of the painting and did not go into the concept of painting.

According to Michel Foucault, painting has been governed by two principles. According to Michel Foucault, painting has been governed by two principles: the separation of figural representation repre'sentation platique and linguistic representation repre'sentation linquitique. He points out that this was abandoned by Klee and Kandeinsky. Furthermore, he discusses the fusion of modeling and linguistic representation using Magritte's "This is not a pipe" Cecin'est pas une pipe as an example. In Japan, however, these two concepts have been fused since the Man'yō period, and they belong to the medium of painting. Yabashi's paintings took me out of my infant experience (when language and phenomena were still in their infancy) and led me into the labyrinth of painting. At that time, based on my own judgment and prejudice, I recommended his paintings for the Excellence Award, and as one of the judges (Tadayasu Sakai, Koji Kinutani, and Morio Shinoda) at last year's Hokuriku Jinzu-kyo Biennale Exhibition, I recommended his paintings for the Excellence Award, and they were awarded each time.

Morio Shinoda, Professor Emeritus, University of Tsukuba

Shotaro Yabashi

Kesaran Pasaran, Udonge flower. It was the beginning of the Showa era (1926-1989), and it is said to bloom once every 3,000 years, making it a kesaran pasaran. It is said to bring tremendous happiness. It was 80 years ago. Whether it is a plant or a living creature, even its existence did not satisfy my curiosity as a child, and I became an adult without having solved the problem.

In 2010, the "New Generation of Contemporary Art" exhibition was held at a tiny art museum in Ogaki, and young artists in their twenties were selected to be part of the jury (Masahiro Aoki and Morio Shinoda). When I judge something, I go from intuition (with little or no recognition) to intuition (recognition but no judgment) to thinking to analysis. It was at this stage that I became interested in the works of Yabashi Odotaro. The infantile experience that I had at the beginning of this article was the entry point for me to develop my interest. In general, Yabashi's works are neither figurative nor abstract. Philosophically speaking, it could be called materialistic painting or pure painting. In the 1970s, there were works of conceptual art that were framed with a canvas frame on the front, but they only showed the structure of a painting and did not go into the concept of painting. However, they only showed photographs and had them painted by a Sunday painter in "Custom Paintings by Pat Nelson" (1969). Here, even "choice as a part of art" has been diminished. I like to create my works efficiently and complete them in a short time. The quicker the process, the better, because you are taking something that is already in your mind and making it tangible. In Japan, however, we find satisfaction in suffering. It is a masochist theory. It takes more trials, pains, worries, and dilemmas to assemble a work in one's mind than to materialize it. The reason why this is harder than the physical act of creation is because it is free. If we start discussing this, we will be involved in the big thesis of "What is art? So I will focus on "choice," which is a part of art.

In this exhibition, I have selected Western antiques as the main components. These are things that are impossible or unimaginable with my skills, and because they are complete as parts, they have many advantages, such as saving time and allowing me to change my mind. Above all, I am satisfied with the outlandish results that I obtained, which can be called a three-dimensional collage.

The Art of Choice

The Art of Choice Morio ShinodaOur art begins with choice. We draw pictures, carve wood and stone, and print plates. After acquiring each skill, we proceed to modeling. But not all of them become works of art. In fact, more often than not, not all of them become works of art. Many contemporary artists go through this process. If we think of this process in terms of efficiency alone, we first have something we want to create, and then we acquire the necessary skills in parts. This will save you a lot of time. Then you select something that already exists, or something that has been created for another purpose. This is Marcel Duchamp's Ready-Made, Picasso's "Cow," a bicycle saddle with handlebars, etc. A long time ago in New York, a painter prepared a new canvas and his pet, Orm, walked on it to make a pattern. When he exhibited it, there was a big controversy. One side argued that it was not a work of art because Ohm had drawn it, and the other side argued that it was not randomly exhibited by the artist, but had passed through a filter of selection. Furthermore, in the late 1960s, during the era of conceptual art, John Baldessari, an artist from Los Angeles who was also a friend of mine, took his own

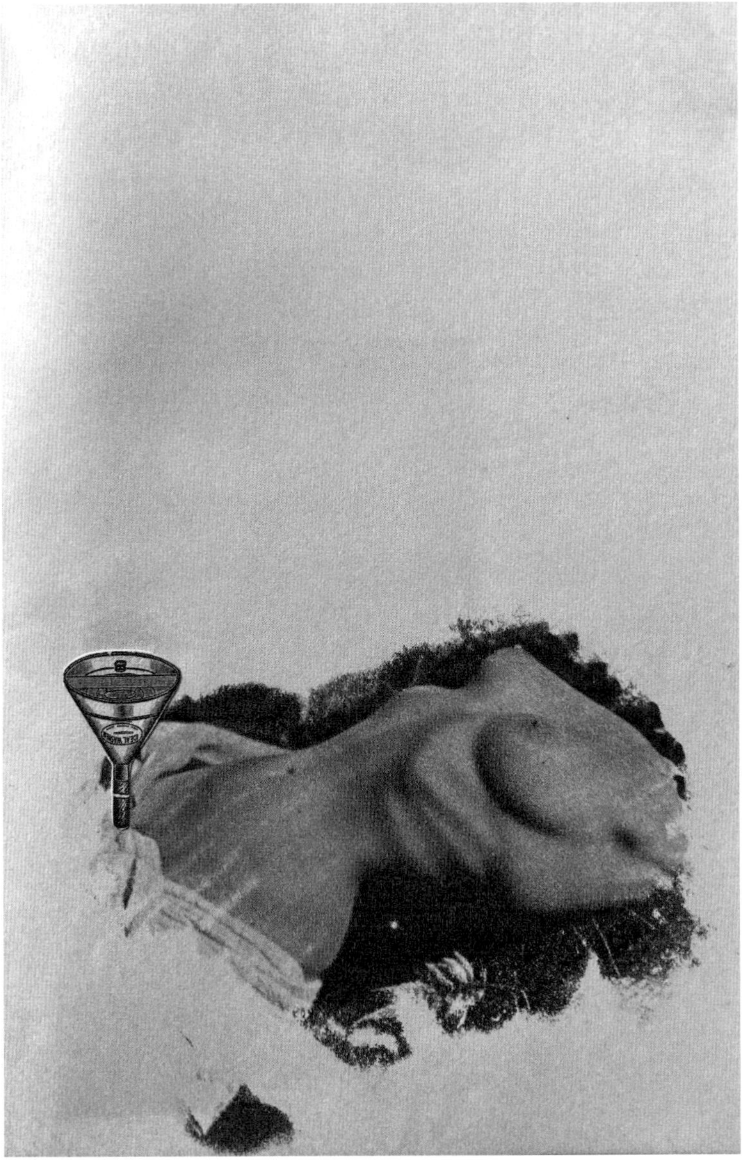

Memory and Now

Memory, in a sense, is data that is already in the past when we recognize it. I've been living in the "now" since I can remember. I don't remember my parents ordering me to do anything, even during the war. I have never had the experience of studying or preparing for anything in anticipation of the future. This is because the values that were instilled in me during my most important years of embryonic development in elementary school, middle school, and high school collapsed overnight.

A three-dimensional work has one more dimension than a two-dimensional work, so it contains more information. Therefore, I have not titled my works because a title would interfere with the work. The first two digits are my age, and the next two digits are the number of works. However, after I passed 80, I could not trace my memory with my age, so I had no choice but to give it a title. However, these are keywords for tracing my memory, and have nothing to do with the work.

After many years of work, a kind of system is formed, and I am afraid of creating a work with narratives. I always want to create with the ideas of the present and evolve my work. When this continuity is interrupted, he will retire. I want to live the rest of my life freely and unrestrained.

November 16, 2008 Morio Shinoda

Liberation of the Earth

I have been thinking about the liberation of the earth for many years, and since I was appointed as a professor at Tsukuba University in 1979, I have been studying it as a concrete research, and have been giving back to the class with my theory of environmental domination. In particular, I was attracted by the beauty of the environment of the Mount Tsukuba National Water Park during my tenure there, so I gave up my personal fortune to purchase a 1,000 tsubo plot of land, which enabled me to conduct various concrete experiments. Part of this project is this NIIHARI PROJECT. Liberation here means liberation from human beings. Basically, the environment I want to live in is to be as far away from the surface of the earth as possible. According to my current calculations, the distance from the earth's surface for a single human being is 20 to 30 meters. Three years ago, we secured 300 square meters of land in the vicinity of the site and started the experiment. Some say I am childish, but I am in my eighties, and I am bringing back the sensibility of a five-year-old. Everyone has a secret base! If I am five years old now, even if it takes me 30 years, I will be a 35-year-old man. I would like to enjoy this part of my life with you.

Morio Shinoda
Representative of Morio Shinoda Laboratory

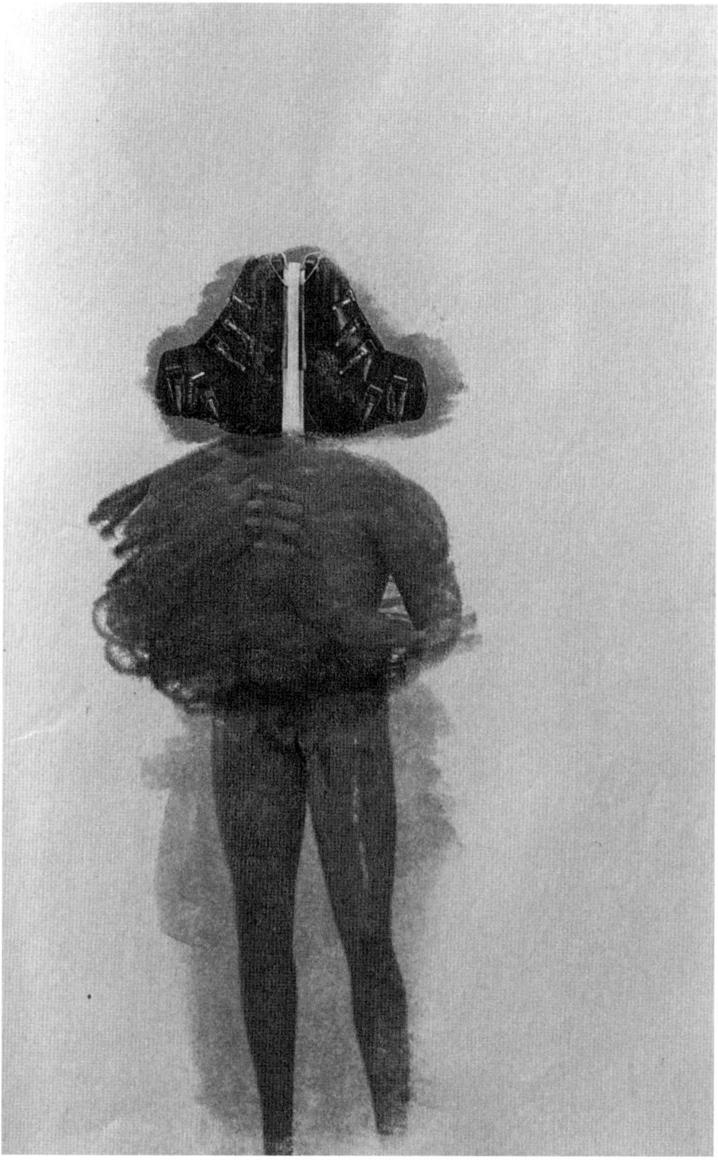

or rather three-d • 1mens1onal-modelling, and opened the next door can understand this world. This is because Mori and Shinoda, who know the pain and I P easure of making, deeply acknowledged each other's works.

T his solo exhibition will display things from the early d ays to the latest works presented in recent years. It is an exhibition that should b e called a retros pective. In terms of knowing this artist's process it is an unparalleled project.

These are intellectual and constructive works with a rare kind of formative power. The footprints of Shinoda's art are themselves the walks of the few pioneers who have shown sculpture the way to contemporary three-dimensional expression. Furthermore, regarding such ingenuity, there can be no objection to the praise of Morio Shinoda as a symbolic artist who represents the Showa to the Heisei era.

Director of The National Museum of Modern Art, Kyoto
Masaki Yanagihara

about solidly condensed things and hollow things with just a surface. Additionally, they exchanged opinions about works in micron units.

As if a matter of course, Mori knew of Shinoda's works to date. Shinoda also knew of Mori's works, but those were his past works and not the now current ones. Mori gave Shinoda a tour of his studio. What he saw there was a work made of steel. A mass that emitted a cold light made of machine tools of computer innards, in which cavities were drilled and grooves carved. It was a work whose shape was formed in micron units.

Morio Shinoda had also been making precise works, but in front of Mori's works, he mumbled. 'I have been making precise sculptures until now, but from now on I won't use that word,'he said. It is not an exaggeration to say that this author, who was witness to that situation, was present at a historical scene. At a later date, Mori spoke to this author of how highly he valued Shinoda's work.

These are two artists who represent contemporary J apaneseart. That meeting and conversation were moving. Only those who have opened up the potential of sculpture,

Thus, his works are created with light metals such as aluminium and stainless steel, and based on geometric forms like structures or delicate equipment. Showing inorganic and cold f future space cities. However, these are not the cold-blooded equipment of mechanical devices; there are organic as parts-that show sensitivity. In other words, the works are formed as both these parts oppose each other and are indivisibly intertwined.

Now, in April 1995, Shinoda held a solo exhibition at Nizayama Forest Art Museum, Toyama prefecture. It was the inaugural exhibition of this museum. At the same time, in neighbouring Kurobe city, Bushiro Mori(l923-2004), called the silent sculptor, had constructed his studio and was immersed in creating. He was uncommunicative and avoided meeting people to the utmost. Even so Shinoda wanted to meet Mori. When this author acted as a mediator and relayed the idea, Mori agreed to meet Shinoda. After a few days the two met. They exchanged simple greetings, and it began with a wandering talk. Then they reached a talk about'」apaneseswords and cast goods.'It was a talk

For the exhibition Open the Next Door

I have been participating in the strange world of art for a long time, but artists who are this dandy, and who have such a great charm to attract people, are rare. The people of the world call this artist a sculptor, but probably Morio Shinoda is outside of that category.

Originally in sculpture the volume and form of things was considered the subject, and regardless if it was concrete or abstract, expression as quantity and mass was the concept of sculpture. This artist however has no such definition or theory. His works tightly pull physical bodies with wires, and are created from structures of tension that are made to float in mid-air. The power for sustaining a subtle balance becomes condensed energy with a feeling of tension and rocks the space.

The essence of physical objects as three-dimensions gives tension to the space established by the works, vibrates the space, and how it exists as life in the space becomes the subject. Yet Shinoda's works'sharpened sense of space is truly magnificent, and further create a unique outlook on the world with a grand scale.

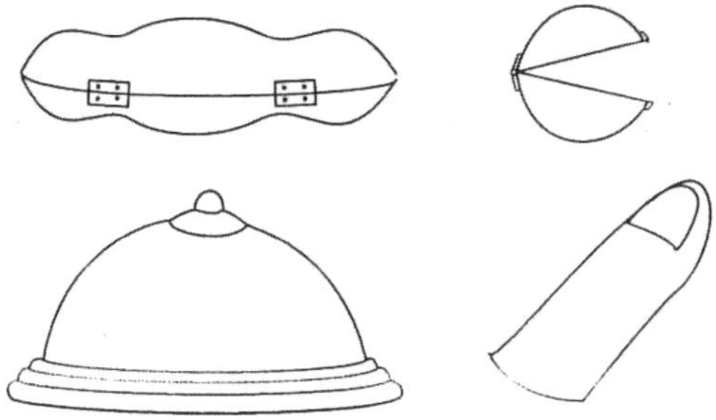

(Body part case)

developed and we will be able to stretch our height as much as we want, and our skin, organs, and muscles will be able to do the same.

In this age, your sense of beauty will not be questioned. In the 21st century, however, your beauty and ugliness will depend entirely on your sense of beauty. In the 21st century, your beauty or ugliness is entirely up to your sense of beauty. This is where my theory of body sculpting comes into play for the first time.

In the 21st century, your beauty and ugliness will depend on your sense of beauty. I don't have it either. However, since it is a part of my body, I don't want it to be missing, so any part of my body needs a nice case. It should be made of metal, either gold, silver, titanium, or aluminum.

The time will soon come when you will carry several cases like the one shown above, and you will be on an important date with your girlfriend, listening to pleasant music in a luxurious hotel, but at the last moment, you will have left your cigar-sized silver case at home.

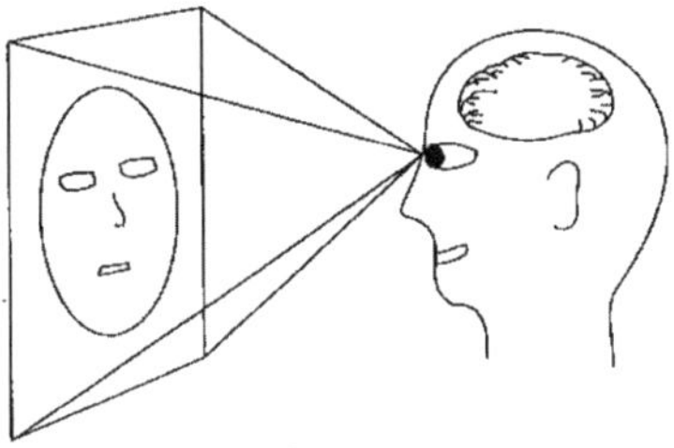

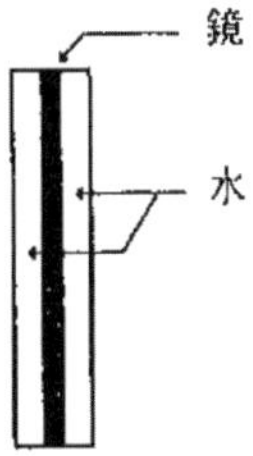

Can we get a patent?

When you look at your own face in the mirror, you are looking at your face from the inside (brain). Therefore, when you look at your face in the mirror, you are looking at the correct image, not the reversed image.

This is what I came up with in the bath.

Let's take a closer look at the physical body.

I haven't used soap for several decades. The first thing I do is to take a bath in water that is a few degrees above my resting temperature for at least 30 minutes. This is similar to what is often said about swimmers who sweat profusely in the pool. Sweat pours out from all over the body, the pores open fully, and water (sweat) sprays out from inside like a muddy stream, pushing dirt out of the hair follicles. Later, homemade virgin oil will make your skin. If you think I'm lying, just touch the skin of a 66-year-old man!

Section 4:
Further to the body

As we approach the 21st century, plastic surgery has developed and height can be increased and decreased at will. As we approach the 21st century, plastic surgery will be

Section 3:
From physical objects to the body

The most inconvenient thing for me in the bathroom is that the mirror becomes dull when I look at my beautiful body. I want the mirror to be a mirror. --In the bathrooms of modern hotels these days, there are mirrors that are electrically operated and do not fog up. I have experienced this, but I just can't get used to this mirror. Rather, I feel anxious that someone might be peeping at me from behind the mirror. Therefore, for me, the mirror I need must be a thin sheet of paper. However, in the vertical direction, it would first become dull! So, what about the vertical direction? Furthermore, why not seal the mirror in water? Isn't there a way to keep the mirror from fogging up when it is set into the floor?

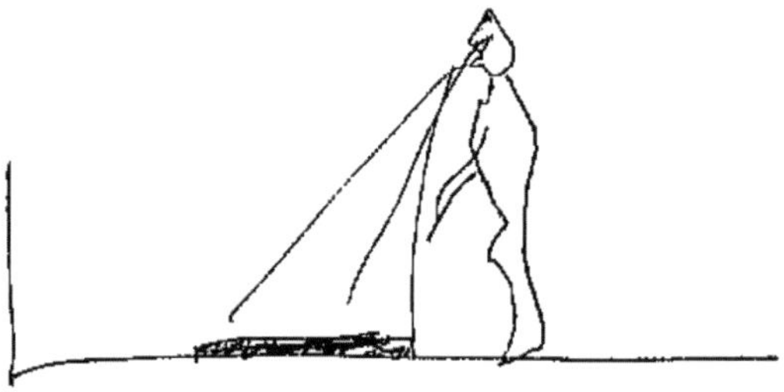

Speaking of mirrors, why are left and right reversed and not up and down? The answer is no. It is not reversed in the mirror. This is because, as you can see in the figure below.

saint, or maybe not even a human being. And so on. • • • • • •
A stone! --After all, hundreds of years have passed without knowing anything. The disciples decided that they should choose two, not just one, and if they were going to choose, they should choose the opposite poles, so justice and evil, peace and war, not as opposites, but in the sense that one phenomenon gives rise to the next. Therefore, it is different from Western dualism. (For example, Hegel, Kant, Marx, etc.) Lao Tzu in China is a collaboration of seven people. Just as Shakespeare in England is a collaboration of seven writers. (There was a theory in the 1940s that Shakespeare was not an individual.

When I take a bath, these thoughts come to me.

Next issue!

After writing this far, there are still many things left to be written in the physics section, and I cannot go on without giving more characteristic physical considerations in the next half of the issue. In the next half of the article, I will describe more characteristic physical considerations.

Section 2:
From Physical Considerations to Somewhat Physical and Mental

In the first section, I was talking about matter, or an object, or a substance, which I still don't understand. It's only the first chapter, so please forgive me. I will definitely try to figure it out as I write. However, I have to decide for the moment that the body is an object. There is an Eastern proverb that says, "A healthy mind resides in a healthy body. So, can a healthy mind have a healthy body? Is this reversibility possible or not? No. It is impossible for me to measure it with my immature 66 years of experience. Therefore, while I think the title of this second section is incorrect, let's start with it.

In the first section, I wrote about the reactions that affect the body based on a very simple action, taking a bath, as I felt them. Cold, hot, painful, itchy, pleasant. But are they permanent or not? And is it eternal? (Persistent and eternal should not be understood on the same level. A few days or a few seconds in the bath can certainly have a faint persistence of these, but conceptually speaking, the moment you think about it, it is strictly a kind of past that none of us can deny. I'm sure you're right. Happiness is good for physical preservation above all else. Unhappiness transcends everything else, and there is no such thing as unhappiness alone.

The temperature of the bath neutralizes both happiness and unhappiness in the body and mind. The contradictory nature of the body and mind will be discussed later in this article. The Indian philosopher Bhagwan, commenting on the Chinese Lao Tzu, said that when he saw an old man doing nothing, seven philosophers said that he was a god, a Buddha, a cripple, a

Section 1:
Material Space and Quantity

As I mentioned in the last issue, the bottom is cold and the top is hot. This gives extreme stimulation to the lower half of the body, and the person concerned is unable to appreciate the outdoor scenery. Naturally, the eyes are focused on the lower part of the body, and although it varies from person to person, if the person remains motionless for 90 seconds, the difference between cold and warm should disappear. There was plenty of time to admire his penis. In the midst of all the stillness, only his penis wavered. The reason for this is that in a split second of movement, the initial baptism of cold water must be repeated.

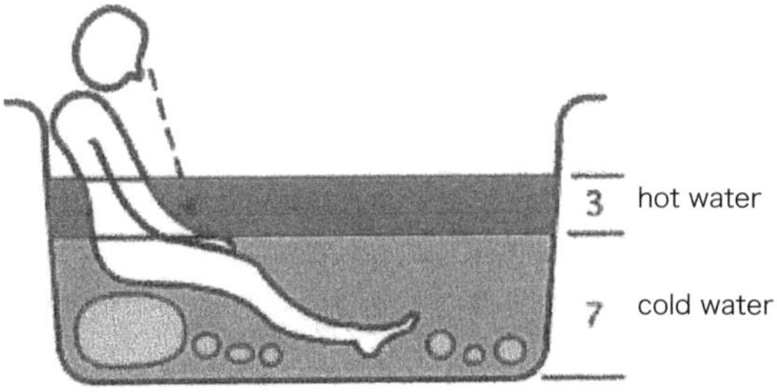

The standard: 327,214,000 mm
3 of cold water versus 90 seconds of 50°C hot water.

Chapter 1: Material Considerations in the Bath

In the previous issue, Vol. 69, I presented the first part of my theory on baths, but I lost track of it several years later. Reading it over again, I found a serious mistake in the first section of Chapter 1, "Material Considerations in the Bath," "Material Space and Quantity.

The dimensions were different. The reason why I insist on this dimension is that it may cause the subsequent theory of baths to collapse from the ground up. I sincerely hope that the readers will listen to these boring dimensions for a while. First of all, I would like to ask you to modify the space you call a bathhouse.

(See the figure on the previous page)

It is shameful that I, a precision-oriented person, should have misjudged such a rudimentary measurement, but in fact space is as vague as that. It would be irreverent to inscribe such vague space with integers such as 1, 2, and 3, but unless the reader can create a bathhouse that is close to these dimensions, this discussion of bathrooms will not go any further. So, I would like you to put this dimensional image of space into the drawer of your mind.

Now we can finally get to the main point.

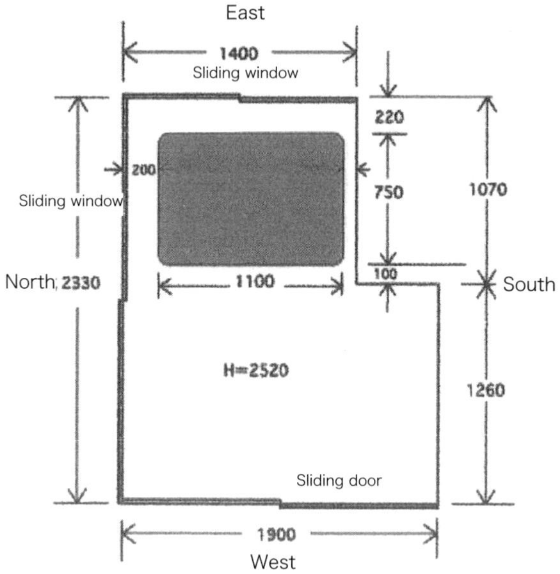

Bathtub.
Volume=327,214,000
Installation of bathtub > 355 - on the floor, 255 - under the floor

This physical space is the minimum space, and more would be preferable. However, this proportion does not mean that enlargement is a good thing. This is a very delicate proportion, and although it is physically possible to accommodate one, two, or even three people, the emotion is lost.

Bath

Morio Shinoda
Professor Emeritus, University of Tsukuba Sculptor

Start of bathing

When I heard the news about the Yamba Dam, I thought that it would cost a lot of money to dismantle the dam if it is cancelled. We would like to keep the facilities as they are and reuse this huge object as a place for art and culture, as well as a base for ecological communication to the world. Therefore, how about inviting world-famous artists to the first exhibition and holding an international competition as a way to reach out to the world through the exhibition? In the future, the museum will be based on the concept of ecology, and will communicate this concept to the world.

More than ten years ago, I was involved in the renovation of the Hokuriku Electric Power Company's dam power plant in Nyuzen Town, Toyama Prefecture, which was built in 1925.
He is also the artist of the inaugural exhibition. He is one of only two museums in the world to have reused a power station, the other being the Tate Modern in London, England. Since then, more than 10 years have passed and visitors from all over the world have come to see the museum.

If this project is completed, it is sure to be registered in the Guinness Book of Records as the museum with the world's largest monument.

Proposal for the Yatsuba Dam International Art Exhibition (tentative name)

Morio Shinoda + Space Art Institute
Representative: Shinoda Morio
Professor Emeritus, University of Tsukuba

Mr. Seiji Maehara, Minister of Land, Infrastructure, Transport and Tourism

I have been involved in the field of spatial art for more than half a century, and in 1960 I was invited by an American university to teach at the University of California, the University of Colorado, and the University of Minnesota. In 1985, he received the first Art Educator Award in the East from the American Sculpture Center (one person per year is selected from around the world).

In 1963, under the tutelage of his teacher, Dr. Buckminster Fuller (architect, philosopher, and author of Spaceship Earth), he began creating spatial and ecological works.

Talking Iron: Metal Sculptures of Today
Tokyo Metropolitan Art Museum Catalogue
Morio Shinoda (1931-)

It has been more than 30 years since I started tension sculpture. Tension now pervades every corner of my brain and is semi-automatically controlled. In a cycle of one or two months, I hardly need any sleep at all. I have held five solo exhibitions in the past year, and the three-hour sleep has become a fixture, or rather, a physical part of my life. For me, it is a contradictory logic that the continuous tension during this period eases the tension, but it is a fact and I cannot help it.

I used to think that it started from my encounter with the tension structure, but it must have originally been in my soul. I now think that the tension desire that emerges from this is what makes me create tension sculptures. The earth is soft, people are vague, life is thin, and so on. After affirming everything, I put tension on my mind and body. He prefers emergency over routine, instability over stability, and abnormality over normality, not because he finds them comfortable in themselves, but because he loves the tension that arises. The result is these tension sculptures. Finally, I am often asked whether or not I have a title for my work, but I do not, because I want to leave the creation to the viewer more than to the artist.
(1992.8.21)

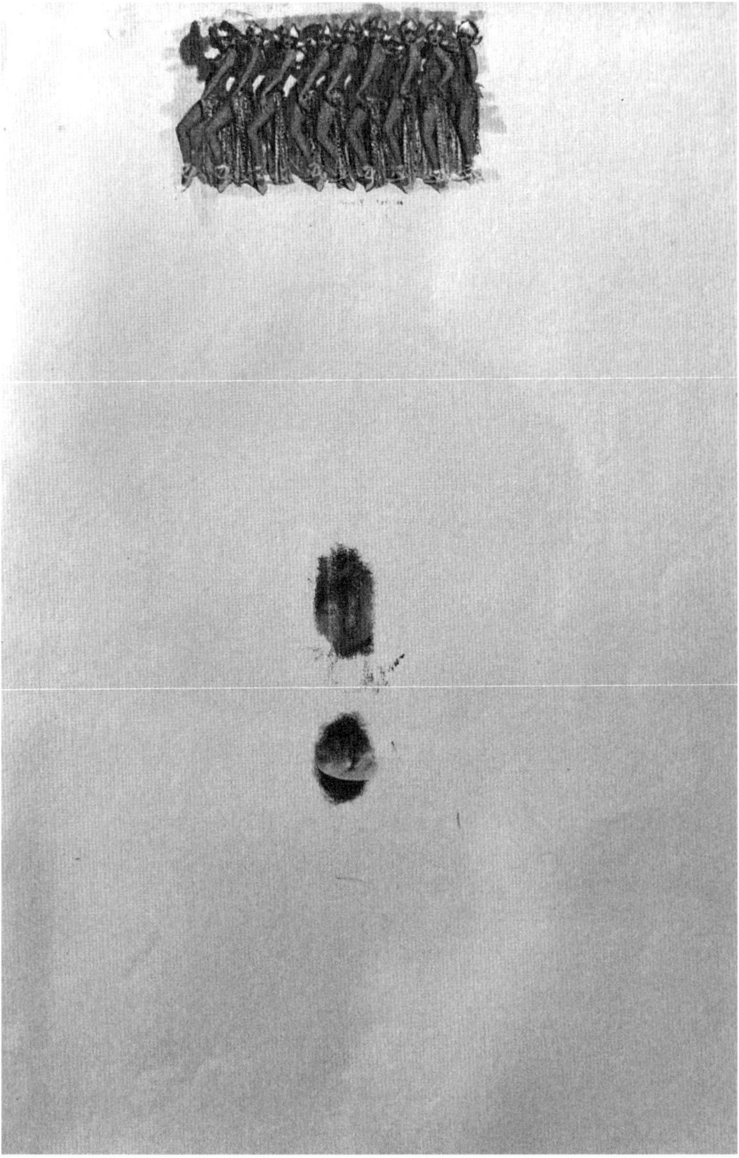

"Corbusier's Savoy House is beautiful, it's art," and I said, "It's not art. I said, "That's not art." We had a dispute about that. I said, "That's not art." "Wouldn't it be beautiful if you made something in Pronz that looked exactly like the Savoy and put it there? "I think it's beautiful in proportion, but it's not art. I think that art has a certain message, or at least the message of the artist. If it doesn't have that, it's not art. I think this is still the case in Europe, but the biggest problem is the idea that beautiful things are art. I think that has changed since at least Duchamp. Beautiful things are not necessarily art. However, when it comes to architecture and art, I think they exist in the same category. If Shinoda-san's "TC5801" was built in the middle of a forest, I would immediately call it a folly. Because it's architectural. But if you ask me if it's a Folly then, it won't be a Folly, and I don't want it to be. I feel that the concept of a Folly is defined as something that has no purpose made by an architect, something that has a certain message, something monumental. If that is the case, it would be boring if this is what it turns out to be.

good at writing. I can't even decide on a title (laughs). (laughs) I don't like the idea of putting on makeup afterwards.

Nakahara: The most annoying thing for the viewers is when literary expressions are attached to the title. When something literary is attached to a title, you can't help but be drawn in by it. There are a lot of cases where I wonder if that's what the work is about. But in your case, "Tension & Compression" is a clue, isn't it?

Shinoda: "Tension & Compression" is the first title, but it's not a message or anything, it's just a structure that I have, or in science, a technology. It's a title, but it's not a title, much less a generic title for the work. After that, the title is always the numbering of the TC.

I do a lot of word games, where I write down 20 or so words for "sculpture" and then put the other media on one side. For example, "literary sculpture," "theatrical sculpture," and so on. That's when interesting ideas start to emerge. The opposite doesn't happen at all. The interesting thing is that there is no reversibility at all. "Sculptural literature" and "sculptural architecture" don't make any sense. If you play with words too much, you end up asking what sculpture really is, which is a contradiction in terms.

Nakahara: I think that the definition of sculpture is quite complicated, especially when I talk to people in the architecture field. When I talked with a German critic, he said, of the world of Kabuki. I've always wished that this kind of expression would appear in situations where people evaluate art and design. In Japan, we don't get many critical reviews, do we? In other words, you don't know whether a work is good or not because it has received a bad review. In the New York Times, there used to be a reporter named John Canady who worked on the arts and crafts section, and he used to beat up on the works more often than not, but I think that writers rebel and grow up by being criticized. In Japan, the only way to get praise is to have your work published in a newspaper. In Japan, just because something is published in a newspaper, all you can do is praise it.

Nakahara: That's true. I sometimes write as a freelance writer, but I once had a book review job where I gave a book a bad review, and it was hard when I was writing the manuscript. It was hard when I was writing the manuscript. I would rewrite the manuscript until just before I finished it and handed it over, thinking that I shouldn't have said this much. So, I don't know about professionals, but I'm a bit of an up-and-comer when it comes to writing.

However, in art criticism, there are definitely mistakes in reading. Shinoda: Do you always read your own critiques?

Shinoda: If we talk about critiques in terms of messages, even when I introduce my own work, as a recipient I read the text again. On the other hand, I'm not very good at writing. I'm not that was on the table with my hand. When I did that, it turned out to be a work by Chamberlain (laughs). That work cost about $500, but at that time, art has a problem of where to put it, but more importantly, as a recipient, the fact that I could not receive the image that he was transmitting will remain with me when I look at the works of various artists later on. On the other hand, it may be that because there are works in the museum that can be paid for by hand, we receive them under an illusion. I feel that there are a lot of works that if it weren't for the probability of art museums and other media, I wonder if they would really be art.

Nakahara: It could be said that the art museum is the place where art is created, isn't it?

Shinoda: In my case, the issue of place has nothing to do with it. This is the first time I have shown my work at Yamagiwa Inspiration instead of a gallery, and unlike a gallery, there are no preconceived notions about the space, so I can exhibit freely and relax. I would like to continue to work in spaces that are free and not fixed.

What is required of contemporary art?

Shinoda: I happened to be reading a newspaper yesterday, and there was a person who wrote a very scathing review why I don't title my books is that the title itself can become a message, so I just use the number.

Nakahara: I have one of Shinoda's works, and when I visited his atelier for the first time, I found something incomprehensible among all the works lined up. It looked like a series of boxes stacked on top of each other, and I had an image of a huge architectural structure, so I was looking at it while saying, "If you scaled this up, it would look like an aircraft carrier. However, I suddenly began to wonder how this could be a work of art. Clearly, it was a work of art. The two boxes were not touching each other, but the top box was floating in the air. The two boxes are not touching each other, but the top box is floating in the air, and it looks strange, like it's transmitting information. That's why I thought this was good.

Shinoda: What made me really happy was that the first person who recognized the box was Nakahara-san. No one thought of it as art. It was a work that I made at a time when people were moving away from the idea of something clearly floating, but people didn't even notice that it was floating, and even if it was, they weren't really interested in that kind of thing.

Nakahara: Art, in a way, requires an active attitude on the part of the reader, doesn't it?

Shinoda: Yes. There was this one time. When I was showing my work at a gallery in California, I rolled up a piece of paper be an outdoor monument, and I don't want to be too conscious of that when I make it. I don't want to be too conscious of it when I make it. It usually ends up as a monument called sculpture, so now I'm separating the term pure sculpture.

When I look at the work of other artists in sculpture, I feel that the monument itself has a thesis, as if the monument is a large work and the rest are small works that are put together in a solo exhibition or something.

Nakahara: Shinoda-san, you mentioned that you would like to create this work in a forest in the future, but at that time, you didn't intend it to be a monument, did you?

Shinoda: Yes, I do not.

Nakahara: That's where self-fulfillment comes in, isn't it? I think that's why it can have a message. It's quite a difficult problem to consciously have a message, isn't it? If that's the case, you can create a message by writing.

Shinoda: That's right. When you say "monument," it has a message. I wanted to eliminate as much of that extra stuff as possible. I don't need a message. I want to think that the work itself is the message.

Nakahara: In the end, art is not about what the creator thinks the message is, but about the reader's desperation to read it. I think that the depth of reading determines whether or not the reader can survive for a long time.

Shinoda: That's right. I want people to read it. The reason

Up to that point, I think that was the time when architecture and art were at their happiest.
Shinoda: In a 1982 lecture by I. M. Pei, there was an explanation of a building project that he and four other artists were working on together. It wasn't a case of me doing the building and you doing the interior, but an artist named D. Frevin was also participating, and he made a proposal of what he wanted to do with the light, and then the architects started at the same time, saying that they needed a room like this for that purpose. It spreads from the inside to the outside.
Nakahara: It's a very unusual project, isn't it? It's quite interesting.
Shinoda: In my case, the building is already completed, and I attach it to the monument. As I wrote in the pamphlet for the upcoming exhibition, what exactly is a monument is what I have been wondering the most lately, especially for the upcoming exhibition.

The work itself is the message, and it is up to the recipient to read it

Shinoda: I wonder if there is a difference between the attitude of a sculptor making a sculpture and that of a monument. I am making a sculpture. I am making a sculpture, and it happens to all of his paintings are of dead creatures. He is a conceptual artist, but I thought he was a kind of ecologist. Ecologist is not the right word, but I wonder how the earth will change in the current situation. Isn't the human race going to die out? It seems to me that he is thinking up to that point. I think that the work of an artist is very much a tactile way of reading the future.

Shinoda:In my case, I think I've been very lucky in my encounters with people. Meeting people like Max Ernst, Meret Oppenheim, and Buckminster Fuller, who were pioneers of their times, was very stimulating and nourishing for me. The work I did in 1958, inspired by Fuller's lecture, is the start of the tension. I was also influenced by Paolo Soleri. The stimulation I received from sculptors and artists had already ended for me in the 50's. After that, I was mostly looking at architecture, starting with Fuller. From then on, starting with Fuller, I was mostly looking at architecture. There was a time when I was running around all over the United States looking at the early American architects such as Louis Kahn and Eero Saarinen.

Nakahara: I think architecture used to exist in unison with art, and in the 1920's New York Art Deco architecture, when you walked in the entrance, there were sculptures and murals, and you thought, "Oh, that's beautiful. However, when I look at today's architecture, I don't think it necessarily matches the art.

An artist who is quick to read the times with his delicate sense of touch

Nakahara: Mr. Shinoda, you mentioned that you were influenced by Buckminster Fuller, and a collector I met in New York said something that I actually agree with. "A collector I met in New York said something to me that I actually agree with: "When you're on the side of the artists, you're the first to see how they change with the times. So when I think of Fuller, I think of him as someone who read the future of the earth on Spaceship Earth. Shinoda-san brought that into the world of artists and expressed it in the most radical way, I think. There is a balance in the social relationships between people living on the earth, isn't there? I think you were the one who captured and expressed that tension, that dangerous balance, in the 1960s.

Shinoda: There was a time in the 60s, when Dali was still going strong, when he said that his beard was an antenna from space. He happened to see my work at that time and said, "Shinoda's tension is kind of like my antenna. I heard him say in a magazine, "Shinoda's tension is almost like my antenna. Coincidentally, I suddenly remembered that what you just said about artists having tactile senses is interesting because it has something in common with the fact that Dali had a beard.

Nakahara:There is an artist named William Wegman, and

Inspiration

"Morio Shinoda: Document Exhibition
July 24 - August 31, 1991

An Art Philosophy that Produces "Pure Sculpture"

Morio Shinoda is one of Japan's leading sculptors. Through "TC (Tension and Compression)," a metal sculpture incorporating a suspended structure that he has consistently presented, he talked with Hiroshi Nakahara, a good friend of his work, about his attitude and thoughts toward art.

Special Conversation:
Morio Shinoda and Hiroshi Nakahara

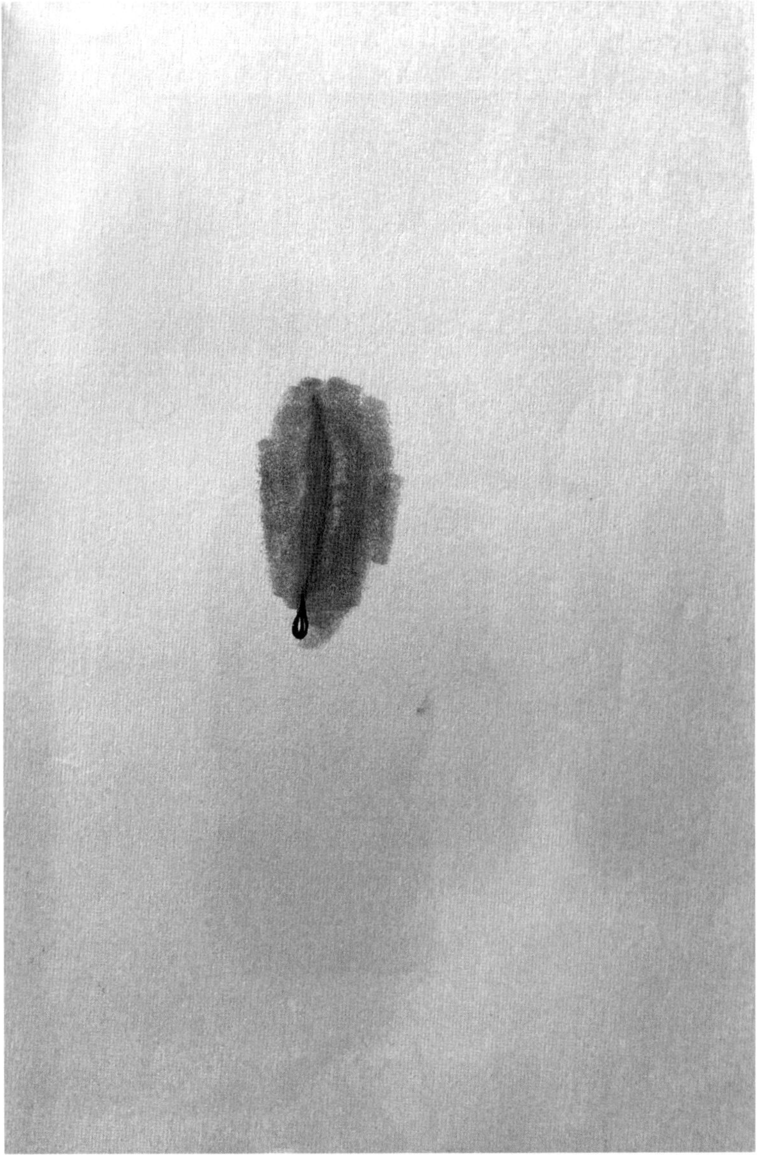

civil servants.

This is not because of the taste of the furniture or the quantity of things, but because the space is different. The same volume of space can change depending on how things are placed, how colors are handled, and so on. This is what I call spatial communication, and when people start living, they unconsciously create their own space. A crab digs a hole in the shape of its shell.

Moholy-Nagy, a Hungarian-born painter, sculptor and designer, said, "Space is the reality of human sensory experience, and perception of space is a physiological function of human beings. I believe that a good living environment is one in which this space is personally and actively incorporated. The German psychologist Metzger proved that by shortening the height of a flat surface by a quarter, it looks the same. This means that we can use an extra quarter of the actual space. Is space also governed by gravity? Furthermore, by adding psychological space utilization such as color, pattern, shape, etc., it will be possible to change the residential space considerably.

S&E No.7 Autumn 1990 Mitsui Fudosan pamphlet

Spatial Life

In the 40 years since the end of World War II, I have lived in 12 different places in Japan and 13 different places in the U.S. There are certain advantages to living in a rented house. There are certain advantages to living in a rented house, especially in my line of work, where I often move to be near the relevant factory or to find the environment I need, depending on the nature of my work. Since I was young, I have always had a bohemian streak in me, and I feel as if settling in one place would dilute my future, so I keep moving. In the worst cases, I moved because I liked the location. There's also the freedom of not having to be nervous about buildings. It is because I am a rootless person without a house that I was able to go out with an invitation from an American university out of the blue.

The living room and dining room are on a four-story skip floor with a five-meter high ceiling. The living room and dining room have four skip floors, and the higher ceiling is a five-meter vaulted ceiling. The difference in height between these four levels is immeasurable in how much effective space and comfort it gives to the residents. I applaud the bureaucrat's design. It is interesting to note that although the exterior of dozens of houses are exactly the same, the family composition of the people who live in them varies so much that it makes you wonder why there are so many differences in the same

Spatial Illusions

Right-Handed and Left-Handed Spaces

In the late 1950's, the Housing Corporation built an experimental full-scale reinforced concrete apartment building for bachelors in Hiyoshi on the Toyoko Line. At that time, apartments were usually wooden two-story buildings of cheap construction, so the concrete construction was quite modern and was enough to attract the attention of the young people of that time. I remember that if I pushed myself, I could somehow afford to move in with my starting salary. However, it was a single room of 3.5 tsubo with a small sink, gas stove, and a single bed. Each building had five floors and 100 units. The competition was quite high, but I won and ended up moving in. In this kind of one-room apartment of the same size, supporting walls and partition walls are placed one after the other to support the ceiling, and equipment is built into these supporting walls, so the neighbors have to be in the same shape. The space differs depending on whether the facilities are located on the right or the left. In other words, there is a difference in the sense of space. It may have something to do with right-handedness or left-handedness, but for me, a space with equipment on the left and no equipment on the right feels at least a few centimeters wider. This may be the same sense of space that I have when I walk into a movie theater and the seat I relax in is located to my right.

OLDSMOBILE
NOW SHOWING
YOUNGMOBILE
THINKING 1969

A walk in the countryside

The monument was created to commemorate the opening of the Denentoshi Line in 1966. At that time, people were interested in the moon, and I started work on it with the theme of "space family" in anticipation of the coming age. Incidentally, it was three years later that the first man stood on the moon.

The original idea was to bury a 50-meter section of the monument in the pond, which is now a roundabout, and light the monument at night when a small wave rises in the water. The idea was to bury a 50-meter section in the pond and light it at night so that the monument would glow when a small wave formed. However, it was difficult to maintain, so when the shopping center was built in front of the station, the pond was turned into a small hill and ginkgo trees were planted to give it its current shape.

We made 12 of them, and six of them are now standing in front of the station as a family.

Tokyu railway line and town information magazine "THE GROWING" vol. 9, 1990.7

atrium, there are metal pipes running from the ceiling to the floor, and you can slide down them. However, there is no other way out except by using these pipes, so please refrain from doing so if you are not confident in your physical strength. This building is the place where I put the most effort as a space, and the interior aspects are designed topologically, so you cannot see this mysterious space unless you stand on the floor. The main house is no longer a problem if you've made it this far. Fear and momentum increase or decrease in inverse proportion, so your energy should increase with familiarity. Finally, the reason why I built such a house is because, for me, life is both a fear and a pleasure, a place to study the body and mind, and above all, I wanted to live a life that was convenient, free of rationality, hot in summer and cold in winter.

"Tsubasa no okoku" (All Nippon Airways), June 1988

into the forest, you will see a white staircase with about 50 steps. You will have to climb them. This is because it is part of the minimal exercise. However, please note that the width of the first staircase is 3 meters, while the upper staircase is only 1 meter wide. The top step is 8 to 9 meters high and there is no handrail, so if you fall, you are not safe. At the top of the stairs, there is a 50cm gap between the stairs and the approach to the main house to make them independent and to digest the next exercise. This is the distance I think I will be able to fly when I reach the age of 80, and it was the most difficult decision to make. I had the hardest time deciding on these dimensions, because when I become too old to fly, I will lose my home like a vagrant living under a bridge girder. Now, fly with all your might. The approach is three meters wide, so you won't fall. Fly as hard as you can. The approach is three meters wide, so don't worry, you won't fall. The approach to the building is also tapered. This is to make the distance look longer by using perspective so that you can fully enjoy the nature around you. On the way back, it will seem shorter. On the way, you will see a small entrance on your left that looks like a doorway to a tea ceremony room. This building is a private museum that displays my works and collection, so if you are interested in that area, please take a look. The gap here is one meter, but you can get down to the porch of the museum by putting your hand on the top of the doorway and doing a little pull-up. Even if you fail to do so, the ground is three meters high, and there are pushers below, so you won't injure your feet. Inside the

A message of 1000 words

The "Sky Museum" of Illusion. Sculptor Morio Shinoda

For the past few years, I have been thinking about my own place of residence (Sumika). Dwellings, even private residences, are subject to various restrictions and legal regulations. In addition, we are also constrained by the private restrictions of our personal life and family structure. Even for people like me, who do not have and will never have a so-called family or home, we tend to get caught up in the general concept of a house and start by choosing a compromise to the restrictions.

The starting point is a fully functional dwelling place for me alone to live. Based on the principle that it must be more comfortable than anything else in my lifetime, I constructed a house called "Kukki Kan" in my mind like a fantasy. The name "Kukki-kan" was given to the house with the meaning of an object with a strange space, or a sculpture with the function of a dwelling. I wrote it down from three perspectives: my own spatial desires, a structure that requires the minimum amount of movement for my body, and a daring to coexist with physical nature rather than sensory nature.

Now, let me take you all to the Sky Museum. When you get off your car at the Kita-Tsuchiura Interchange, you will see a pale yellow house on the hillside to the right of Mount Tsukuba. If you get off the car and drive 50 meters, you will find the entrance to the museum in the woods at the intersection where the village road splits into two. As you step it is used more than when it is manufactured.

My Porsche 356SC1964 is getting closer and closer to perfection after 26 years. And after living with it for more than 20 years, it has become physical and completely part of my body.

After that, I got a used 911T 1972, but I couldn't separate the parts of my body, so I had two of them, and then I had three with the 1984 911 Carrera. It's like a child, you can't leave it. I am thankful that my personality doesn't change every year like a normal car, and after driving a car for 20 or 30 years, when I look at old photos, I have many memories, but when I see myself getting old, I feel horrible. When I see my students again, who I used to give rides to when I was a student, they have families and children of their own, and it is as if they have gone back in time.

Also, just as plants react to humans, cars also react after decades of being together. If you say to them, "I think I'm declining these days," they react immediately and their dandruff becomes worse. The reader may find this hard to believe, but it is a fact that I have encountered this phenomenon many times.

Morio Shinoda

(Professor, Faculty of Art and Design, University of Tsukuba)

Porsche

The Porsche 356, a soft sculpture because it cuts the wind.

Porsche 356 --- A man must feel a strange tingling coming from the bottom of his stomach. It seems that when this car was born, what men were looking for was not just speed. The mysterious beauty of the unfinished mechanism and the smell of the times. Once again, it tickles the human heart.

Currently, at the heart of Porsche's headquarters in Stuttgart, the company is unable to reach a conclusion on whether or not to build a car for super-demand. The super-demand is literally a car that will never break down. All the design work is done and they are just waiting for the go-ahead, but it is clear that the completion of the car will result in a loss of income.

However, I like this positive attitude. In Japan, there is an ancient concept of "usage," and things that have been used for a long time increase the value of the product. In the old days, uchikake, a bride's wedding kimono, was used as a nightgown before the bride's wedding to make the silk supple, and on the day of the bride's wedding, it was said to have a beautiful luster. It can be said that a product is closer to perfection when

Today, the one
chooses

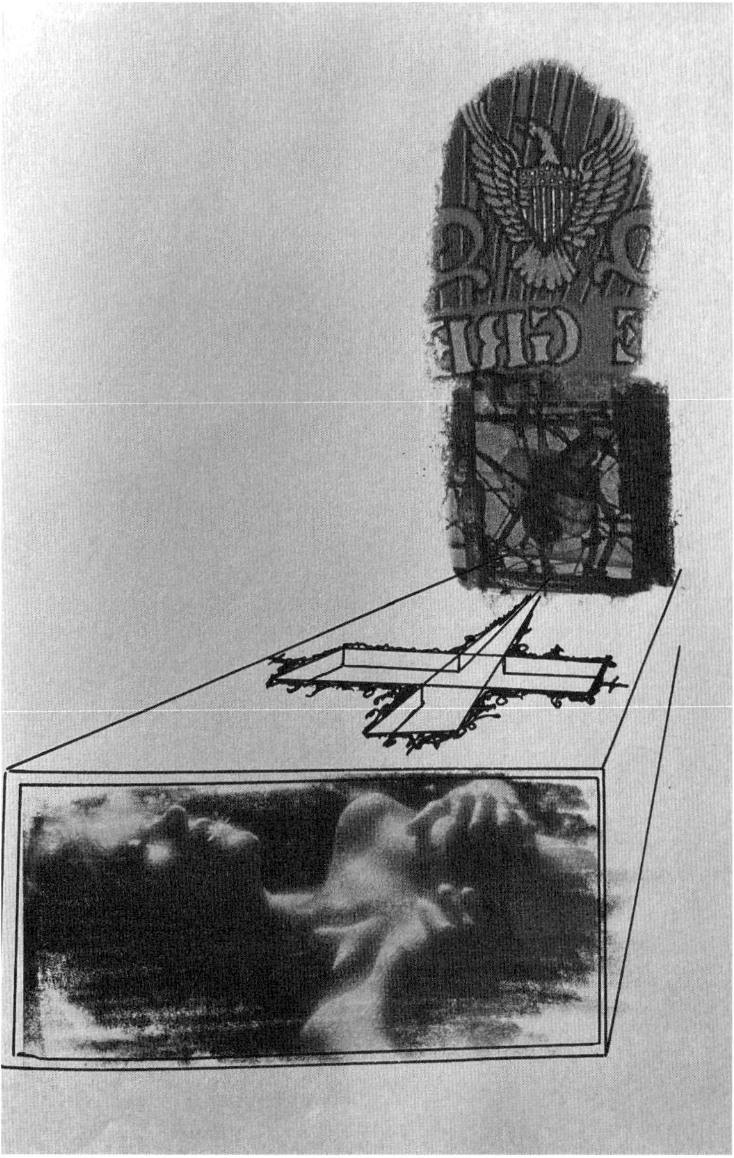

■ Health

"I have a desire to spend a night in a hospital.

■ A book

yunosuke Akutagawa's "The Words of a Confucian Actor"

■ Favorite words

Philosopher Ebiquiel's "Pain is pleasure.

■ Pleasure

Being afraid is a pleasure. If there is no fear, the concept of avoidance cannot be born. Because the Japanese people have been poor until now, we have entered an age where everything is computerized and comfortable, just like now. However, someday, people will start to think that they need to move their own bodies to live. However, people cannot live long enough for society to change. There is no other way but to do it yourself. ......

■ Compromise

In life, compromise is up to 80%. However, it is too lonely to end up with that. After all, my own world is ....

Professor, University of Tsukuba

Composition major. Comprehensive Plastic Arts Course. In English, it's called Plastic Arts and Mixed Media. In the past, there was a division by material, such as sculpture, stone carving, wood carving, etc., but I decided to divide by media itself.

■ What should students do after graduation?

Become an artist. Or they can work for an agency like Dentsu, or a design company. They can also work in architecture or as curators at art museums.

"Tsukuba-no Tomo, No. 39 (October 15, 1989)

■ When you are depressed

I stay at home and think for two or three days without eating or drinking that there is no other man on earth with such bad luck as me. "When I get to the bottom, even if the next day is normal, I feel like it's better than yesterday.

■ Cigarettes

Eighty packs of "Peace" light cigarettes a day. I used to cut up both cans of peas. "I can't find them anywhere now. But I can't just buy a year's supply of something harmful in a can.

■ Dream

If a private art museum is established as part of the Shinji project, I would like to display all of my large-scale works in museums around the world, just once, before I die.

■ Untitled

The works are numbered only. If it is an abstract work, it is better to give it a title so that people can look at it with a sense of precedence.

■ In order of number

Just in order. The work I'm working on now is 5801.

■ Book

The Declaration of Pleasure" (Nan Tenko Gallery Publishing Department) - when I had my first solo exhibition in Japan in 1972.

■ Reading glasses

When I was young, I was farsighted. When I was young, I was farsighted, but when I was over forty, my eyesight suddenly became so bad that I could not live without my glasses. My mother is 85 years old and in good health. She reads the newspaper without wearing glasses.

able to study.

■ Test

"He said, "Well, whoever you are, raise your hand if you don't think it's me. I also said, "No, originally, I was too brazen. A foreign teacher came and we had a conversation and everything, and I came out on top. I was the only one chosen to go to the U.S.

■ The Art Institute of Chicago

The class was held in a world-famous art museum, and I got to see the real thing. It was a great learning experience.

■ My teacher

I had no teacher. Rather, it was the environment.

■ Drinking history

My father could not drink a drop. My mother was so drunk that she was knocked over by slaughterhouses. I also didn't drink at all when I was a student. As soon as I became a government official, I was forced to drink. Especially after I was assigned to the design department.

■ My pace

I don't drink heavily, and I don't drink at parties unless I have to. However, if I want to drink, I will have a bottle of whiskey right away.

■ Moderation

When I don't drink, I don't have a drop for a week. If you don't want to drink, don't drink; if you don't want to eat, don't eat. A moderate life is no good.

■ Have a strong stomach.

It's rare that I get sick the next day. After a night's sleep, you'll feel refreshed.

consistently got one every month.

■ To the Design Department

The head of the department said to me, "You may have gone to a different school, but you have the ability. Come to my place. This was the first time I had a real job.

Until then, I had only seen things from the outside. I didn't see things systematically. "I was taught the basics by my section chief, who told me, "This is not a drawing.

■ Work

I would take my designs to Akita or Yamagata and ask the craftsmen to make prototypes. I would then redesign it to make it more modern and exportable to foreign countries, and promote it for them.

■ The 1960s

When I first started sculpting five or six years ago, I was sometimes called an order artist. If the image can be reproduced, it doesn't have to go through my hands. I would draw a drawing and order the necessary parts from a foundry. I just assemble the finished product.

■ Six tatami mats and one room

At a time when everyone had their own studio, a single drawing table in a boarding house was all that was needed, no studio, no machines, no tools.

■ Business trip to the U.S.

It was like a half inspection. Most of the time, it was the head of the department. However, I couldn't speak the language and became neurotic in a foreign country away from my family. On the other hand, the other side complained that if I didn't send younger people with better language skills, they wouldn't be and writers from all over the world to give lectures and spread the word to the general public. The library had all the latest magazines in art and design from around the world. --The library had all the latest art and design magazines in the world.

■ What a joke.

There were artists and architects all around me. Eighty percent of the staff came from the design department of Chigyo University's College of Engineering or the current art college. As I learned from them, I started to follow their ways.

■ Curiosity

I like to watch things. Even now, I can watch a construction site for an hour without getting bored.

■ There are many competitions.

It was a time when the word "design" did not exist. The only way for Japan to make money after losing the war was to sell Japanese products to other countries and make money. The Ministry of International Trade and Industry (MITI) pushed export promotion measures as its main project, and local product and industrial associations competed to solicit designs with prize money.

■ Prize money

The amount of prize money on the blackboard was 50,000 yen for the first prize and 30,000 yen for the second prize, an amount comparable to my salary.

■ Third Prize: Specialization

The specialists were desperately trying to win the first prize. The experts were desperate to win the first prize, and I was aiming for the third prize to make some extra money. I

From now on, it will be the age of English, so he told me to go to an English school.

■ Pillar

My mother worked, and I helped her by buying food and cooking for her from junior high school to college.
I helped my mother by buying food and cooking from junior high school to university.

■ A sense of life

I had no dreams at the time when Japan had lost the war and what would happen next. It was natural to live in poverty. ......

■ English Literature

I majored in English literature, chose Chaucer, and wrote my graduation thesis.

■ I dropped out.

It was a time when people praised me just because I could speak English. I thought this would ruin me.

■ Part-time job

Before the Peace Treaty, there were good jobs for people who could speak English. At the Ministry of International Trade and Industry (MITI), there was a job to translate bills into English and obtain permission from the headquarters.

■ After the Peace Treaty

After the peace treaty was concluded, the section was abolished, but since I was a civil servant, I could not be fired. I was secretly hoping to be assigned to JETRO (Japan External Trade Organization), but my boss took the liberty of assigning me to the Industrial Arts Research Institute.

■ Library

The purpose of the institute was to invite profound scholars was injured. From a young age, I grew up discovering that this place was dangerous.

■ Now it is

Too much convenience. I think we've lost sight of what's dangerous for us.

■ Father

Born in Nagano Prefecture. The second son of a farmer who used to be the headman, he was first adopted.

■ Mother

Born in Gifu Prefecture. I left for Tokyo when I was about five years old, and later joined my father.

■ His eldest son.

My mother's family name. There are many Shinoda surnames in Gifu.

■ Brothers

Four. The second and fourth died prematurely of pneumonia due to a lack of medicine during the Russo-Japanese War.

He was five years younger than me.

The third son, under my influence, graduated from Musashino Art School and became a full-fledged graphic designer. He made much more money than me in Tokyo.

■ Workers' mobilization

As a junior high school student, he used a lathe to cut the legs of the Zero fighter plane.

■ Father's death

One month after the end of the war, when I was 14 years old, he died of intestinal typhus or something. He was forty-five years old.

■ Last Will and Testament

Who's who in Tsukuba

Morio Shinoda, Professor of Art and Design, University of Tsukuba

■ What is comfort?

The first thing I hate is air conditioners. I sweat when it is hot, and shiver when it is cold. I rarely use the central heating system in the public servants' quarters.

■ Airtightness

In a building made of aluminum sash and concrete, if you close the door in winter, you may wonder what is going on outside.

■ Drafts

In Tokyo, I live in an old wooden house. In Tokyo, I live in an old wooden house, where the wind blows in and the rain makes noise. Such a life is my dream.

■ Land

I have never owned my own land until I reached this age. I've never owned my own land until I reached this age, because I thought I might leave that environment at any time.

■ I'm on the edge.

But I don't know if I can live for another fifty years. I don't care where I live, I just want to realize my own world and live in it, even if it's only for five or ten years.

■ Shinji Project

I want to keep the mountain forest as it is, but build a sculpture 20 meters above the ground, and live there literally in harmony with nature.

■ Idea

I hope that the daily life I lead here will provide some ideas to people all over the world.

■ Identity

When I was born, there was still the Dopu River in Meguro. We could catch cicadas. There were cliffs with no fences. I

The Saturday Evening Post

so many people here, you can probably tell from the outside that something is going on. I wondered how such a thing as a work of art could be established. An art museum is basically a system for showing works of art as works of art, and although this may seem like an abstract topic, I wondered if I could say that about each of your works in concrete terms. That's what I was thinking today. When you try to appreciate a work of art in a tatami room, you usually stand and look at the work, but you can sit and look at the work. The level of the works is of course much higher here, but I felt it at that time as well. There was one good one in Osaka, too. I was also surprised by the paintings of the children of Tentokuin Kindergarten, which is the same as the last story by Professor Ota. That's about it.

Moderator Suzuki: Thank you very much. Thank you very much, teachers and the monk of Tentokuin. With that, I would like to conclude the symposium.

I'd like to conclude my talk briefly. I'd like to talk about what you've said so far about the relationship between artworks and space, specifically machiya (townhouses) as a space, but also the relationship between environment and people, or to put it simply, between a container and its contents. Personally, I think it's a question of how meta is established in the context, and I've been thinking about it for a long time. What I mean by this is that yesterday I was following Sakamoto-sensei and watching the installation of his works. The whole "machiya" is the meta of the machiya, and meta means transcendence, and the opposite of transcendence is immanence, or at any rate, "machiya. The opposite of transcendence is immanence, or at any rate, "machiya." No matter what you do, if you look at it within that context, it looks like a machiya. Today, we have large posters, but yesterday, we just put up small pamphlets. Yesterday, we just put up small pamphlets. But even if I tried to write that, it would be buried in the townhouse. Yesterday, I was thinking that there was a strange power of the town houses, or the townscape, or the temple town. When I looked at it today, there was a little more than that, but there was an easel-like sign on it. Returning to the topic of meta, the meta is, in other words, a work of art. The fact that there is a work in itself and the fact that the work appeals that it is a work of art, that appeal is meta. Yesterday, I couldn't find any such element that appealed to me that this exhibition was an exhibition venue. I was already overwhelmed by the power of the machiya. Today, I don't know what to call it, but if there are life for a living person, as well as the necessary space for a social community. In other words, how to make the best use of the material itself in the space that human beings have created based on the material, I think some of you said it intuitively today. I think this is the kind of space where you can be a little more sensitive to the light itself, and the materials themselves, just as they made you question the quality of your works and made you create them, I think the light of the human space of the past can be a force that brings your works to the surface. I'm not suggesting that we should go back to the past, but I would like you to think about what kind of light is appropriate for this space even now. Today's museums are called white cubes, aren't they? Instead, I would like to create a space with light and artworks that are appropriate for the material space of this machiya, a space that returns to the human being and to the material. The work of Tentokuin, who is raising his children with great care and respect for nature, and who has great potential for the future, was a surprise to me. I felt as if I had been shown a real example of how such sensibilities are naturally nurtured and how such works can be created by being in such a living space. If only all of those people could come to art school, I think it would be great. The last part of this article is a bit of a ramble, but that's how I feel. Thank you very much for showing me your good works.

Dr.Takahashi:My name is Takahashi. I have a few things I want to talk about, but I'll try to be brief. I have a lot to say, but townhouses, including today's work. I would like to summarize one or two things based on what the three of you have said from an artistic perspective. If you look at the map, you will see that there are very few machiya houses on this side of the Saikawa River. The Saigawa River is a river between two castle towns, and the town space where people live is spread out like this. The period from the middle of the Edo period to the pre-war period is considered to be a good opportunity for the stable development of machiya in Kanazawa. As the machiya developed, there were various forms of cooperation as a living space community, which is now called a school district. In the last semester, we read the literature together, and Professor Sakamoto brought us the basic documents, but the research is still in progress, or rather, it is difficult to progress, and it is difficult to understand. It's hard to know when it was built, how many there were, what it was for, and what it looked like, but from my point of view, it still exists in this town. It may or may not be alive because it was not burned, but it still exists as a space. The fact that it was used by people who needed it in the past, and that it has been preserved even now, makes me think that there is something hidden in it that is connected to something fundamental to the basic human community. The townhouse we are talking about here does not have a hallmark, so the question of which hallmark this townhouse is connected to is a private one. Machiya is just like that. Machiya is exactly like that. They are made of wood, plaster, paper, and earthen floor. They are also equipped with all the basic necessities of differently on my way to and from school, so I always look for a change. I thought that Hiromi and machiya were human spaces and felt that it was an attractive town, so I suggested that we study Hiromi for a while. So I suggested that we study Hiromi for a while. If we chose Hiromi, we would be looking at the town of Kanazawa and the space of the machiya, so the other professors raised their own issues with the students.

Moderator INOUE: I think it was still in spring or before summer.

Dr. Ohta: After the Golden Week, we went out to the town, and Dr. Sakamoto prepared a map, binoculars, and footing, and we went out to the town several times to conduct surveys. Actually, I should thank the mayor for this, but in reality, I was not the one who submitted the paperwork, but Mr. Tajima and others cooperated with me to submit it, saying, "If you are working so hard, we will give you a little budget for the exhibition. But when we did that, we got the money. It was only 200,000 yen, but I think they were able to pull it off. In addition to that, Dr. Sakamoto made a lot of effort, and we also received support from other sources. I am very happy to be here today. I would like to express my gratitude to all of you, including senior and junior members of the town, who came to see the exhibition or came to see how it was going. Thank you very much. I have to converge on the topic of townhouses, but I think you can understand that I am interested in Hiromi and don't know, including art school professors and students, so I would like to give a brief explanation of the process that led us to this point, and thank you. As some of you may know, the Kanazawa College of Art established a doctoral course a little more than eleven years ago, which was very rare for an art university. Since then, the faculty has been working together with the incoming first-year doctoral students, through trial and error, to see what we can do to increase the power of the program. So there is a strange class. This year, we are fortunate to have eight new doctors. Fortunately, eight new doctors joined us this year, and it's amazing how much manpower we have. In other words, we could pose a problem, do research on it from various angles, and then summarize the results and link them to the work. After several years of teaching this class, I felt that it would be strange for a doctor's class if we gave the students problems, they had to make some effort to answer them, and then they had to submit a report and receive a grade. So I raised the issue. So I raised the issue. At that time, there were six of us each, and two teachers in the field of arts and crafts who are not here today are also part of that group, so there are quite a lot of teachers committed to the project. This year, we mainly worked on a certain problem from April to September in the fall, and then tried to connect it to the work. When I came to Kanazawa from Tokyo about ten years ago, I found that the townhouses were not damaged by the war, so they are still very attractive. I don't like to walk the same path every day because I have to walk many paths. I always walk a strange building called "Chi-meikan," which was named by Professor Yukimura, and I wrote an article about it in the Art Techo of that time. It is a steel-framed structure on the bank of the river, but of course they keep collecting scrap iron to build it. It is about three stories high, and there is no separation between the floors, so you end up on the observation deck on the top floor while touring around inside. Moreover, it is an architecture that multiplies day by day. There is a theory called "Metabolic Architecture," which was advocated by Kiyonori Kikutake and others during the Okinawa Ocean Expo. Of course, it was an illegal building, and he continued to build it, ignoring the guidance of the government. If he had built it on his own land, it would have become as famous as the Watts Tower in Los Angeles as a world-famous amateur building, which is a shame.

This is a bit long, but I would like to end my talk here. Thank you very much for your time.

Now that we have talked about machiya (traditional townhouses), temples, and architecture, I would like to ask Mr. Ohta and Mr. Takahashi if they would like to share something with us based on what they have just said. I would appreciate it. First of all, I would like to ask you, Professor Ohta.

Dr. Ohta: I was running away from the symposium because I was forced to do the work of three people, but it turned out to be a good thing for the symposium, so thank you very much. Looking at it this way, it seems that there are some people I accompanied her. But once we got inside, it all changed. The beauty of the structure was astonishing. Perhaps Maupassant was as comfortable with the beauty of the interior as I was.

I have to get to the point here, but to conclude, there are different dimensions to living and seeing. There is no shortage of tourists in the Chaya district in the east, but no matter where you go to explore, you will never get beyond the dimension of seeing. "To live in a space is to breathe in it, for better or worse. In 1990, I bought a 1,000 tsubo plot of land in the village of Niiharu in Ibaraki Prefecture and decided to build a huge sculpture with a floor space of 200 tsubo and live there. I wanted to create a perfect eco-circle with the surrounding nature, and the exterior of the sculpture would be a work of art, so it should be worthy of appreciation. So I thought of this as a nano-sculpture or molecular sculpture, where the whole is one work and the interior is also an independent work. I think the same thing applies to the machiya and Katsura Rikyu that I mentioned earlier. "In the case of sculptures, we look at the whole and see it as a single work, but on the scale of a residence, we can appreciate the whole and its parts in a comprehensive way. However, on the scale of a dwelling, the whole and its parts can be appreciated in a comprehensive manner. If this is taken in reverse, it requires a great deal of sensitivity and strong modeling ability for the creator. Last but not least, I would like to talk about the keyword "dwelling" that I was most interested in and wanted to share with you. When I was at the University of Tsukuba, I conducted a research on a newspaper called "Le Temps" asked, "Is the city of Paris going to be irreparably disfigured and disfigured by remaining any longer attached to the bizarre and money-grubbing ideas of a machine builder? After all, the Eiffel Tower is something that even commercialistic America is unlikely to want, and is undoubtedly a disgrace to Paris. When the foreigners come to visit our World's Fair, they will exclaim in amazement: "My God! "How dare they! Is this the horrible thing that the French have devised to show us their much-admired taste? The last part, "This horrible thing? This is the sentence I wanted to emphasize, but among those who joined the opposition were Guy de Maupassant, Charles Garnier, Alexandre Dumas Fiss, and others. Roland Barthes wrote about it in his essay, "Maupassant, among others, often lunched at the Eiffel Tower restaurant, though he was not fond of the place. "Because this," he said, "is the only place in Paris where you can't see the Eiffel Tower. In fact, in Paris, you have to pay infinitely more attention to avoid seeing the Eiffel Tower." That's what he said. Well, Barthes seems to be an opponent, but later he says, "It connects me and all my friends who I know are looking at the tower, over Paris. The Eiffel Tower is full of friendship. And so on. This has a lot to do with my idea of "living". For example, when I think about Maupassant eating in the restaurant of the Eiffel Tower, it must have been very comfortable. I am not a big fan of visiting historical sites, but I once took two of my students to Paris for the first time. One of them was a young girl and she really wanted to see the Eiffel Tower, so I

Next, I would like to talk about the space of Japanese architecture. In 1903, Tenshin Okakura published a famous book in the U.S. called "The Book of Tea", which was not translated but written in English by Tenshin himself. The architect Frank Loyd Wright (1867-1959) was greatly influenced by this book, and although he had been building gothic style houses, he was able to create a number of new buildings, including the Unity Church in Chicago in 1906, the Robie House in Chicago in 1909, and the Imperial Hotel in Tokyo. He began to focus on the differences in height within the same space, such as the stepping stones, veranda, main room, and alcove of Japanese houses, and began to design floors with various differences in height within Western architecture. This further influenced Eero Saarinen, Louis Kahn, and others, and was conceptualized as the skip floor by Paul Rudolph of Yale University, which became a major inspiration for American architecture after World War II. Just as the ukiyoe prints influenced the Impressionist painters in painting, there was an epoch like this in architecture.

IV Living

Before I talk about living, I would like to share an interesting episode. On February 14, 1887, the Eiffel Tower, built by Gustave Eiffel, an engineer, was criticized by Parisians. On February 14, 1887, during the construction of the Eiffel Tower, this is the spirit of service that they wanted their guests to fully enjoy. Also, when you leave, you are naturally in reverse perspective, which makes you feel the length is short. In fact, this kind of consideration is given everywhere.

To give you a couple more examples, the handrail in front of the toilet looks straight when you stand in the corridor, but when you look at it from the side, you can see that the cleats of the handrail are slightly angled, and the extension of the handrail is connected to a point in the ground, just like a fan. There is more. The shelves in the living room of the chusyoin have a slight perspective in depth, which gives a sense of space. These shelves are called Katsura-dana, and together with the Kasumidana in the Shugakuin detached palace, they are called the three shelves of Japan. This is called the "Nihon nani nani" or the "eight sceneries of Omi," which was advocated by the beauty leaders of the past. This is the case with old temples, private houses, and machiya in Japan. These pleasant beauties are not limited to the Japanese, but also include the golden division and the pleasant sounds of Mozart's music, which is mostly composed of the chords do, mi, and so. One sound researcher claims that the sounds of nature, such as the touch of trees, bamboo, and bamboo grass, are all chords of do, mi, and so. Perhaps the sense of beauty resonates with the heartstrings of vibration in relation to the realm of human physiology.

III Space in Japanese Architecture

Bruno Taut (1880-1938) lived in Sendai and Takasaki for four years starting in 1933, and traveled around Japan to discover ancient Japanese tools. Katsura Rikyu was built as a villa for Tomohito Hachijomiya, and the first phase was built between 1620 and 1625, which is the present Koshoin. The first phase was built between 1620 and 1625, which is the present Koshoin. The second phase, from 1645 to 1648, included the construction of the Chushoin, Shinshoin, Shokintei, Laoiken and other tea houses. Although this detached palace must have been a place of hospitality, the introduction is so simple that it does not seem to be the home of an important person. Furthermore, the more you are invited to the entrance, the less you can see the thoughtfulness and concern of the house owner. But for some strange reason, I felt at home. Further on, there is a long corridor with a width of two meters, and on the left side, there is a moon viewing platform made of round bamboo, which is really simple without a handrail. To my surprise, the corridor, which is fifteen to six meters long, narrows by about one meter toward the end. In other words, it has a perspective. The purpose of this is to give a view of the garden of Katsura Rikyu, which is called a circular garden, from the building. The building is built on stilts to avoid the flooding of the Katsura River, so the eye level is more than twice as high as usual. In the case of serving guests, the reception room is located at the far end of the building, and you can see the garden from the corridor leading up to it, from the perspective I just mentioned. It may not be apparent at first glance, but

Dutch people in Nagasaki in the south.

After I retired from Tsukuba University, I worked at Nagasaki University for two years, and when I got on the streetcar at 3 o'clock in the afternoon, I saw many high school girls getting on, and they all looked like Rie Miyazawa. Some of my students were of Miyazawa descent, and I would ask them, "Do you have any Dutch or Portuguese ancestry in your family? But they all said in unison, "No, we are pure Japanese. No, we are pure Japanese. They hardly notice it. In Western Europe, people put their ancestors' names in their names. For example, Picasso's name is so long that it looks like Jugendanashi in rakugo. I am convinced of Chiba Shigeo's theory that the Japanese people are a hodgepodge.

Next, I would like to talk about Japan's back culture.

Next, I would like to talk about the back culture of Japan. For example, there is a famous sentence in Zeami's Fuushikaden, "If you keep it hidden, it will become a flower. It is an aesthetic that comes through concealment. Buddhist architecture that came from China is very gorgeous, and Toshogu is a perfect example, but architects criticize it for being too harsh. However, architects criticized it as being too harsh. Well, I am talking about the time after Katsura Rikyu, and even Katsura Rikyu was not that famous, but it became a world-famous building by the German architect Bruno Taut. What I am trying to say is that Katsura Rikyu is truly the "back culture" of Japan.

function of daily life, creating a structure unique to merchant houses. For example, the function of the kitchen, food storage, and storage space was completely separated from the interior space of the tatami room, which was used as a place to live and interact with others. Also, from this time on, the tatami mats that used to be tatami mats (* today's zabuton) on the wooden floor were replaced by shiki mats, and the prototype of today's Japanese houses was formed. This is where multiple spaces with diversity were completed, rather than spaces with different functions as in the West. In other words, it could be a bedroom for sleeping and a comfortable reception space for entertaining. Then came the tokonoma (alcove), and I think that's when art came into play. This was not a fixed style, but rather a way to express the dignity of the owner of the house through seasonal hanging scrolls, accompanying flowers and food. In a modern sense, the creator and the receiver of a work of art have become equals. Moreover, it is not just a single piece of art, but a total work, an installation if you will. Even the fashions, movements, and gestures of the people present were works of art, spaces, and the nature of the seasons. Today, however, I think that we have abandoned this wonderful culture of life due to importism. That's what I think.

According to him, "The Japanese are not a single race, but a hodgepodge, and I don't know where they came from or where they developed. I think this is very true. I think this is very true. My next theory is that there are Ainu people in the north, who may have some Russian blood in them, and Portuguese and graduate school sculpture program at Kanazawa University of Art. Actually, when I received this proposal, my name was at the end, and I was thinking that since there were architects and Edo literature professors in front of me, I would listen to the professional lectures of the other professors and share my amateur impressions and little knowledge, but to my surprise, I was deceived. (Laughs) I'm not an expert on machiya or architecture, so I'll just share my own thoughts.

As I wrote on the whiteboard, I would like to talk about four key words: "the origin of the machiya," "the culture behind Japan," "the space of Japanese architecture," and "the meaning of living.

I. The Origin of the Machiya

The predecessor of the machiya was the farmhouse. In the caste system of "samurai, farmers, artisans, and merchants," merchants were at the bottom of the hierarchy, but after the establishment of machiya, they started to sell their products here. Especially in the Muromachi period (1336-1573), when townhouses were first built and the houses were linked together, merchants began to display their goods in the wider entrance instead of in the dirt floor. In the Heian period (794-1185), most of the main streets of shrines, temples, and castle towns were located on the east and west sides of the city. So, this "Dori-Doma" was the perfect passage for the wind. Later on, the earthen floor came to play an important role in the an impression painting. In the case of the fish, he sketched and sketched the real fish in front of him. As for the chabo, I raise them every day, so I touch them. Sometimes I even hold them and raise them. I feel that their ability to supervise and express themselves is born out of this constant repetition of their lives. As for impression painting, I read to the children a long story based on a Russian folk song and folktale, and asked them to draw what impressed them the most. They are six years old, so I don't think their drawings are fully formed, but in their own way, the composition and colors are very frank and honest, and I think they are interesting. What I'm trying to say is that I think the environment is very important for children's growth, especially for human beings. In this respect, I would like to cherish nature and things made of wood, so that children can come into contact with them. As I mentioned earlier, wood is very comforting to the heart. I think it is important to incorporate this into our daily lives, without any logic. I've talked about a lot of random things, but I'd like to conclude. Thank you very much. Thank you very much for your time.

Moderator Inoue: Thank you very much. I had the opportunity to work part-time as a teacher at a kindergarten, and I was amazed at the difference in their skills. I was amazed at the difference. I think that environment is really important. Now let's continue with Mr. Shinoda.

Dr. Shinoda: I am Morio Shinoda, a sculptor in charge of the that temples have an important role to play in this respect as well. I also think that wooden buildings, whether machiya (traditional townhouses) or ordinary houses, can create a calm and relaxing space. I also believe that the environment, or the way the environment is, is very important for personality development. I don't mean to prove this, but if I were to tell you about the situation at our Tentokuin Kindergarten, we try to incorporate as much nature as possible into the school, so that the children can live in direct contact with the trees and flowers that are planted inside the school every day. The school building, where the children learn and play, is also made of wood. I think it is important to create an environment where the children can come into contact with nature as much as possible, and to create something that they can work on by themselves. I think it was a physiologist who mentioned the importance of children living in a wooden structure, because trees emit waves called beta waves. I heard a theory that these waves have a very positive effect on the physiology of children, especially young children. So, I think it was a good thing that our kindergarten building was made of wood. Another thing is that I always want to give my children the real thing. I always want to give my children the best things possible. This is also mentioned in the Declaration of Human Rights for Children, and I believe that these children will nurture that kind of power because they will be carrying the nation of Japan on their shoulders in the near future. Now, I have a little piece of evidence. I have a picture of a fish, a picture of a chapeau, and this point. In any case, maintaining and managing traditional buildings, Buddhist statues, and other such things is expensive, to put it bluntly, and we are struggling. How can we maintain them? To tell you the truth, it was a private conversation, but at one time, there were various opinions such as, let's destroy everything and move it deep into the mountains, or let's destroy the garden and build an apartment. There is also the Hyakumangoku Cultural Park or Edo-mura, which is located in the back of Wakuha and Yuyu, and there was a suggestion to move it there. In this way, Tentokuin had many dangers. The important thing is to protect it. If they are not taken away, we have to protect them, and if they are damaged, we have to repair them, so we have been playing a weasel for a long time. Otherwise, cultural properties cannot be protected. I have visited the city and prefectural governments many times to ask for financial support for these cultural assets. However, since the lives of the citizens of the prefecture are directly involved, it is difficult for the government to give priority to the preservation of traditional cultural assets.

The other thing I would like to talk about is the importance of wooden architecture. It is my imagination, or perhaps I am still in the early stages of my studies, but I think that wooden architecture has been accumulating and evolving since before Japan existed. And I believe that this is something unique to Japan. I think it is important to protect these unique Japanese wooden buildings, and to nurture a rich spiritual culture among the citizens of the prefecture who live there. I believe the same as before, and it has to be maintained. Recently, technology has advanced considerably, but it is still very difficult to repair and preserve old things. At the same time, it is a fact that the preservation of Buddhist culture or traditional culture and temple architecture is becoming more and more valuable. At the same time, it is a fact that the preservation of Buddhist culture or traditional culture is becoming more and more important. Under such circumstances, what should we do with Tentokuin and how should we protect it? As long as it is a temple, it is important that many people come and go. Originally, a temple was a place where many unspecified people could enter, heal their own minds, and get together with each other. In addition, there are Buddhist statues and paintings in the temple. In addition, there are Buddhist statues and paintings in temples, and these statues and paintings play a role as Buddhism. I think these things have a certain place or role to play in human society. Another thing is that Tentokuin was built by the third lord of the Maeda family, Toshitsune, for his wife. It was built under the power of the Maeda family, or the Tokugawa Shogunate, which was a major power behind the Maeda family. It was built under the power of the Maeda family and the Tokugawa shogunate. In addition, in the case of Tentokuin, it was given the role of controlling many temples by the Maeda family, or rather, it was ordered to do so. Naturally, there was also politics involved. In addition, temples have their parishioners, some of whom live in townhouses. I think the relationship between machiya and temples is also related to machiya today, but I think that this space of machiya is really a characteristic of Japanese architecture, a space that is flexible and free. When you take away all the sliding doors, a large space appears in front of you, or a small space, etc. Machiya is a space that is very much connected to the surrounding climate, customs, and seasons. Through this exhibition, I hope that people will think of machiya as a place for new discoveries. That's all for now. Thank you very much for your time.

Moderator Inoue:Machiya in a word has various differences and characteristics, Kanazawa has Kanazawa machiya and Kyoto has Kyoto machiya. In Kanazawa, there are Kanazawa machiya, and in Kyoto, there are Kyoto machiya. I learned a lot. Thank you very much, Professor Sakamoto.

Next, I would like to hear from Mr. Genku Arai, the monk of Tentokuin. Thank you very much.

Kazumasa Arai:As an outsider, I feel that it is very out of place for me to speak, but I would appreciate it. As Sakamoto-sensei mentioned earlier about the preservation and maintenance of machiya, it is difficult to maintain and manage Tentokuin as well as machiya. As some of you may know, Tentokuin is located in such an environment, with buildings, halls, and trees planted on a site of about 24,000 square meters (8,000 tsubo). It has been more than three hundred years since I was involved in this project, and it is very difficult to maintain and manage such an old building. So of course, it has to be house. The "dori-doma" was used as a passageway to carry the waste outside. That's why it was not possible to lay boards there. However, now that sewage pipes run along the street side and flush toilets are installed on the front side, such passages are no longer necessary. In addition, some machiya in large stores have "earthen storehouses". In Hokuriku, there are also "sedos," which are open spaces in the back of the house where people can hang their laundry, play with their children, or work. Another important part of the house was the courtyard. In the old days, houses were built in a row of eaves, so there was no light leaking from the neighbors. In the old days, houses were built in a row, so there was no light leaking in from the neighbors. It also served as an air vent. They are like chimneys that let the wind pass through. Also, especially in the northern part of Japan, you have to dump snow. In the old days, the courtyard was used as a place to dump the snow that accumulated. As you can see, machiya houses are made in a wide variety of ways, and of course there are many people who work on them. Carpenters, plasterers, tatami-mat makers, fusuma (sliding door) makers, tile makers, and many other craftsmen work together to create a single space, and in that sense, I think it can be said that the machiya itself is a work of collaboration. Last but not least, the number of machiya in Kanazawa is gradually decreasing. In 1999, there were about 11,000 machiya houses in Kanazawa, but in the spring of last year, there were only 9,500. Calculated on a yearly basis, about 300 houses have been destroyed. They have been turned into parking lots or rebuilt. I don't know how you feel about the teahouse type, and these are collectively called "Kanazawa machiya. Machiya itself is a modern term for a townhouse or a house with stores, and you can still find many of them in the city. Machiya is a style of building from the Edo period, with stores underneath and people living on top. The average machiya in Kanazawa has a frontage of about three and a half to four rooms, and when you enter, you will find a dirt floor, and at the back of the floor, there are rooms of about six tatami mats connected vertically, and next to the rooms, there is an extension of the dirt floor called "dori-doma," where you can enter with your feet on the ground. In the case of Kanazawa, taxes were determined by the number of frontage spaces in the old days, so that's how it was done. So basically, the first floor is for stores, and the back of the first floor and the second floor are for houses. In addition, machiya houses have tatami rooms and Buddhist temples, which have tokonoma, or alcove, which is a space for displaying seasonal items or hanging scrolls. This display space is the most sacred or important place in the house, and although there is a Shinto altar in the house, it is also the place where the god of the house is said to be. It was also a place where the god of the other house was said to reside. Also, a house that has been closed down is called "shimotaya. Of course, there are many ways to use such a space, but in the old days, the water supply was located at the back of the house, and all the drainage was done at the back. In the old days, the water supply was located at the back of the house, and all the drainage was done at the back of the

Draft of the Machiya Exhibition Symposium

Moderator Suzuki: Thank you very much for coming to the "Teramachi Kokoro Machiya" exhibition. We would like to hold a symposium, "Let's Talk Art in Machiya...What's in This Town, What Was in This Town," which will be held at the same time as the exhibition. I'd like to start with you, Professor Sakamoto.

Dr. Sakamoto: As the first speaker of the symposium, I would like to talk a little bit about machiya. Actually, there is a group called the Kanazawa Machiya Inheritance and Utilization Study Group, which is working to preserve and renovate vacant machiya houses in Kanazawa and to actively utilize them. This place, the venue for this exhibition, is one such machiya. We have also coined a proper noun, "Kanazawa machiya," although it is not a common term, with the aim of preserving the pre-war wooden houses of Kanazawa. Machiya was originally the residence of merchants and craftsmen, and this house belongs to that category. However, the building we are in now was built in the early Showa period (1926-1989), so it is not that old. Therefore, the ceiling is high, as is the second floor. There are many machiya with very low ceilings that are much older. In the old days, there was a letter that went around stating that it was prohibited to build a second floor, so people used the second floor as a kind of hidden room. In Kanazawa, there are samurai residences and samurais' residences in the Nagamachi area. In Kanazawa, you can find these in the Nagamachi area, and they are surrounded by earthen walls and gates, such as samurai-style machiya. In addition, there are also machiya of

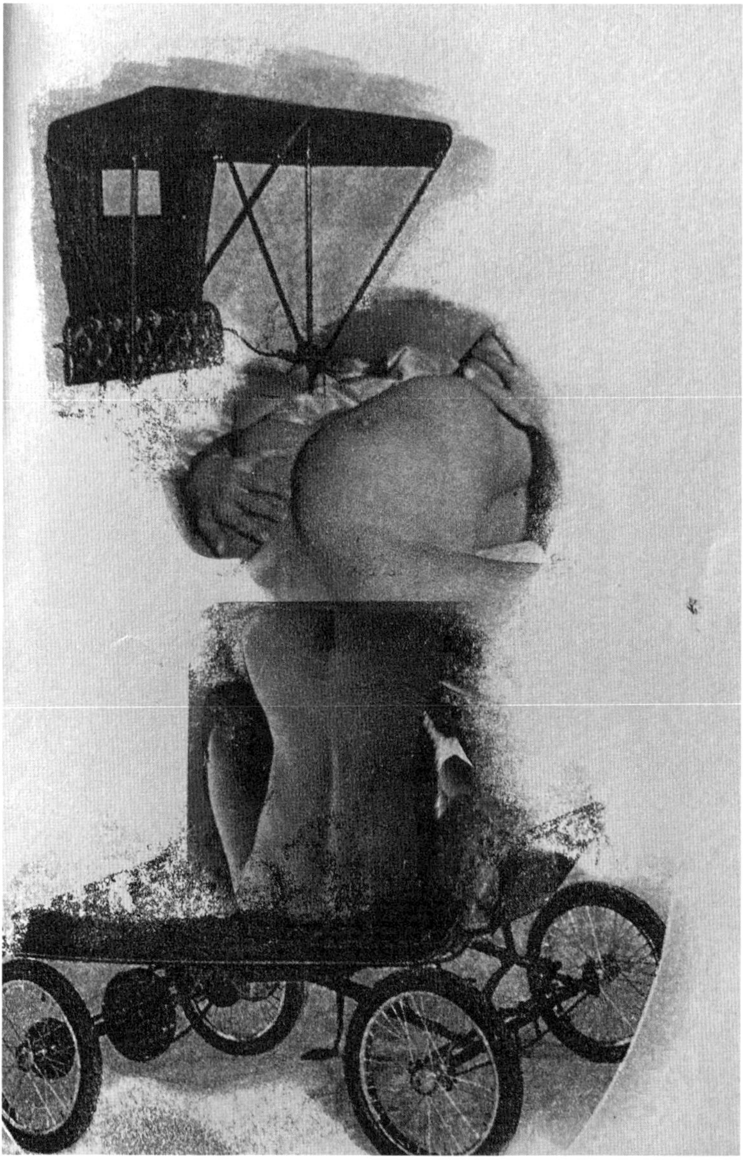

While Jones' sadism is bright and humorous, Grossman's is full of abnormalities. Most of her works are male figures, and many of them have only the head, without the neck, and are displayed like a watermelon. Even the life-size works were missing the knees and arms from the elbows down. They could be seen as a kind of torso, but they were not in the proportions of the classic torso. On the surface, the figure is always covered with black tanned leather and connected with zippers. In this way, we see the essential difference between men and women. Furthermore, although not sculptures, the hard texture of steel, as in Motoi Sorayama's illustration of a robot, combined with the female form, promotes eroticism. The photographer Shinya Gondo, who was also introduced in the French edition of ZOOM, has been looking at these expressions from the eyes of a man like me.

From "Camille Claudel Album" (published by APT International, Inc.), 1987.

and the pose of the legs slightly twisted and bent at the inner thighs are the figures of beautiful male homosexual boys.

John Cassell, a hyper-realist artist who has been painting women's buttocks for years, seems to have produced art from an even more refracted physiology. A few years ago, while I was in New York, I had a chance to meet him and he told me something interesting about his work. His motifs of beautiful buttocks are not intended to depict buttocks, but are merely materials to accentuate silk and satin underwear. His collection of women's underwear and thin nylon fabrics was impressive in quantity and quality. Furthermore, I noticed a certain consistency in Casale's choices. It was the feel of the cloth. He is almost charismatically passionate about visualizing that touch on canvas. It is fetishism. In contrast to this, Allen Jones looks at women in a very direct way. On the surface, it takes the form of sadism toward women, but it can be seen as a variant of love for women. This is evident in the publication Allen Jones Figures, published by Gallerie Micro in Milan in 1969. It is a kind of pictorial magazine that contains Jones' works as well as magazine clippings, advertisements, and posters that he had collected. Their cartoons often featured women. Their cartoons were sadistic in their treatment of women, yet loving in a way that made them seem playful. As Allen Jones himself has stated, he is mostly influenced by these two artists as motifs for his work.

Another writer who uses sadistic themes as motifs is Nancy Grossman, a woman who looks at men from the side of women.

For a long time, I have been making sculptures that could be called mechanics. For a long time, I have been making what are called "mechanical" sculptures, which have been evaluated as mechanical works made of very detailed mechanical parts. However, many people say that they are very sexy when seen from a woman's point of view. While the former is clearly for the eyes of men, in the communication of the latter, I should think that a part of my inner feminine gradation is connected with female viewers. In fact, there is a part of me that spends a great deal of energy trying to change the surface of aluminum, an inorganic material, to make it tactile. While most of my work is done by chance, this is the only manual work I do. When I first came into contact with Michelangelo's sculptures during my stay in Europe, I was astonished by the licking marble stone statues, which were completely different from the works I had seen in gravures, and at the same time, I was impressed by the homoeroticism of the male figures. The homosexual element that had been faintly present in a part of my body was suddenly magnified, and I have memories of traveling all over Europe in search of Michelangelo. This trip turned out to be more of a trip to satisfy a truly impure and anomalous desire than to appreciate art, but in this trip I saw the beautiful boy David and marveled at the sexiness of Bacchus. I vividly remember that my thoughts went back to the Renaissance era, and I had the immoral idea that Michelangelo was creating a male statue as a homosexual object. It is true that the plump body of Bacchus in Florence, the clothed hands of the dying slave in the Louvre, installation, equipment, or device, but was later transformed into a device by combining several pieces of work - it suddenly came into the limelight. What these women artists have in common is that they have incorporated the realm of craft and handicraft into their sculptures, as opposed to the traditional, very masculine sculptures. There was a time in the 1970s when potters on the West Coast of the United States, led by Peter Baucus, created ceramic sculptures that were called "punk art," but the works of today's female artists are even more craft-like and hobbyist. However, even if the materials and details are handicraft-like, they are still quite convincing as art. In 1981, I once organized an exhibition of new artists at Project Studio One (P.S.1) in Brooklyn, New York. P.S.1 selects up-and-coming artists year after year and gives them grants to work on their works at the venue and have them exhibited there at the end of the year. Among the female artists who left a lasting impression on me at this exhibition were Theodora Skripitares, Lydia Han, Nancy Grossman, and Sheila Klein. In addition, I was able to meet Linda Pengrez and Liran, who are active in New York, and they are also artists who create works based on feminine ideas. Later, under the influence of these Western women artists, new artists such as Nobuko Tsutsumi, Mayumi Terada, Miho Hirota, and Tomie Seto grew up in Japan. This so-called feminine art is now a worldwide trend. And what is characteristic of all of them is that they have given a different meaning to the hobbyist handicraft form by enlarging it.

these two have their own subtle gradations. The creation of art, which is a very personal and internal work, is greatly influenced by this gradation.

I once gave an assignment like this to my art students. I once gave an assignment like this to my art students: "You are to create a three-dimensional object without thinking of art as such, but rather as your personal hobby. What was apparent here was that no matter how many times I repeated it, there were certain characteristics that differed between men and women. This is the fact that everyone can see that the work is made by a woman or a man, and that it is made from a part of the body that is close to the physiology. In the past, when a writer was called a "woman writer," it was assumed that she was the same as a man. Therefore, the adjective "feminine" was used. The adjective "joryu" was used to imply that the writer was a woman, but in the same way as a man. After the Women's Lib movement of the 1960s, gender equality was established, and from the early 1980s, the era of women's rights was reestablished. In contrast to the former, in which men were the darget, women's art is based on the fact that they are women. This, combined with the emergence of installation art in the latter half of the 1970s, which originally meant "installation," "equipment," or "device," and which combines several works to create a device, has suddenly come into the limelight. In combination with the installation art that emerged in the latter half of the 1980s - which originally meant

Women's Eyes and Sculpture

When I talk about women, I always have to be aware that I am a man first. This is because although women are familiar to us as human beings, they exist as far away from us as perspective viewed through a wide-angle lens. In biology, there are two pyramids, one for females and one for males, and we males at the top of one pyramid understand male dogs in order to understand females at the other top. It seems to me that we men can communicate with each other much better with male dogs than we can with women, and that we can communicate with male pigs, and even amoebas, by descending the mountains, crossing the plains, quickly moving to the next mountain, opening the gates of genetic modification, and understanding the female reptiles, all the way to the top. I believe that only then will we be able to understand the human female in any way. The popular belief that women think in the womb is also a self-satisfied theory developed by men in the male pyramid. Thus, the title "Women's Eyes" refers only to the feminine perspective through the eyes of men, not to the eyes of women themselves.

I don't know what the editor's intention was in giving me this title, but I would rather focus on the male and female eyes. In other words, I would like to look at what men make and what women make, and the men and women who appreciate them, through my own eyes. At the beginning of this article, I used the metaphor of two pyramids, one male and one female, but just as Weininger said that the male and female seen as individuals are a mixture of the male and female as an idea,

Chapter 1

Morio Shinoda

This is the first time that Osamuga Ueno has appeared on Face Book. I have been posting all my personal information on FB for a long time. I've been posting all kinds of personal information on FB for a long time now, because one piece of information can reach the whole world. It's a very convenient world we live in. I don't know why, but for some reason he refused. I use FB for everything from announcements of my solo exhibitions to trivial musings. I don't use Twitter much at all. I don't have any particular reason for doing so, and I think it's fine because it has worked for me. Perhaps that's why Osamu Ueno didn't use FB, but it's too short to exchange information in whispers. I was surprised to find that it had recently appeared on FB, but at the same time, I can't deny that it has become very convenient for me.

The reason is this! A few minutes later, I saw a photo sent to me on Line, and I understood. It was Hemingway himself, with his long fishing rod on his shoulder, who hadn't caught a fish all day. And when I saw his preface, I knew I was in for a big surprise.

Shinoda

@Taku Tamehiro

Preface

"For Whom the Bell Tolls (Ernest Hemingway)

In this white book, the spatial perception of white may be the white that asks how I perceive the blank.

Yuval Noah Harari says that the dawn of the modern age is the recognition of a blank map.
In this age of human supremacy, it may be time for the cognitive space that Shinoda created 40 years ago to blossom.

Is Shinoda's art of conceptual space too early?
Or is he an outlier in the IT age?

Will the expansion of my existence as an individual of experience and perception continue into the next generation?

How will you express the gap in your mind, the white of space, through this book?

"I want to ask you.

An invitation to the white world.

Osamu Ueno

Preface

I've been thinking about this for about forty years. If there was a pure white book on the shelf of a bookstore, it would be the first thing to stand out! I proposed this idea to various publishers, but none of them took me up on it. I'd like to deal with that in this book.

I believe that the memories of thirty years ago have become physical, but forty years ago will become historical knowledge. For example, if we divide the history of emperors by thirty years, physicalized memories will emerge.

Therefore, in the case of fashion, if you look back thirty years, you will find designs that have been passed on. Art, on the other hand, is a world of the individual, a kind of invention. Even if you take a piece of art from 30 years ago, it will be easily discovered, but if you take it from 40 years ago or earlier, it will be less likely to be discovered. This white book is a book with a sculpture. This white book is a book with a sculpture, or you could say that the sculpture has a book. And it is co-authored with Osamu Ueno. Normally, co-authorship is a matter of proposing issues based on the same or similar concepts, but here it is a strange book that seems to be connected somehow, if at all randomly. It is a strange book.

Morio Shinoda

Chapter 2 Osamu Ueno

Contents

$$\mathcal{H} = \sum_{n=1}^{N-1} + \sum_{n=N}^{\infty}$$

Happiness Equation

August 30, 2020

Theorem 1. *Happiness $\mathcal{H}$ consists of two parts, one is the term that build up step by step, the other is the term cannot be obtained by the extention. Here we represent the first term as a finite sum and the second term as an infinite sum.*

$$\mathcal{H} = \sum_{n=1}^{N-1} + \sum_{n=N}^{\infty} \tag{1}$$

$$\sum_{n=1}^{N-1} : \textit{Material wealth, Science, Logic} \tag{2}$$

$$\sum_{n=N}^{\infty} : \textit{Spiritual wealth, Art, Intuition} \tag{3}$$

On the theme "Happiness Equation", I see the structure (1), which is the structure between finite and infinite. A Finite N cannot be enough for infinity, but the finite part is necessary for the infinity

Analogies can be found in various situations. We build the material wealth (2) for happiness, but we cannot reach happiness only by material accumulations. The rest to happiness is to change the way you think, that is, to stop counting what you don't have and to be satisfied with what you have(3).
The above example is the relation between material wealth and spiritual wealth. I think science and art have the same relationship for happiness..

Naoki Wada (Mathematician)

Naoki Wada ● Born in 1986.Studied mathematics at Kyoto University and at the Stekulov Institute of Mathematics in St. Petersburg, Russia.He completed his master's degree at Kyoto University's Graduate School of Informatics in 2009, and withdrew from the doctoral course in 2013.Currently, he is engaged in supporting data utilization in companies and government agencies at VALUES Corporation.

The White Book

Morio Shinoda ／ Osamu Ueno

白い本　篠田守男／上野オサム

2021 年 10 月 9 日　初版第 1 版発行

著者　篠田守男　上野オサム

挿画　篠田守男
写真　上野オサム
　　　Taku Tamehiro（P12、P492）
数式　和田尚樹
画像監修　鈴木昌実
編集　本多隆彦
ブックデザイン　TWworks
翻訳　IT 自動翻

発行者　本多隆彦
発行所　株式会社ギャラリーステーション
　〒 111-0053
　東京都台東区浅草橋 1-23-5　飯島ビル
　電話　03-3865-0088
　ファックス 03-3865-0233
　URL https://www.g-station.co.jp
印刷・製本　ベクトル印刷株式会社